Warning: this book delivers hard truths. Jess Brady shows you how to get more life from your money and create a plan for your future. It will challenge how you think about money and yourself. A must-read for anyone wanting to get serious about their finances.

— **Glen James**

Author of *The Quick-Start Guide to Investing* and host of the *money money money* podcast

Finally — a money book that ditches the jargon and shows women how to grow wealth on their own terms. Jess makes finance feel like a glass of bubbles with your bestie: real, relatable and totally doable.

— **Molly Benjamin**

Founder, Ladies Finance Club and author of *Girls Just Wanna Have Funds*

GET GROWING

GET GROWING

A no-nonsense guide to cultivating
wealth and financial freedom

Jessica Brady

WILEY

A catalogue record for this book is available from the National Library of Australia

NATIONAL LIBRARY OF AUSTRALIA

Registered Office
John Wiley & Sons Australia, Ltd. Level 4, 600 Bourke Street, Melbourne, VIC 3000, Australia

For details of our global editorial offices, customer services, and more information about Wiley products visit us at www.wiley.com.

Wiley also publishes its books in a variety of electronic formats and by print-on-demand. Some content that appears in standard print versions of this book may not be available in other formats.

Cover design by George Saad
Cover and figure background images: © Léo Alexandre/Adobe Stock

Set in 11/16pt and Utopia Std by Straive, Chennai, India.
Printed and bound by CPI Group (UK) Ltd, Croydon, CR0 4YY
C9781394352661_060226

The manufacturer's authorized representative according to the EU General Product Safety Regulation is Wiley-VCH GmbH, Boschstr. 12, 69469 Weinheim, Germany, e-mail: Product_Safety@wiley.com.

To my wild, witty and whip-smart mother, Deniece, who once shaved her head in an act of defiance, whose favourite word rhymes with 'hunt', and who drives like she's stolen it. Mum, you are never scared to have or share your opinion. Thank you for leading the way.

WHAT'S INSIDE

Before we grow: Grounded in Country and context xi
Laying the ground work: Your money growing guide xv

1 Roots 1
Detangling the mess of young Jess and my relationship
with money

2 Dirt 15
Dishing on the systems and structures that stifle our
growth and feed us fibs

3 Dig 33
Unearthing what shapes our money beliefs and
behaviours beneath the surface

4 Shed 73
Letting go of shame and perfectionism to make space
for more helpful money habits

5 Plot 97
How to set money goals that matter and
make decisions on what to grow

6 Weed 127
Ditching bad debts and patrolling the
doubts that are slowing your growing
(creepers, crowders and resource suckers)

7   Seed   161
    Building a conscious cashflow plan that feeds your
    goals and seeds your future

8   Sprout   193
    What to know before you grow: the risks and
    rewards of investing

9   Grow   217
    How to cultivate long-term financial freedom through
    investing and super

10 Winter   249
    Your plan for financial shit storms: insurance, savings
    and frosty relationships

Flourish: A love note to your growth and everything it
makes possible   285
Acknowledgements: Giving my gardening crew their flowers   289
Keep the garden party growing: Meet Jess and join
the community   295
Notes: References and research   297

BEFORE WE GROW
Grounded in Country and context

I wrote most of this book on the traditional lands of the Gadigal and Darkinjung people and acknowledge that sovereignty was never ceded. 'Always was, always will be, Aboriginal land.'

I also feel compelled to acknowledge the context and times we are living in. The world feels hard and heavy right now and, at the same time, we must never underestimate our ability to make a difference, even when it seems tiny and inconsequential.

I am acutely aware as a white, straight, middle-class Australian woman that many people right now are not afforded opportunities that I often take for granted; opportunities that many who have gone before me have fought hard to get.

I am lucky and I know it. My fight for a fairer, more equitable world will continue until we have made the meaningful structural change needed, or until I take my last breath — whichever comes first.

It is not the critic who counts; not the man who points out how the strong man stumbles, or where the doer of deeds could have done them better.

The credit belongs to the man who is actually in the arena, whose face is marred by dust and sweat and blood; who strives valiantly; who errs, who comes short again and again, because there is no effort without error and shortcoming; but who does actually strive to do the deeds; who knows great enthusiasms, the great devotions; who spends himself in a worthy cause; who at the best knows in the end the triumph of high achievement, and who at the worst, if he fails, at least fails while daring greatly, so that his place shall never be with those cold and timid souls who neither know victory nor defeat.

—*Theodore Roosevelt*

LAYING THE GROUND WORK

Your money growing guide

So you want to grow your money? Well, you're in the right place. My hope is that this book becomes your money go-to guide. That it lives on your bedside table, dog-eared and covered in tea stains, notations and highlighted sections—from the bits that really speak to you, to the ones you need to read again.

I hope you reach for this book when you are having a wobbly money moment and need to realign. The one you return to when you reach a new milestone, or your life has pivoted and you're ready for the next level. I want it to be the book that you rave about, gift to a friend in need or add to your list of top reads—because it's genuinely created change in your life.

Ambitious? Fuck yes.

But I promise you, if you do the work, it *will* work. Because here is the beautiful thing about the power of education: no-one can ever take it away from you. And its value grows over time.

Before you race to the bits in this book you really want to know, I first want to mentally and spiritually prepare you for the fact that some parts of this book might make you uncomfortable—quite uncomfortable. What I've learned from two decades in financial services is that these areas of discomfort—the areas that we flee the fastest from — are normally where we need the most help. I get it; no-one wants to feel personally attacked by a relative stranger through a series of words on a page. It's natural and normal (and actually really clever from a survival perspective) to want to move far away from things that make you feel uncomfortable.

But when it comes to uncomfortable feelings and money, you generally need to do the opposite. You need to sit with those moments, because often, deep down, you know those are the things you need to change.

Through the chapters in this book, I help you understand what has shaped your belief system with money so far, what parts you need to focus on and what financial pitfalls to avoid. I offer ideas for your next steps, based on where you are right now. As you get more comfortable doing one thing, you can then come back and take the next step. Because a one-size-fits-all solution for how you build your money plan doesn't exist (much to the dismay of some people). My job is to give you options, ideas and insights to help you feel confident in making your next money move. Your job is to show up and do the work.

The important thing to remember is that 'money know-how' is not a line of genetic code that you're either born with, or you aren't. It's not passed down through bloodlines via your DNA. It's a skill, and it can be learned. And, as with any new skill, the first few attempts to do anything new with your money might feel hard or awkward or daunting. Remember when you first learned to ride a bike? If you were anything like me, you were wobbling all over the place. (I never wanted my training wheels off; I was sure I could never master it.) Or the first time you drove a car? Fucking terrifying. But you kept going, right? And now you probably drive without even thinking about whether or not your hands are in the correct spot, or if you've looked in the rear-view mirror. Those behaviours are now second nature to you. That same 'muscle memory' will happen if you keep at it with your money — it just takes practice.

Money, as a concept, has no agenda. Each of us gets to determine how we deploy it. So this book is all about helping you feel more powerful and in control of how you think, behave and invest your money — because in most instances, these actions will dictate the outcomes of your life. Recently, I heard someone refer to money as being like a hammer — it can help you build something, but it can also smash walls down. It's how you use it that matters.

This book covers the most important money themes, topics and concepts, so you can leave with a clearer understanding of exactly what areas you need to consider when growing your money.

The first few chapters take you through my own history with money, as well as the historical context of systemic inequality (and why it matters). We then dive into identifying your own money beliefs and what shaped them. Along the way, I outline ideas and concepts to help you build strong beliefs and habits moving forward.

Then, I give you science-led insights on how to build financial goals that feel right for you, show you how to weed out what's not needed and use your income to set yourself up for success.

The last few chapters are where you'll learn how to grow your money by investing it and how to protect yourself when it comes to managing financial risks. I warn you: there are swear words and bad jokes throughout — so be ready.

This book draws on many concepts from gardening, nature and the natural world more broadly to help you build your own thriving money ecosystem. So why the gardening and nature metaphor? Well, thriving with money is similar, in many ways, to how the best ecosystems on the planet survive. But Mother Nature is also wild and tempestuous — just like our lives. She is beautiful, complex and contradictory. Working *with* her is generally advised over trying to work *against* her. The same goes for your money. It can afford you all manner of things, and working with it will yield a far better outcome than burying your head in the sand and hoping it all works out.

Yes, nature is full of flowers and rainbows, but predators are also lurking in the bushes and violent storms can erupt without notice and destroy everything in their wake. The same disruptions happen in our financial worlds too. Money can enable amazing things in life, but I'm not going to promise you that you can eradicate *all* the bad stuff from your money world forevermore — and you should run from anyone who says they can. However, I will teach you what to look out for and how to best stay protected and safe, while not just surviving but also flourishing.

Messy money (or had I just messed up?)

I've spent more than half my life in finance and helped thousands of people feel more in control of their money. But, honestly, when I first started giving financial advice, I was too nice. Clients would come in after over-spending and not sticking to our goals-based financial plan and tell me a well-constructed (and, in some instances, pre-rehearsed) sob story of their latest mishap.

They would tell me how they were just so busy, or tired, or that they just, kind of, 'accidentally' slipped and bought a brand new (and very fucking expensive) car. And I would be there to soothe them, amend the strategy and give them their next steps.

They would leave feeling relieved (probably) that I hadn't raked them over the coals, and I thought that meant 'job well done' on my part. Then I started to notice that this was a pattern. They would rinse and repeat the same stories and reasons, and I would once again realign their plan. I then realised I wasn't helping them at all. They were flushing their goals down the toilet, and the only thing I was helping them do was to feel okay about it.

I decided that wasn't the kind of financial adviser I would want, so it wasn't the financial adviser I was going to be. I enrolled in a program to learn about acceptance and commitment therapy (ACT), which focuses on helping people behave more consistently with their values and apply mindfulness skills to their actions. I became obsessed with what a greater understanding of neuroscience could do to the way we manage and think about money.

When I began applying some of my newly learned techniques with clients, I started seeing amazing results. I realised my job was actually very little to do with numbers and much more to do with helping people build better and more productive beliefs, habits, techniques and rituals to support their growth. Of course, financial stuff went with this — including cash flow plans, debt-reduction strategies, investment plans and financial protection plans — but this foundational work needed to be completed first.

What I realised was fascinating (and now quite obvious): helping people build a financial game plan started with the person, not the money. Talking about different investment options is futile if there is no money to invest. Giving people a perfectly risk-profiled retirement strategy without first addressing their fears and hopes and dreams means they will never actually implement it.

So, I started more human-first financial coaching with my clients, and it worked so well I was embarrassed (and honestly a bit angry) that I didn't do it sooner.

Initially, I was hesitant to dish out tough love when my clients came in with their tales of financial snafus and excuses, but do you know what I learned? They loved it. Sure, it didn't always feel good for them right then and there. But once they realised that they could no longer get away with the BS they once could, our relationship grew stronger and deeper.

I told them that their goals would either need to be thrown in the bin or seriously reduced down if they kept going the way they were. I told them it didn't bother me if they never achieved their goals; it wasn't my life they were playing with, but theirs. Only they would need to live with the consequences of their actions. Harsh, but this ignited the fire and the fight in them.

They were not okay with me striking through their goals, or writing 'on hold' or 'not a priority' next to things they longed for. It was honestly fascinating to watch their whole being change. Instead of excuses, they started looking for ways to get back on track. They got more focused and committed to doing the (often hard) work.

Sometimes, my tough love didn't work. For some, the idea of financial freedom not just happening overnight wasn't an easy pill to swallow. Some of them thought engaging a financial adviser meant I would bring out my magic wand, wave it around and make everything better. How I wish I owned that wand. And so, a tough decision would have to be made: step up or step off. I couldn't, in good conscience, keep charging them fees for a strategy they were not implementing.

The idea of firing my first client was one that made me sick to my stomach. They had turned to me for help and I was releasing them back into the jungle, often without the strategies in place that we had agreed to achieve together. I wondered if I was failing them. Maybe I wasn't cut out for this?

I didn't sign up for an emotional roller-coaster when I studied financial advice. I signed up for investment modelling, tax minimisation strategies, meticulously detailed cash flow plans that showed *exactly* when a goal would be attained. Clean, sterile strategies that lived in a Petri dish within a temperature-controlled lab — or some mythical place where plans are executed perfectly. Ah, but that is not real life.

What I encountered instead were clients facing redundancies, unexpected pregnancies, income changes, divorces, illnesses and left-field inheritances. Once the oxygen of real life hits that lab-controlled Petri dish, you don't always have the predictable outcomes you planned for. But that *is* what you are working with — a life that crisscrosses down unexpected paths. A life that sometimes sees you take a step back to go forward or go down a shortcut you previously didn't know was there. It's a journey that can be messy, unpredictable, contradictory and sometimes even dangerous. And the only person who holds the map is you.

Taking control of the money map

Sure, experts can show you the common paths and pitfalls that may lie ahead of you. We can explain how to navigate that icy crevasse safely without plunging into financial ruin, or show you the fastest route up that mountain to stability and freedom. But we don't control the weather. There will always be things that are unforeseen and mean and dirty, and you need to be able to pause and decide on your best course of action. And, honestly, when the weather is rough and you're wet and cold, and in need of a nice hot shower and a good long rest, forging forward can feel hard. But *this* is the exact moment you need to dig in.

Some people think they want what's up the mountain but they expect to be airlifted there, with no effort required on their part. I mean, let's be honest, some people *are* effectively airlifted there — be it through good luck or generational wealth or both. But that isn't the case for most of us. And so, if we aren't willing to pull our metaphorical money-making socks up, we may as well hang up our boots. We can tell ourselves it's too hard, that we're too busy, and it was probably unrealistic anyway. We can talk ourselves out of even trying to build the life we want often before we've even started!

Why? Because habit change is bloody hard. It can feel wildly uncomfortable to hold a mirror up to yourself, and sift through memories and heartache as you hunt for the lessons and learnings. It's terrifying to know you're never going to have all the information on something, or know exactly what the outcome will look like. You feel like you're giving up control, or you're worried you'll fail.

Yes — God forbid you try something that doesn't work out, or muck something up along the way. Too many of us have been conditioned to see our decisions as resulting in either success or failure, where failure = bad. We see mistakes, mishaps, errors in judgement or 'failures' in life to mean that *we* are a failure. We want to bury them as quickly as possible.

The human brain isn't very good at detaching itself, and our self-worth, from the thing that we fucked up. Remember: what other people think of you or the decisions you've made is not worth one *brass razoo*. (Brief side-quest incoming — a 'brass razoo' is the term for a non-existent coin of trivial value birthed into everyday slang by Australian WWI soldiers. A brilliant analogy for when we are worried about being judged, or feeling like a fraud or failure with our money.)

Okay, back on track. Of course, most of us don't want to meander through life feeling like a complete failure, so we decide the whole money management caper is not for us. And we settle.

Now I have no problem with people who choose this path. It's yours to decide. But, in reality, it's incredibly important to be able to see where you've made a mistake — because that's how you learn and grow. And sometimes when we share our mistakes, it helps others learn and grow from them too.

To feel less alone on this journey, I put a call out to my amazing money community. I asked people to share their financial experiences — from their 'oh-shit' moments to their proudest moments with money. Throughout the book, you'll find various 'money in the wild' profiles, offering additional insights on the specific areas covered — because we're all on this path together. (These are their real stories, just not their real names.)

Inevitably, like the people who share their stories through this book, you will have times in life when you cannot carry on as planned and need to make unexpected pit stops, or take a different trail to the one you started out on. Sometimes the best thing you can do is pause, get out your compass, have a little snack and a long sleep, and mull over your next move. This can be especially the case after a hugely emotional event has occurred (like a death, divorce or illness), because they create emotional fog.

Research from Princeton University[1] shows that during times of acute stress (like, you know, financial disasters), our IQ actually drops by about 13 points. 13 points! That's equivalent to the loss of an entire night's sleep. Ever tried to make sound choices on no sleep? Disaster. Ironically, at the exact time when you need to navigate a financial fog or veritable shitstorm, your brain is less able to show up for work. This is clearly some sick evolutionary joke.

But the fog or shitstorm must be navigated. You will need to dig into areas within you didn't even know you had, find your grit, and keep going. And it will be hard — because the most frustrating part about the concept of resilience is that, in the bright lights, it sounds like a positive and exciting thing. Yet, when we are called on to actually be resilient in life, it feels fucking awful.

A gap exists between knowing and not knowing, or doing and not doing, and that middle ground often feels shaky. But it's in this messy middle where you learn the most. So, as hard as it is and as frustrating as it may seem, the more unsure you are, the more you need to take a deep breath, pat yourself on the back and say, 'I'm feeling like this because I'm in that shitty, messy middle space on the journey to knowing'. Remember that.

You are going to have frustrating moments with your money. But I also know that, no matter where life takes you, and no matter the changes to where you live, what you do for work, who you date or even who you consider a close friend, money will still be there. It will endure the seasons and changing tides. So, if you're going to be in a relationship with money forever, shouldn't you make it a great one? Hell yes you should. Great, then let's get started.

ROOTS

Detangling the mess of young Jess and my relationship with money

Life is either a daring adventure, or nothing.

—*Helen Keller*

Now, before I get into the nuts and bolts, let me rewind just a little and share some of the money moments that shaped my life—because I want you to know that my own journey with money has, at times, been rocky and windy. And if I'm going to ask you to be brave and vulnerable with yourself, I think it's important that I am with you too.

So let's go back to 1987, a year before my arrival. My parents have just been handed the devastating news that my father has an aggressive brain tumour, the size of a tennis ball, and it was going to kill him. Never one to waste a crisis, my then 24-year-old mother hastily makes plans to wed her sick beau amid his radiation therapy and create a keepsake in his memory—me.

When I was four months old, at the ripe young age of 28, my father took his last breath, leaving his then 25-year-old wife widowed and alone to raise me in the big, wide world.

Now I am sure it's obvious, but in case it isn't — they hadn't had a huge amount of time to set themselves up financially. My mother was still training to be a nurse and my father was a builder. They spent their money and time going to gigs, dyeing their hair black (like many an '80s rockstar wannabe) and having fun. Suddenly everything got very adult-y, very fast.

Thanks to some sage advice from my grandfather, my dad did have income protection insurance. But he either didn't want, or didn't think he needed, life insurance. He was young and seemingly healthy so what was the point? Alas, no pile of cash appeared in his wake. (Although a large funeral bill was delivered.)

So, in case you thought this was another finance book from someone with oodles of generational wealth, I can assure you that, growing up, my life was much more wooden spoon than silver spoon. I had plenty of privileges, but being born into money was not one of them.

Tight squeeze childhood

Money was tight when I was a child. I lived in second-hand clothes, often gifted from Julie, a wonderful lady up the road whose daughter was about a foot taller than me. Rolling my sleeves up was my go-to fashion lewk for a good chunk of the '90s. Mufti days or 'free dress' days (where you don't have to wear your uniform to school), are the archenemy of poor children. For primary-school aged Jess, these days created unnecessary extra stress and pressure. At least in my second-hand uniform (hemmed by Mum with medical tape), I was the same as everyone else. I could hide in a sea of sameness. In mufti, I felt exposed as the poor kid I was.

Then came the fads and trends of the 1990s that I, as a Spice Girls loving, *Sailor Moon* watching child, desperately wished for. Don't get me wrong — I always had food on the table, clothes on my back and toys strewn all over my bedroom. But I wanted the stuff that 'everyone' else had. I craved the latest Polly Pocket, the newest Impulse spray deodorant scent, a Tamagotchi — yes, I dreamed of keeping a blob of black squares on a tiny screen alive, fed and cleaned up after it had shat everywhere. I begged for the newest, latest and greatest shiny thing.

The words 'we can't afford that Jess' were commonplace.

By the time I was seven, my Mum had remarried and birthed two more humans. My brothers, Chris and Ben, and I have very different relationships with money. Sure, we grew up in the same household, but by the time my youngest brother had started school, my parents were starting to see some financial rewards from their hard work (both my parents worked fulltime, plus my Mum completed a master's degree and somehow kept all three of us kids alive), and some strokes of good fortune. Plus, you know, house prices were not as diabolical as they are now.

They say all clouds have silver linings, and while I am sure a younger version of myself would vehemently disagree, growing up without a bunch of cash had its benefits. If being cool was off the table, I could instead be creative. And smart.

I'm naturally curious and inquisitive. As a child, most evenings found me curled up in bed, reading. Reading allowed me to escape to far-flung places, to make friends with characters on the page and to dream big. Sure, you might have the latest, cutest, glittery butterfly clips that I really want, Sarah, but did you know that Beatrix Potter was an accomplished sheep-farmer and Peter Rabbit was inspired by her bunny, Peter Piper, that she used to walk on a leash? No. Didn't think so.

Learning to me was exciting. I was thirsty for knowledge and always scouting out the next literary adventure at the local library. Libraries are one of the best societal equalisers — I didn't need money to get knowledge, I just needed my grandmother's blue and white library card and I was away.

I learned from an early age that newer isn't always better. I spent many a Saturday morning with Mum on a garage sale pilgrimage from one side of town to the next. I couldn't wait to get the weekly paper and map out our route. Wealthier suburbs were top of the list, as were deceased estates. If I spotted a deceased estate in a wealthy suburb, we knew we had struck metaphorical second-hand, garage-sale gold. We'd wake at 6 am to ensure we arrived as soon as they flung their garage door up, ready to sniff out a bargain. We meant business.

Traipsing for treasure in other peoples 'trash' got me curious about the stories and history of things — I boldly would ask where something had come from, how old it was and who owned it. (Much to the surprise of the bleary-eyed stall or home owner, who no doubt was bemused by a young red-headed kid wanting to know the history of their discarded items.)

Our finds were special to me, not because they were plastered all over the pages of *Girlfriend* or *Dolly*, but for exactly the opposite reason — because they were rare and unique. No-one else could easily (in the days before the internet), just go out and get exactly the same thing. And something about that really soothed me and my quest to 'fit in'.

Instead, I was learning that it's okay to stand out, to be different, and to not buy (literally) into all the hype of fads. And while I wouldn't say that I *never* got caught up comparing myself to others, it started to teach me to lean more into the things that I liked and give less fucks about what other people were chasing.

My second-hand finds also taught me a very precious money lesson: cost doesn't always equal value. Some of the most precious items I found cost me next to nothing and, yet, I loved them. The lower the cost and the rarer it was, the more excited I got.

I once revelled in wearing an electric blue, vintage boob-tube dress purchased at my local op-shop for $1 to my cousin's wedding when I was in high school — much to the dismay of some family members, who thought daring to even admit that it was second-hand, let alone cost a mere dollar, was both unladylike and mortifying.

The girls at school thought it was 'gross' that I wore vintage earrings or that my bed was second-hand from a deceased estate. (They may have been right with that last one, but I was assured that the old lady who'd had it before me didn't *die* in the bed.)

Even today, you can often find me scouring for bargains in my local op-shops, or trawling through council clean-up piles in swanky areas near me. Once you've discovered the rush of finding treasures, it's hard to see mass-manufactured stuff as alluring. There is reward in the struggle, the stories and the search.

She works hard for the money

Now, I don't know about you, but I wasn't taught a damn fucking thing about money at school. I didn't even like maths at school — even though I was quite good at it. I endured it, rather than enjoyed it. Maths felt boring and esoteric. I mean, when would I ever need to remember theorems from ancient Greece? (Turns out, never!) I didn't even do maths in year 12, opting for subjects that were going to be much more helpful when I entered the real world, such as dance, drama and ceramics. Yeah — adulthood hit *hard*.

But, I was also hell-bent on being 'successful' (defined then as having leftover money after all the bills were paid), so I hatched a plan: I was going to work hard. I decided, based on little-to-no research, that if I focused on working hard, everything would sort itself out and then (surely) my life would be perfect when I grew up. How beautiful is naïveté?

Part of this truly cooked scheme was to ensure that I did everything correctly, as often as possible. If a right way and a wrong way were possible, I would do everything in my power to ensure I didn't have to endure the humiliation and torture of being wrong. *Ever.*

This instinct went way back. In kindergarten, my parents were called into the school to have a meeting with my teacher. Fearing the worst for their 'spirited' young lass, my mother sheepishly walked into my classroom to learn that I had been completing my full week of homework and handing it back, one day after it had been given out. That way, I thought, the teacher could check it and provide feedback, before I needed to formally hand it in for marking on a Friday. Surely the most brilliantly hatched plan by any five-year-old — like, ever?! In my mind, this guaranteed I would get 100 per cent of my homework correct 100 per cent of the time *and* get to take the class silkworms home for the weekend as a reward. Genius. My teacher (and my mother) didn't agree.

They tried to explain that I couldn't get it checked ahead of time. (*Why?* I wondered. *I've done the work, and you know the answers. This is basically foolproof. Check my work for mistakes now and then give it back to me, please!*) I was told the point was to only have it checked once, and that it was okay to make mistakes. My brain didn't compute. Here I was trying to hack my success in kindergarten and I was being met with unnecessary, bureaucratic red tape.

I cried and decided you can't trust adults. The bastards always change the rules — and especially when they've worked out that you've worked them out. And let me tell you, as the eldest and only daughter, you best believe that I knew the rules.

Despite the seemingly unjust roadblocks, my plan remained unchanged: work hard, have success.

My predominately low-socioeconomic, blue-collar community (which was statistically one of the worst in New South Wales for unemployment, youth suicide, teen pregnancy and intergenerational poverty) was full of beautiful, kind, caring people. People who genuinely would give you the shirt off their back if you needed it more than they did. They showed me that you don't need to have a lot to help someone else. I was constantly surprised and inspired by their resourcefulness and care for each other, something many others (hello, billionaires!) could learn from.

I also come from a strong, matriarchal lineage, which I don't take for granted. It helped me see what working hard meant as a woman at a time where most of my friends' mums didn't work (outside the home) after they had kids. The women in my life knew how to get shit done. And they didn't prescribe to traditional gender norms. Neither my mum nor my grandmother would be put on pedestals for their cooking skills. (Mum's few attempts are all now family fables.) They didn't keep pristine houses, or keep up with the latest trends. Instead, they always worked (outside the home), so when I got to my teenage years, I quickly followed suit.

I had three jobs in school, saving my pennies like a bear preparing for the winter. By the time I finished high school, I had saved $9000. And I was very, very careful about how and where I spent it.

Myths, mirth and money musings

Okay, let me cut to the chase. It turns out, I was wrong. Working hard does not, in fact, guarantee your plans will work out perfectly. The brochure for adulthood is entirely misleading. I thought all my hard work would mean I could eat ice cream all day in my perfectly clean house and everything would be, kind of, fun?

Instead, it felt a bit like that scene in that book about a wizard by she who shall not be named, when thousands of Hogwarts admission letters fly at full force out of the fire place. But instead of letters confirming I was a wizard, it was rent renewals, reminders to get the car serviced, alerts to book in the dog's vaccination, electricity bills and rate notices. It was reminders about Pap smears, medication scripts — or have I still got repeats? — bank cards close to expiry and new car insurance premiums. And then the mental load stacked on. Have you got milk? Booked your haircut and the council hard rubbish pick up? Did you order Mum's birthday gift yet and RSVP to that event? Are you getting enough protein? Have you cancelled that gym subscription, bought blueberries, got that baby shower gift, booked flights? Have you got milk? When are you going to pick up your dry cleaning, call back your very patient aunty and go to the dentist? Is there washing in the machine? Have you got those heels resoled and ordered that new shower curtain? *Why is there no milk?!* All without any cute owls anywhere in sight!

Honestly, now I think I get why Vernon Dursley bolted the post latch shut and threw the letters into the fire. Like me trying to get to grips with the realities of adulthood (with, at the time, undiagnosed ADHD), he probably thought if he ignored them, they would all disappear. If only...

I didn't even have kids and I was fucking exhausted by the mental load. I felt like I was failing at being an adult. Surely 'adulting' wasn't meant to feel like this. The pressure was never-ending and exhausting — and I didn't even *want* to eat ice cream for breakfast like I had once dreamed of, because I knew it would make me feel bloated and sick all day.

Well, I thought, *this is shit. I'm not living like this forever, with life admin following me around like a dark cloud hovering overhead.* So, I did a few important things that changed my life.

First up, at the tender age of 21 years old, I got my first financial adviser. He worked in the same bank I worked at and, honestly, probably took me on as a charity case because I had nowhere near enough money to be considered his ideal client. He looked older than my dad, and was kind, gentle and patient. He really wanted to make sure I was set up for retirement. *Retirement?* Steve — I've just started working. That's the last thing on my mind. But, he wisely advised, if I thought about it now, I wouldn't have to again for a while. So I started making (tiny) extra contributions from my entry-level income to superannuation, and kind of then forgot it was even happening. I now (in my late 30s), have more in super than the average woman in Australia retires with (which is both exciting and horrifying simultaneously).

Another colleague at the time lovingly (yet forcefully), made me get my personal insurances sorted. *What? I'm young, fit and healthy. Surely I didn't need it yet?* She rightly pointed out that now was the perfect time to get insurance, exactly because I *was* young, fit and healthy. (Honestly — you'd think I would have learned from what happened to my dad.) But I was about to go on a girls' trip and I really didn't want another expense, so I assured her I would finalise it all when I was back. Next thing I knew, she was pulling me into a meeting room with the paperwork ready to complete before I went on the holiday, saying if I did it now, I would be fully covered should anything untoward happen when I was on my trip.

Honestly, I felt a little ambushed, and I don't like being told what to do. But I knew she always had my back. Deep down, I also knew that I — working in the insurance division of the bank — needed to practice what I preached. Given that only a year or so later I had my first medical issue (which would have affected me being able to get those insurances in place), I am eternally grateful that she made me do it. Without her insistence, insurance probably would have stayed up in that mental load cloud, hovering ominously, waiting for the right moment to rain down on me.

At the time, I owned some employee issued shares, but I wasn't investing my own money. I was hoarding it. I liked it right where I could see it, in my savings account. See, I didn't know *anything* about the share market and it felt daunting and like I was giving up control of my money. If I kept it in the bank, I could be assured that if I didn't spend it, it would be there waiting for me when I next needed my emotional, check-my-daily-balance fix.

But somewhere along that journey, I lost my way.

Firstly, I did what everyone else did and bought a car via a car loan (that's what you do, right?!). Next, more medical issues popped up and I saw a world-leading specialist, which ended up costing me about $10 000 in out-of-pocket surgery costs. Then I started dating someone who was both older and wealthier than me. Never wanting to be accused of being there 'for the money', and instead of having an honest conversation about my budget, I found myself trying to keep up and pay half of everything, *all* the time.

Quickly I found myself swimming in personal debt. Debt! I, the brilliant saver, was now...not.

Being in debt felt like I was lugging around a large, heavy, invisible boulder. Thank the Goddesses this weight was invisible, because it needed to stay a secret. I was the proud 'frugal saver' of our friend group, and I wasn't prepared to fall from grace. I was deeply embarrassed. Ashamed. I worked for a bank and I now was in debt. What the hell was happening?

After some trial and a fair bit of error, I got all my debt paid off. And do you know how I celebrated paying off my credit card? I, the person who approximately 90 per cent of the time dresses like a dishevelled pretend farmer, decided (for reasons that I genuinely cannot explain), to purchase Chanel earrings. *On my fucking credit card.*

That's right, folks. I celebrated paying off my debt by purchasing something completely fucking farcical, with debt! Oh, what a joy and delight it is to have that put on a page. I guess I thought I had 'made it'. And that's what people who've made it do, right? Really, all I had 'made' was another hole in my budget.

Finding my feet

Thankfully, my brief run-in with vanity was short-lived. I returned to my frugal ways and got more financial advice, this time to help me start investing and to put together a roadmap to save $100 000 to start my first business. I said no to things more than I said yes — because I realised I was wasting money on things I didn't value.

Secondly, I started to notice a pattern within myself. I was working hard and setting very ambitious goals. Again, this had always been my plan: work hard and success would come. I had sorted out my budget and set my goals — and I was continuing to believe they should now, like, magically manifest themselves into reality.

After a few years of feeling like I was making some progress, but also still feeling a bit stuck, I engaged a goals coach to help me take things to the next level. I've worked with her ever since. See, what I didn't realise is that most goals require actions beyond 'work hard' to be achieved. Alas, you don't just rock up to your front door one day to find your goals on your doorstep with a red ribbon around them and a congratulatory note perched on top. It takes time and effort. Bummer, right?

Again, this now is obvious to me, but at the time it was the missing ingredient in the goal-attainment elixir. Small, seemingly insignificant and boring, admin-y tasks are what help you achieve your goals. They're the tasks I really didn't feel like doing when I got home from work — the ones that didn't light me up, spark joy or look *anything* like what the influencers touted from their #livingyourbestlife posts. I wasn't frolicking on the beach with perfect hair. I wasn't in an aesthetically pleasing, colour-coordinated designer kitchen. It was just me, with messy hair, in my decrepit blue kitchen that was weirdly part of our hallway, wearing an old shitty pink fluffy robe that looked how I felt: tired.

11

Before I got someone to help me, I always found the perfect reasons why I couldn't do these tasks. And those reasons were real. By that time, I was working at an investment bank that was notorious for working you hard. I didn't 'have time', I told myself. I was too tired. I needed to get groceries, or see my friends (which is good for my mental health, I assured myself). I needed to go to the gym (good job prioritising my physical health), and I needed a bath (self-care — obviously).

I looked and found all the perfectly socially acceptable reasons to assure myself I couldn't possibly do the 'mundane, non-urgent but actually quite important if I *actually* wanted to achieve any of my fucking goals in life' tasks.

The annoying thing I learned was this: if you're looking for reasons to not do the thing, you will find them *everywhere*. These will be great reasons. You'll find the perfect excuses — and trust me, between myself and the people I've worked with, I've heard them all. Time and time again. You could spend your entire life listing out all the valid and sound arguments not to get onto it — life is littered with them.

But I now had a goals coach, and suddenly I was being held to account to get them done. I was having to add life-admin tasks to my diary like some sick game of Tetris. Attention that could have been focused on critiquing the latest *Grand Designs* episode now had to be focused on follow-up emails, paperwork, application forms and reach outs.

It all felt like such a chore — until it started to work.

Now, I am not here to pontificate on how perfect I am. I still struggle to wade through my endless to-do list. I'm still not a highly organised human. I don't now run to do admin tasks with gleeful delight. My hair is still messy and, despite a public plea, the threadbare pink (not at all fluffy) robe is still in my possession.

Nothing about my life is perfect. But, by the time I was 34, I had already started, scaled and sold my first business, been on my first mini-retirement and purchased a teeny, tiny terrace in a capital city in

Australia, on my own, without any financial support from my family or a partner.

My investment portfolio has been bubbling away for close to two decades. I've set up investments for my nieces, so when they grow up they will be given a financial leg-up in life, and I've boosted the bejesus out of my super. Money has afforded me opportunities I would never have been able to have without it.

And I haven't just secured my own financial future. I've helped thousands of people pay down millions of dollars of debt. I've helped them save to buy first homes, investment properties and homes for their single mums. They've started businesses, paid for IVF, or started or expanded their families. I've helped them get out of fear state and build healthy and positive money beliefs — so they can start investing and retire early, send their kids to the school of their choice, help their ageing parents, go on extended holidays, leave their shitty partner, leave their shitty job, write books, build a gimp room (yep!), be able to buy a yacht and sail around the world indefinitely. Stop feeling stuck. Start feeling excited. Get a game plan together and get moving on it.

We've all had moments of doubt, felt stuck and made mistakes. But, I promise, if I and all these others can do it, *you can too.*

2

DIRT

Dishing on the systems and structures that stifle our growth and feed us fibs

The one duty we owe to history is to rewrite it.

—Oscar Wilde

It is easy to pretend we live in a world where all is fair and just. But that's simply not true — especially when it comes to money. And you don't have to dig down far to see this reality. And the more you uncover, the worse it gets. Money, power and greed lead to murky decisions.

This book is designed to help you set your money world up for success, but it would be remiss of me to sell a story that we live in a world where everyone is on a level playing field, and everyone has equal access and opportunity to thrive.

If you're reading this, you probably already know that. But maybe you're not sure why, or whether it's even possible to change it. This chapter shows you how and why finances aren't just personal; instead, they're part of a system that affects us personally. By understanding how we've got where we are today, you can understand what you want to do about it tomorrow. You're boosting your financial literacy so you can change the future for you, your family and your community. To be able to do that, it's important to know what you're dealing with — and let me tell you, some of it is pretty dirty.

The roots of social injustice, exploitation and inequity spread wide and deep. And for too long, we have demonised poor people. We've treated poverty and being poor as if it's a choice, and something that's easy to avoid. The underlying assumption here is that if you wanted to be wealthy, you could be. So if you're not, either you were too lazy or stupid to make it work, or you didn't want it badly enough to make the necessary sacrifices. That's on you.

Margaret Thatcher infamously stated that poverty was simply a money management problem because 'people didn't know how to budget', and due to a 'personality defect'. Yet, history is bursting with examples of systems, laws and norms that were carefully designed to lock certain people out of opportunities to accumulate power and wealth, while offering and enabling those opportunities generously to others. And when I say 'certain people', I mean most people — the majority, in fact. But especially women, First Nations peoples, people of colour, the working class, migrants, queer and LGBTQIA+ folks, and people with disability. Basically, anyone who's not a straight, white, aristocratic man faces systemic obstacles. And that's without taking into consideration the compounding impact of having more than one of these intersecting identities.

While money is, on face value, neutral, in reality it's far more nuanced than that. Money and the systems that support its flow reflect our priorities and vision, and who and what we value — literally. On one side of the coin, some of the biggest businesses get billions in bailouts, tax breaks and government loans, justified due to the need to 'save jobs' or respond to shocks such as the pandemic. Or governments may consider them 'too big to fail' and so offer support to ensure they don't collapse and trigger broader economic issues. Yet, on the other side, people on welfare are being made to account for every dollar (Robodebt, anyone?). In the still too recent past, First Nations peoples were having their wages stolen and 'redlining' was commonplace (this was the creation of US federal government maps that prevented predominantly Black communities from accessing mortgages based on 'risk'[1]).

So strap yourself in, because we are going on a brief (but important) exploratory dig into how our economic systems (that is, the rules and institutions that decide who has power, who gets access to resources and who doesn't) deeply harm people's ability to access financial independence, especially women. I cannot cover all of these obstacles — that in itself would be its own, large, book — but the bits I narrow in on make for uncomfortable reading. Yet, we must talk about them, because gaining this knowledge is a critical part of seeing our money stories for what they are — not personal failings, but ones shaped by the world that is and was. A world that has created collective and harmful unconscious bias that's hard to shake.

Trouble and strife through the ages

About two decades before England colonised (invaded) Australia, decision makers (men) were busy putting ideas into common law that limited women's rights in marriage contracts. This theory, known as *coverture*, was quickly enshrined in other English colonies, and most strongly in the laws of the United States.[2] Like all the other patriarchal bullshit ideals, it was touted as 'care' and 'support' by ensuring women were 'under the protection of one's husband'. The reality was far less rosy. Jurist and politician, William Blackstone, renowned for describing the doctrines of English law in the 18th century, famously stated the coverture laws meant 'the very being or legal existence of the woman is suspended during her marriage'.[3]

Yes, you read that right — as if after the 'I do' bit, *bam*. She spontaneously ceased to exist right at the altar, vanishing up and into the (no doubt), caring, noble, well-meaning wings of her husband. Conveniently for him, marriage meant any property, earnings, rent, investments and even personal belongings that were once hers would be passed to his control.

According to the law, a woman would need her husband's consent to part with anything, but (predictably) he could overrule any bequests she had made. While women were busy ceasing to exist due to marriage, they were still required to do all the domestic work — including all the cooking, cleaning, child-rearing tasks and supporting of their husband's needs. (Of course, if she helped with any of his farming or business work, any profits made belonged to her husband.) Doesn't that sound exactly like the kind of 'protection' you're after, ladies? While some women were able to find ways to start businesses and make a living, in the grand scheme of things, the law wasn't on their side.

Of course, power and money have long been considered a match made in heaven. The perfect power couple if you will. For most of history, marriages had very little to do with love and much more to do with strengthening strategic alliances, building dynasties and preserving or creating wealth. Matches motivated by moolah. Some parents, desperate to make 'good use' of their offspring, had their children enter engagement contracts as young as seven[4] and married off in their early teenage years to secure property, money or status, or to pay back debts.

Catherine of Aragon (King Henry VIII's first wife) was famously betrothed at three years old. Fucking three! Just think about that for a minute. Most of us couldn't even spell our own name by then, but tiny Catherine already had her fate decided for her by a bunch of royals keen to strengthen alliances between countries. Her life was used to play out some real-life game of Battleship or chess.[5]

Of course, not all strategic moves turn out like you plan them. Catherine and Henry's infamous marriage didn't last (neither did another three of Henry's marriages). Yet, it took almost 450 years from then for Australia to recognise that forcing people through emotionally and financially taxing legal systems to prove who was responsible for the marriage falling apart wasn't the way forward, finally passing 'no-fault' divorce laws in 1975. This change resulted in a massive spike in the divorce rate in 1976. Seems the 'good old days' the *manosphere* (usually young, white, 'Christian', single men who've swapped real life experiences for a mic and a podcast) are obsessed with wanting us to return to wasn't always a peachy partnered paradise after all.

Remember: the whole idea of women having agency and autonomy wasn't always a legal right. (We can save our conversation about what's legal and what's reality for another day.)

Let's jump forward to when women did start to win more legal rights. Yes, white women in Australia could vote and stand in federal elections from 1902, a right they'd held in South Australia since 1895. (First Nations peoples were excluded from federal voting rights until 1962.) But even the wins in South Australia only got across the line thanks to a miscalculated blunder. In an attempt to shoot the whole 'women should have rights' thing down, a (not so gentle) man named Ebenezer Ward thought he would be clever. See, the original Bill they were trying to get legislated included a clause that prevented women from becoming a member of parliament. Ebenezer thought by taking that clause out, the entire bill would surely now be so preposterous, it would get thrown in the bin. (*Can you imagine giving women the right to vote and allowing them in parliament? Scoff. Scoff. Perfect plan, this will totally work. Clever us.*) Alas for Ebenezer, the whole thing spectacularly backfired — and the bill was passed. I would low-key love a time machine to take me back to the exact moment he and his co-conspirators discovered their cunning plan to keep women seen but not heard, became a colossal cock-up.

From there, many may have hoped that these 'wins' for women would mean further progress would be swift and effective. Surprise — it wasn't. Other laws and societal expectations kept the handbrake on most women's ability to access economic independence — because, what happens when someone gets it? They get choice. With access to their own money, they have the choice to stay, but also to leave. They aren't stuck in quicksand anymore. The women before us had to fight hard for rights that were given to men at birth.

Why the accidental gender studies history lesson? Because laws, prejudices and societal expectations left strong underpinnings, like deeply burrowed roots that stay in place long after the tree has fallen. The mark of these expectations can still be seen generations after the initial pain was inflicted — especially when it comes to money. Too many women are still being told the very idea of even wanting money is distasteful and unladylike. Instead, women have been told for millennia that their greatest marker of success in life has little to do with personal achievements or accolades from effort, education, perseverance or creativity. Instead, success is if a man chooses to marry you.

If you aren't picked, you've failed. In a fate worse than death, you'll surely wither into a haggard old spinster who, given you aren't going to make babies, is of little societal value. You'll be an embarrassment to your family (who worked hard to make you marriage material!) and you'll probably wind up being eaten by your cat colony after your death.

Alone.

All of this messaging feeds into a primal fear for us tribal creatures — the fear of being alone. And it's a clever marketing tactic. Don't find a partner and have kids? You'll be lonely, miserable and sad forever. Jesus. What if I fall and no-one is around to help me? Who will look after me when I'm old? What if I really want the chocolate that's in the cupboard, but can't be assed getting off the couch? What if I die alone? Fuck. Interestingly, data has shown that unmarried, childless women are actually the happiest subgroup of them all — them and their cats.

Now I don't care who, or if, you marry. I don't mind if you have kids or not. I attempted to start my own cat colony in 2020 with a one-eyed feline named Frank and, like mine, your choices are yours. Aren't they? I mean, *are* they?

Give it up for the women who came before us

It might be easy to forget that women alive today (maybe even your mum, your grandmother or that lovely old lady up the street) lived in a time where they had little physical or financial autonomy. Hell, millions of women all around the world today *still* have little to no autonomy. The fact that women in Australia can have a bank account in our own name, decide what career we want, who we shag and how we invest our money is a relatively new phenomenon. I grew up truly believing I could have it all. I just needed to work hard and it would happen. The world was my metaphorical oyster, and I just needed to dive deep enough to get it.

Of course, as I outline in chapter 1, it wasn't exactly as simple as that (and I am not quite sure you can have it *all* at the same time, without serious stress and overwhelm). But the women before us faced systems and laws that *literally* locked them out of having financial independence. These laws limited their choices and kept them stuck. They were fed horseshit ideas that women aren't as smart or capable as men when it came to managing money. They couldn't open bank accounts, apply for a credit card or take on mortgages without a male signatory. Their lives were controlled in a way I don't think many of us could really understand today.

Decisions on aspects such as marriage, work and babies profoundly impacted their financial future. You might already know it was common practice for women to give up their paid jobs when they got married. But did you realise that getting married could mean women were actually forced out of the workforce? Not that long ago, being married meant women were automatically deemed 'retired' and ineligible to keep their position. Some went to great lengths to hide their status, slipping their wedding ring off on the way to work and being careful to not accidentally reveal their nuptials so they didn't get the sack.

The 'marriage bar' existed for women employed by the Australian Government until 1966.[6] Once you said 'I do', you said 'I don't' to keeping a job in the public service with an income of your own. Your career prospects, and any hope of having wealth of your own, went down the toilet. (But you should be so happy — someone chose you! Now, when are you going to have kids?)

Having children still disproportionately impacts women's financial futures. It affects their income capacity, careers and retirement funds — even today, women take a massive financial hit if they start, or expand, their family. This is much more so than for men.

Societal expectations continue to put most of the (unpaid) caring responsibilities on the mother. Although more men are now taking on more responsibilities, on average women and mothers are still doing the lion's share of unpaid work.[7] Even today, the 'motherhood penalty' sees earnings for new mothers drop by 55 per cent in the first five years after a child's birth; men's are unchanged.[8]

Older women today, who are likely to have spent a large part of their life in unpaid caring roles, are likely to retire with considerably less to live off while also statistically being likely to live longer.[9] That puts them at far higher risk of ending their life in poverty.

It must have been a breath of fresh air when, in 1961, married women could access the contraceptive pill and finally have some choice over their body. What an absolute luxury—which is perhaps the reason it also came with a 27.5 per cent 'luxury tax'. Yes, making decisions about one's own body came with added expense, and yet it was a small price to pay, providing as it did, the ability to decide if and when you had children.

The women who came before us spent centuries advocating for the same rights and access to financial resources as men. Here are some of their more recent wins in Australia:

- *1969:* Women are granted equal pay in instances where they were assessed as doing *exactly* the same work as men in traditionally roles; all other women received the nationally instituted 85 per cent of men's wages.
- *1972:* 'Luxury tax' on the pill is removed.
- *1972:* Landmark equal pay for equal value ruling, with women and men undertaking similar work that had similar value eligible for the same rate of pay.
- *1973:* Supporting mother's benefit established (with single mothers eligible).
- *1973:* Equal minimum wage granted to all Australians, regardless of sex.
- *1974:* Australia's first refuge for women and children opens in Glebe, New South Wales.
- *1974:* 'Breadwinner' component of men's wage removed.
- *1975:* 'No-fault' divorce added to *The Family Law Act (Cth).*
- *1977:* The *Anti-Discrimination Act 1977 (NSW)* enables women to access banking, insurance, grants, loans, credit or finance.
- *1984:* The *Sex Discrimination Act 1984 (Cth)* passes.
- *1992:* Superannuation is made compulsory (with some exceptions).
- *2017:* The *Marriage Amendment (Definition and Religious Freedoms) Act 2017* passes, legalising marriage equality.

- *2019:* GST on sales of tampons (finally) removed.
- *2025:* Superannuation contributions included on Commonwealth Paid Parental Leave payments.

These gains, and others like them, are rarely won without a fight. Sticking with the status quo — especially for those holding on to power — is still an insidious part of our collective psyche.

Money in the wild: Gemma (she/her)

- **Age:** 42.
- **Situationship:** In a relationship — live together.
- **Income:** $140 000.
- **Current savings:** $2000.
- **Current relationship with money:** Healing, growing, in debt.
- **Money monster's name:** 'Spendy Samantha'. Buying things and experiences makes me feel more abundant. I still give in, but I'm trying to put Financially Savvy Sage in the driver's seat more often. (See chapter 4 for more on naming your money monster.)

What debts do you currently have?
Credit cards/buy now pay later, personal loan, HECS/HELP.

Do you save or invest?
I'm saving $1000 per month. I would like to increase that but debt payments are holding me back.

What's one piece of money advice you wish you knew sooner?
This isn't money advice but — no-one is going to save you! You need your own money plan and to build for yourself. Of course,

if a partner can then help with that, great, but that can't be relied on (and relationships aren't a guarantee).

What was your biggest 'ouch' money moment, and what came from it?
Currently, being in debt. I pay one thing off and then promptly overspend/start the cycle again. I want out!

What has shaped your relationship with money the most?
Financial trauma and growing up in terrible poverty. My family had no money and we relied on charities for food, leading to a scarcity mindset, lots of stress and despair around money. I'm unlearning the messages of waiting for someone to save me. Also, not having any role models at all for financial achievement growing up, I didn't believe in myself at all. I didn't believe that I could buy a house or have financial security. (I'm still working on this.)

What does 'financial wellbeing' mean to you?
Security in the form of owning a home, feeling in control financially, making good decisions that align with my goals, and having the freedom of choice.

Did you have a big 'oh shit' moment that made you realise you had to learn more about money?
I had many 'oh shit' moments, but particularly watching so many people around me get ahead when I felt I had been treading water for so long. I know the people around me have had a completely different start to life, get family support and so on, and the cost of living in Sydney is huge, but it's still hard not to be hitting milestones that I would like to.

Have you ever looked at your bank account and thought, WTF? How did it get this low?

Yes, absolutely. It's so easy to spend. I've often used debt to bail me out (which I then have to deal with later), which is a habit I badly want to break.

Anything else you'd like to share?

It's so important to have a non-judgemental and inclusive space to learn about finances in. I've carried a lot of shame around money, and feeling like this needed to be hidden. So feeling safe to share and be open is honestly so healing. I hope that I also continue to build a belief in myself that I can do it.

You can't sit with us (unless you're already rich)

Even today, learning about money often falls outside the traditional education system, leaving it to be taught at home or in community. But if the ones teaching you weren't even allowed in the gates for most of their lifetime, is it any wonder you might still have serious knowledge gaps?

While some of the clear exclusionary systems that locked people out of opportunities have been dismantled, barriers still exist that have a similar discriminatory effect. One of them is complexity. If you've ever tried to dip your toe into the money world and stumped up enough courage to try to read any sort of financial document, at some point in the process you likely thought, *WTAF does this even mean?!* You may then have convinced yourself that you're the idiot, that this is clearly way too hard and that you're out of your depth.

We've made understanding finances elitist and exclusionary. The industry has created a language all of its own — full of acronyms and jargon that have most people questioning their comprehension skills. For too long, industry insiders have made you feel inferior for not understanding their secret code. They've made money and financial markers seem so complex and bewildering by design that mistakes seem inevitable. In most instances, people are so worried they will get it wrong or miss something important that they freeze with fear and decide it's all too hard. They either do nothing or decide to leave it to the 'professionals'. *Yes*, they think, *that's what I will do. I will call in the financial cavalry to sort it out for me. They can help me make heads or tails of it.*

But here's the catch. Most people can only access financial advice once they *already* have money. Learning how to grow your money—particularly from the ground up—will cost you dearly. The irony that those who can cough up the cash to get expert help are also those who already have the money is not lost on me. But how are you meant to have the money to begin with? You aren't, and so you can't.

And this is all continuing while the wealthiest forge forward, probably with an army of financial experts that help them build bigger portfolios, pay less tax (legally) and, in many instances, benefit from situations that are hurting you—including higher interest rates, increasing house prices and higher share prices.

Many financially wealthy people don't have to worry about the things you and I might. If house prices keep rising, their equity in their properties goes up—which means they can borrow against it to buy more properties. Higher share prices mean their portfolio value has increased, and shareholder profit in the form of dividends can be reinvested to buy more shares. And when interest rates go up, they get more money from their money in cash. The rich get richer.

In contrast, when house prices keep going up, those on the other side take even longer to get a foot on the property ladder. Many are forced to rent for longer, with little security or rights, as increases in rent further reduce their ability to save for a house.

When share prices are high, you aren't able to buy as many units with your money. Owning fewer units or shares logically means a reduced cut of any dividends or distributions. And when interest rates rise and you have been able to secure a mortgage, your required repayments increase — forcing you to find cash from somewhere else to pay for the extra cost. This means you have less to save or invest (which, annoyingly, would make you more money).

This is the reality of the money world. And, yes, it is undeniably unfair.

Now, this is not to say all wealthy people are evil rich bastards who would sell their mother for a good price (although some might). Indeed, this book is all about helping you have more money. However, in order to do that you have to understand the system you're working with. This is a system in which money makes money — and it's really fucking expensive to be poor.

Who wants to be a billionaire? Yeah, nah

There is nothing wrong with wanting money. It's okay to want security, freedom and choice. You're allowed to want holidays, to be able to buy a coffee without feeling guilty and to help people you love. You should be able to look after yourself — so you can say 'See ya!' to a job you hate, a relationship that's no good or a situation that doesn't feel right. And money can, to an extent, buy you the ability to do that.

Most people want a life that is financially secure and gives them their version of 'enough'. And while everyone has a different version of what is enough, most don't aspire to become one of the wealthiest people in the world. But somewhere on the capitalism freight train, I fear we veered onto the wrong track. See, I want you to be wealthy. I'm here to teach you how to do it. But I want to make it really clear with you that this book isn't going to make you a billionaire. It's not. I don't think any money book could make that a reality for you.

We are living in a time of extremes. Some people (billionaires) have more money than they know what to do with, yet others live in poverty. Surely this is an indication that the system is still fundamentally inequitable and unjust. Many of the richest people on earth have benefited from exploitation, colonialism and injustice. It's dirty money.

There is rich and then there is *rich*. A billion dollars is one thousand million. I mean, let's be real — who needs that much money?

No-one.

And yet it's getting worse. Wealth inequality has widened further over recent years. Figures from 2020 reveal the richest 20 per cent of Australians owned 63 per cent of total household wealth, while the lowest quintile owned less than 1 per cent of all household wealth.[10] Anyone who wants to defend the rights of billionaires, while watching ordinary people, on ordinary incomes, still not being able to afford a roof over their head, needs to really pause and think why.

But billionaires, many of whom came from inter-generational wealth, continue to amass wealth using political donations and media ownership to reinforce the systems that benefit them and allow them to hold on to power.

So, no, I don't want you to become a billionaire. But the capitalist system as a whole, and the way it continues to benefit the rich while feeding off the poor, is another barrier to get your head around on your journey to just what 'enough' means to you.

So there's the dirt — now what?

Starting this book with a critical review of the ways systems have impacted (and continue to impact) wealth outcomes across society was important, because for far too long we've been told to accept total and complete responsibility for our financial situation and outcomes — completely disregarding the very real barriers put in place by powerful people. We've been fed the BS narrative that, 'You could have had it all, but you chose coffee and smashed avo instead'. Shame. How different your financial world could have been if you only did better.

Now you can see that it's not quite that simple. The system isn't fair. Fat cats are still influencing the world today. Maybe, just maybe, you can now see that you were probably not given the right conditions in which to thrive. Even if you're young, these impacts linger.

It's time to take back your power — and your patch. If dirt is what everything grows from, the great news is you get to decide what grows in yours. You can decide what serves you and so can stay, and what's toxic and gets ditched. I will not pretend the money world is always easy or fair. Instead, I'm here to give you some gardening gloves, a shovel and the knowledge you need to start digging.

Money in the wild: Saanvi (she/her)

- **Age:** 42.
- **Situationship:** It's complicated.
- **Income:** $220 000.
- **Current savings:** $10 000.
- **Current relationship with money:** Perfunctory, theoretical, sufficient.
- **Money monster's name:** 'F*ck it Fran'. I have systems to help calm her down, especially during sales seasons, but she still bowls me over with 'you deserve it' purchases and wins when booking holidays and travel.

Have you ever had to use your emergency savings, and how did it make you feel?
No, not yet. I've gotten by via luck in the past.

What does life look like right now?
My career is well paying and stable, but not my passion, and I'm scared to leave as I see the cost of living crisis. At home, 'it's complicated' doesn't begin to cover it all, but having that level of income has shielded me from what could be a worse time. I could afford a good lawyer for my divorce (which was amicable). My mental health has really become worse as I've gotten older. (Yay for being a woman and dem hormones messing with our systems.) I have also come from growing up below the poverty line, so I know that I can survive with very little, but once you have pulled yourself up it is very hard to let go of this income.

Do you save or invest?
I have a mortgage so I put money in the offset. I guess that is 'saving' but differently to when I was younger and had accounts for 'future' purchases. I have some shares and I have almost maxed my personal super concessional contributions (including any unused carry-forward contributions). I am now investing in ETFs for investment outside of super. I do have an investment property and sold one recently. I am not sure where to go next. I know I need to work out a future and goals to be able to move forward, but I am in a state of decision paralysis.

What is a past money decision you're proud of?
Salary sacrificing super when I was a graduate engineer 15 years ago—thank you, graduate me.

What's one piece of money advice you wish you knew sooner?

Set up a budget that automates your money for the month—I'm still not quite there.

What has shaped your relationship with money the most?

I think the family dynamic and my cultural background. Finance was something that 'grown ups' spoke about and didn't share with the younger generation, which meant I had to go elsewhere to learn and luckily I did. I had to grow up quickly and that meant I was able to ask questions and discuss money with like-minded people. Unfortunately, the culture I come from and people in my family are also very jealous. They think I 'should' act a certain way with my money now that I have achieved what I have achieved.

What does 'financial wellbeing' mean to you?

Freedom of choice. Freedom of life. Freedom from pain.

Have you ever looked at your bank account and thought, WTF? How did it get this low?

Yes, regularly. I don't really check my account balance.

Anything else you'd like to share?

A lot of guilt can come with money (having it and not having it). I now understand that there is luck—luck in where you were born, and luck if you have generational wealth. I do think that knowing I grew up with nothing sometimes plays on my mind when I just want to quit it all and live in social housing and get a pension.

3

DIG

Unearthing what shapes our money beliefs and behaviours beneath the surface

He who fears he will suffer, already suffers from his fear.

—*Michel de Montaigne*

We money experts love to pretend that money is rational, logical and unemotional stuff. But the truth of it is, money is much more complex—and emotionally charged—than that. So for you to build wealth, you first must dig into what you believe about money, and understand where these beliefs come from and how they might be holding you back.

I call this process a 'money memoir' — a historical look back based on your personal knowledge and experiences. This exercise isn't to shame you; instead, it's the very opposite. It's a chance to critically assess how different influences you have been exposed to help build internal narratives. You can dig deeper and find answers to help you break unhelpful thoughts and patterns that keep you stuck in a loop. It's also your chance to reclaim some power.

Because what you think about money dictates how you behave with it. How you behave with it often dictates how much of it you have. And how much you have often dictates what you can (or can't) do in life.

As you move through this chapter, I invite you to be curious and kind to yourself. You likely have big emotions buried somewhere deep down and away. Like the corner of the yard where your family pets lay, this place might be sad and sombre — but also full of rich memories. Now, this isn't to suggest you should exhume the bones of your dog or family cat (please don't!), but this is the time to dig, vulnerably and bravely, into that metaphorical dark and quiet corner you might have been trying to stay away from. It's time to find answers.

Dirt poor, or poor dirt?

Ever killed a plant? Same. You bring it home brimming with pride and anticipation. You buy a cute pot for it to live in and promise yourself, 'I will look after this one. This one's gonna make it'. But then life gets busy. Soon enough, it's not getting what it needs. You forget to water it, the soil is zapped of nutrients, and it's not getting enough sunshine to give it energy. Slowly but surely, the plant starts to wither. Then it dies.

I'm sure the plant wanted to survive — it just wasn't given the right conditions to grow in. It doesn't matter that the pot you bought for it was really expensive (and perfectly matched your house decor!), or that you set reminders to water it and then forgot. The key ingredients for it to thrive were missing. It didn't stand a chance.

It's exactly the same with your money. Just like with plants, your money needs attention, care, patience, sustenance, energy, a little bit of luck (and, of course, some shit thrown in for good measure) to grow. Without the right combination of these elements, it's very hard for almost anything to thrive.

In this nature analogy, think of your money beliefs being a bit like composting. These beliefs come from years of experiences with money that get piled onto a heap over time. You need to take that pile, no matter how rotten you might think it is, and break it down so those memories and lessons can regenerate into something that will grow stronger and faster than ever before.

What once may have felt like a giant pile of decay and waste (including wasted opportunities, wasted ideas, wasteful spending and wasteful waiting) can now become the basis for new, fertile ground.

This works because the first stage of composting is literally just creating a pile (continuing the metaphor, your experiences and external influences), and then getting clever little organisms to start munching away and turning the contents of the pile into smaller pieces (your brain neurons creating ideas and beliefs that you can rationalise and make sense of).

Then, the heat starts to rise (hello, emotions!) and you can start breaking everything down, or letting go of what you need to and building new neural pathways.

The last stage of composting is called *maturation*, which understandably takes the longest. As you uncover insights and have 'aha' (or, more likely, 'oh shit') moments about yourself in this chapter, remember that transformation, just like compost, doesn't happen instantly. Overriding long-held beliefs and breaking habits takes time — and work. While progress may feel slow, as you keep at it, you'll start to see small, but important shifts. Keep munching. Soon the pile won't feel so heavy.

Trust me when I say that I've worked with many people over the years who want to skip this bit and head straight to investing, but let me tell you: this is the vital preparation work that does (or undoes) all the rest. Promise. So let's start to explore what might have shaped your money beliefs and stories so far.

Where do our money beliefs come from?

Culture Family Friends

Industry norms

Religion or spiritual beliefs

Parents and caregivers

Media Education Values

Money behaviours observed

Workplace dynamics

Trauma

Societal expectations

Location

Colleagues

Loss or grief

Risk tolerance Marketing

Neurobiology

Legal systems

Gender

Cognitive bias

Financial education

Intimate relationships

Global events

Intersectionality or marginalisation

Identity

Social media

Peers

Socioeconomic environment

Government

Accessibility

Like most things in life, no one thing, belief or behaviour is going to be the reason you aren't where you want to be. However, research has clearly shown that the core behaviours that impact how you behave with money as an adult are often formed in childhood. Your beautiful baby brain was like a sponge, absorbing everything quickly and easily. By age seven, you're likely to have already formed some ideas and concepts relating to finance.[1] The experiences and environment you were exposed to set the foundation for you to learn how to feel, think and act in different situations. You quickly learned from those around you, adopting the behaviours, values, cultural norms and practices you saw.

However, a few problems with this emerge when it comes to money. I explore this in the next section, but let's first look at an example.

Money in the wild: Kath (she/her)

- **Age:** 48.
- **Situationship:** Single.
- **Income:** $195000.
- **Current savings:** $38000.
- **Current relationship with money:** Wary, improving, respectful.
- **Money monster's name:** My money monster doesn't have a name, but it does rear its ugly head when my resilience is low — if I'm tired or feeling down. It's been the cause of 'doubling down' on mistakes, but I'm a lot better at resisting it than I used to be. (See chapter 4 for more on naming your money monster.)

Have you ever had to use your emergency savings, and how did it make you feel?

I had a couple of extreme vet bills last year. If I'm being very honest, I was a little resentful having to reach into those hard-won savings. But, at the same time, I was so incredibly relieved that I had the option to do so. Fur babies are family!

Having a little buffer makes 'anxious me' unclench a wee bit. I've been slapped by the universe in the past (hello, consequences of my own actions and bad decisions!) when I had no buffer. This little bit of security has been hard won and definitely makes me feel safer.

What does life look like right now?

I'm in a job that stresses me to the back teeth, but I love it and I love the people I work with! Plus, it pays well. I'm renting, and thinking about maybe (maybe!!) buying a little place of my own in the next 6 to 12 months (but, *goddamn*, it's hard as a single person with cozzie livs and everything else).

What is a past money decision you're proud of?

About 18 months ago, I needed a new car ('need' is only half-subjective; my previous car had been in the family for over 16 years!). I flirted very hard with the idea of buying an electric vehicle. I don't have charging infrastructure in the building I live in, and oh my holy god was it expensive. I came so very close to going ahead with it, before having a very crystallising moment in which I realised I just don't value cars enough to spend that much money on one. I switched tact and got an ex-demo model instead, and I paid about half the price. Still a lot of money, but I'm planning on having this car for the next 16 years, so all in all not a bad decision, I think!

What's one piece of money advice you wish you knew sooner?
I wish I'd been brave enough to start investing sooner so I'd
had lots more years to take advantage of compound interest!

**What is your biggest 'ouch' money moment, and what came
from it?**
I spent my entire career living pay cheque to pay cheque.
(Because you can't take it with you when you die and why
worry about tomorrow?! Yikes.) And then I lost my job — with no
savings and nothing to fall back on. I feel like the universe had
been giving me little nudges to pull my socks up and be a bit
more serious with money. I ignored everything, so it sent a *big*
life lesson. It was brutal, but I learned from it. I now try harder to
listen to my gut when making career decisions (red flags exist
for a reason, people!) and I have some savings tucked away
so if, god forbid, I found myself in the same situation, I'd have
breathing space and wouldn't have to jump straight into full
strength panic.

What has shaped your relationship with money the most?
My relationship with money was definitely shaped by childhood
trauma, coupled with a lack of practical education and the
whole belief pattern that money is somehow shameful or
'gauche' to talk about.

What does 'financial wellbeing' mean to you?
To me, financial wellbeing is rooted in freedom, individuality
and security. That includes the freedom from anxiety and worry,
and the freedom to make choices based on what's 'best'
(whatever that looks like), not based on what I can afford. Being
safe, stable and secure, and not being reliant on anyone, is the
element of financial wellbeing I crave the most!!

What's a financial goal you're working towards right now?
Growing my savings so I can afford a deposit on a little flat of my own.

You win the lotto. What do you do?
I'd buy a terrace house (not a flat!) with outdoor space for a dog and I'd travel. Anywhere, everywhere—my only stipulation would be nothing below first class, thank you very much!!

Then I'd buy myself a little treat (maybe nice jewellery and a holiday?), and I'd make a few anonymous donations to my friends and favourite charities. Then, hopefully, I'd have a little bit leftover to stick in my investment account.

Did you have a big 'oh shit' moment that made you realise you had to learn more about money?
My slap from the universe was the beginning of me changing my attitude towards money. But my realisation that I needed to learn more about money has been more of a slow burn. It's been a gradual realisation that I can't just keep coasting along and hoping for the best; instead, I actually have to open my eyes and get in the driver's seat if I want my future to be different to my past.

'Don't touch the iron, it's hot': Learning from painful memories

Turns out, you can respond to a warning not to touch a hot iron in two ways. You can stay well away from it—the instruction alone is enough for you to know it's a bad idea to go near it. Or, like me at about age five, you can ignore the warning, take fate into your own (literal) hands and decide to touch the iron to confirm it is actually hot.

Either way, you'll likely keep a wide berth of any hot irons in the future. I only needed to grab the iron once to discover why the warning was issued. The scolding from both the heat and my mother made sure I never did it again.

More often than not, the things you remember about money from your childhood are intense, negative and emotionally painful memories. They become your 'hot iron' moments.

Perhaps the only time you remember hearing your parents talk about money was when they were arguing about it. Discussions about how money was spent, why a decision was made without the other being consulted, or why money was being used for something 'unnecessary' or 'frivolous' may quickly have turned into heated debates. As a child, you may have found it hard to reconcile why the people you loved the most were fighting with each other, over a concept that didn't make much sense to you. An internalised belief that money equals conflict can easily come from such experiences. You may now never want to talk about money to anyone, let alone someone you love — because your experiences have shown you that talking about money leads to arguments. So you avoid it.

Or perhaps you (like me) were constantly told that 'we can't afford it'. You became hyperaware of the fact that there wasn't enough money to go round, and now you have a belief system that is fearful and scarcity-driven. You might be scared to take risks or do something new, because you have a deep-seated fear (no matter how much you earn or own) that you'll never have enough. You might feel guilty spending money on things that aren't an *absolute* necessity, because it feels wasteful. These beliefs can stop you from moving forward on your goals, because you are fearful of loss, or they can create spending-guilt spirals.

On the other end of the spectrum, you may have grown up in a world with *plenty* of money. Having more than enough meant you got what you wanted, when you wanted it. Maybe your parents worked hard and felt guilty about it — so they spent money in an attempt to buy back some of the guilt. Perhaps you got used to being the person who had the latest thing, and the person who others wanted to be like — and you liked how that made you feel. You got used to spending and never needing to worry about it, because it wasn't important to get across the finer details. You may have built a belief system that money was limitless, or that you were entitled to have exactly what you wanted, when you wanted it — or even that love, attention or approval can be bought.

I've worked with many people over the years who tell me one 'hot iron' moment stands out for them in their childhood — a moment or experience that shaped their beliefs and behaviours from then on. Like the person who told me she watched as her mum's bank card was declined at the grocery store. She became hyperaware of her mother's humiliation as the shop attendant had to take the groceries back out of their trolley. For her, money equalled shame and humiliation. Or the person who watched their family farm go bankrupt and their life flipped on its head — forcing their parents out of work and their home. For them, money plus financial trouble equals your life being ripped apart. Or the person who was woken unexpectedly in the middle of the night so they could flee a dangerous home, leaving behind prized and loved treasures. Their life lesson? Everything might be taken away from me at any moment.

Some of these experiences are large, life-altering events. Other times, they are small but impactful moments. Do you have a 'hot iron' money memory?

Activity: Your 'hot iron' moment

Reflecting on your own 'hot iron' money moments, what emotions come up for you? What internal beliefs did you create from that experience? How have these beliefs shaped your decisions to date? What do you think your brain was trying to do — for example, keep you safe, avoid discomfort and/or retain control?

Dig a little deeper

You need to dig further into two key issues when considering your early childhood experiences with money. Firstly, you need to uncover what you were shown and, secondly, you need to consider how you are now hardwired to react.

Lived experience

Most money lessons that children (often accidentally) witness aren't great. They see stress, big emotions, relationship breakdowns, hardship, instability and conflict. Even when parents think they are doing a great job of sheltering their kids from financial stress, many underestimate just how much those sponge-like bambino brains are picking up. What they don't often see is good money practices being role-modelled openly. This could be because:

- Their parents don't have those skills to show them.
- Doing financial admin with kids around is (I assume), a fucking nightmare.

But at some point, somewhere, somehow, money admin of some variety happened in your childhood. I'm sure most parents and caregivers would have preferred to eat glass than try to update their budget, explain and pay bills, or hunt for a better deal for their car insurance, internet or super provider, while their children screeched around the house leaving chaos, destruction and deathly-LEGO pieces in their wake. It's hardly a conducive environment for those tasks to get done, and kids generally aren't overly excited about watching their parents do boring, adult-y paperwork.

But that means you may have never seen your parents carefully budgeting out money for different areas of your family life, quietly adding to their savings or paying down debt. Most people aren't shown the work and practical steps it takes to make a financial goal a reality. We shelter children, either as an act of love or as a form of sanity preservation, from the practical realities of the financial world they will one day enter. This often means that when they get there, they feel like they have been dropped on a foreign planet — with no idea what to do or where to go or how to speak the language.

Activity: Your childhood money admin

When it comes to money and life admin in your family, what were you exposed to growing up? Was it done in front of you? Explained to you? Were you included in it? Or did your parents do this kind of admin without you noticing, understanding or being aware of it? What impact did that have? If you have kids in your life, how might you want it to be different for them?

Negativity bias

In every aspect of life, negative experiences are more memorable than positive ones. We are hardwired to not only look out for danger, but remember the experience of it deeply and more acutely than something that felt safe and positive. This makes complete sense — in our quest as a species to survive, our brains had to remember what to avoid in the future. *Don't eat those berries; they killed Marge last year. Don't swim when the water levels are high; Carlos nearly drowned when he did. Be careful storing spears; Li accidentally speared their leg last summer and then died from the fall out.* *Brain makes mental note to remember.* It's a pretty clever evolutionary hack.

Research has shown this learning starts early, with infants more likely to be influenced by negative things going on around them than positive things.[2] Preschool-aged children are already able to draw on past experiences to make sense of a current negative situation, and they are much more likely to consider past events when they are experiencing something negative over something positive.[3] Is it any wonder you might have created strong emotional connections and beliefs relating to negative money experiences you were exposed to as a child? Your brain was doing its darnedest to keep you safe.

But here is the wildly unhelpful thing. While this safety-first factory setting may have kept you from the clutches of a sabre-toothed cat or ensured you didn't dive off a cliff onto rocks below, that threat-alerting, fear-inducing mechanism inside your brain is, more often than not, keeping you *stuck with your money.*

Mumma's ~~boy~~ girl, Daddy's ~~girl~~ boy

What you learned about money growing up is highly likely to have been based on your gender and stereotypical gender norms. Research shows parents are more likely to have money conversations at home earlier with boys than girls, while girls are 'trained to be financially dependent to seek safety and security rather than become risk takers'.[4]

Another survey showed the difference in specifically *what* they were taught — girls were more likely to be shown how to manage money responsibly (budgeting and how to track spending), while boys were more likely to be taught how to grow their wealth (including investing, taxes and credit scores). It also revealed that mothers were likely to teach their daughters about money, and fathers their sons.[5]

This gendered financial-literacy-gap baton is being passed down from one generation to the next. Fathers pass on their knowledge to their sons, and mothers to their daughters. (The survey offered no insights on what happens if you had a single parent, parents of the same gender, if you are non-binary or gender-diverse.) Think about what this means. If you're a woman, you are likely to have learned about money from your mother, and she's likely to have learned about money from hers. The problem with this is her mother (your grandmother) was unlikely to have had much experience with or exposure to financial systems or products. (Remember that whole 'stop working when you get married and don't even think about getting a bank account or mortgage of you own' thing?!) Chances are, your mum wasn't taught financial skills in her formative years, and her early childhood experiences were rooted in the stereotypes of the day. And so the cycle of teaching girls how to stay safe and financially dependent, while boys are shown how to make and grow their money, becomes engrained, intergenerationally.

It's also important to note that other factors beyond gender — including race, culture, education levels and life events (be it illness or death in the family, or events such as natural disasters, war and political instability) — will influence what level of financial education you receive, and what money trauma is passed down from one generation to the next.

Activity: Your gendered learnings

Who taught you about money growing up? What were you taught? What money beliefs did you internalise from this?

Do you know much about what shaped your parents' views of money? Who taught them and what life events shaped their beliefs? How did that manifest in how they did or didn't make decisions with money?

Money in the wild: Lara (she/her)

- **Age:** 26.
- **Situationship:** In a relationship—living together.
- **Income:** $58 000.
- **Current savings:** $14 000.
- **Current relationship with money:** Ever-changing.
- **Money monster's name:** 'Anxious Anne'—she stops me from buying things I actually need and which would save me a heap of time and energy and are definitely worth the purchase. And Impulsive Isla—she tells me to do things because someone else is doing them, and they're usually food related.

Have you ever had to use your emergency savings, and how did it make you feel?
I haven't yet. I have often thought about how it would make me feel. I think I would feel a bit stressed that I needed to alter my plans to top it up again, while feeling extremely grateful that I had that buffer and didn't need to rely on others or debt to get me through.

What debts do you currently have?
HECS/HELP.

What does life look like right now?
Career-wise, I am really enjoying my job. I'm in a positive work environment working closely with many women. I would like to earn more money, and am taking an extra day a week at work. It's time to redo my budget and get a regular investment set up.

I live with my partner who is away a lot, which gives me space to grow, but is challenging with budgeting for changing habits when he is away versus when he is home. I wish I had a tiny bit more money to spend on household maintenance—nothing fancy, just small upgrades.

In terms of money, I update my budget when needed and have taken the base of the Evergreen Money Club spreadsheet[6] and adapted it to better suit my needs, creating my own category system for my bank accounts while retaining the original spending categories, and adding a few simple future-focused tabs. I'm currently updating my spreadsheet so I can put in my before-tax salary, and use the ATO tax tables to correctly calculate the final salary I will receive in my bank account, while also being able to adapt this to take into account the different tax after salary sacrificing money to super. This is a great learning experience!

Do you save or invest?

Yes, I am saving for a house deposit with my partner. I have invested a lump sum that I had put aside and have planned to incorporate a regular dollar-cost averaging (DCA—see chapter 8) investing strategy when I take on an additional day at work per week.

What is a past money decision you're proud of?

Taking the steps to invest some money in a way where I felt comfortable and understood the risks. I did the research first and when I was happy with my decision and 50 per cent scared of taking action, I took action! And guess what? Nothing blew up.

What's one piece of money advice you wish you knew sooner?
Look at your bank accounts. Specifically, look to see where your money is going and then rank your satisfaction with your purchase. This really opened my eyes to things I could do without and allowed me to reflect on my choices and make informed decisions in the future that make me feel good in the short and long term.

What has shaped your relationship with money the most?
Family. My family never really spoke about money. I knew we didn't have heaps when I was a kid, but we had enough to do the small things (like going to the cafe once a week for an iced chocolate *or* a pastry and having nice cheese for our sandwiches). My mum always wanted to spend money (within reason) and my dad wanted to save it, but without a clear purpose, so I didn't really understand much about the purpose of money and what it was being spent on—I don't think I really understood the concept of rent or a mortgage.

What does 'financial wellbeing' mean to you?
Having enough money to not be worried about the small stuff—like getting an extra grocery item if you need it for your recipe. Having a stable income to afford a home for yourself and your family. Having a place for friends to gather and make memories together that is safe and reliable.

Did you have a big 'oh shit' moment that made you realise you had to learn more about money?
I was at a work presentation and they were talking about the risk categories in superannuation, and I thought, *Oh, I can actually learn about this, plan around it and have an impact on my own financial situation.* Then I did that. I joined The Evergreen Money

Club[7] a month later, and now know a lot more than I ever would have imagined. (Although I still need to learn more, people keep asking me questions about how things work because I know more about finance than them!)

What's one outrageous thing you've spent money on, and did you regret it?

What felt absolutely outrageous at the time (and I loved the feeling) was buying the newest style of Sony noise-cancelling headphones. It was 100 per cent worth it. I *love* them so much and they have changed my lifestyle and made busy shopping places more bearable when I must go shopping.

Have you ever looked at your bank account and thought, WTF? How did it get this low?

Yes! But I have a good idea in my head of what money is going in and out, and most times I had missed a transfer. I have mostly fixed this issue by having a dedicated bills and rent account that all automated transfers and debits come out of.

Anything else you'd like to share?

I love learning about money and am considering becoming an accountant. I used to be really angry about money and reframing it as a tool of trade was really helpful for me. The idea that money isn't evil was really critical. I still think some billionaires are evil—but because of their nasty actions, not because they simply have money.

Teaching triangles over taxes

If the experiences you had at home didn't role model best practice money management, fear not—the education system caught you, right? Surely over the almost 13 years or so you spent in school, you were absolutely, definitely, surely taught something to support you managing money day-to-day and investing so it can compound? After all, unless you become a monk or Tarzan, every single child is going to, at some point, have to get across taxes, budgeting and retirement planning in their life — regardless of what they do when they 'grow up'.

As far as I can tell, the experience for many people during their school years was vastly different to this ideal. Broadly speaking, most of us weren't taught much about money at school. The closest I got was my year 9 commerce teacher, who taught us how to write a cheque — a skill that has proved *extremely unhelpful* in my life to date.

This isn't an attack on teachers; they work to a broader curriculum. But if your exposure to money was limited to what you learned at home, then school could, and should, be the place where practical, healthy money skills and concepts are taught.

The great news is it's starting to happen — certainly across the various curriculums now in place across Australia. But while financial literacy is broadly endorsed by state and territory education departments, it still doesn't form part of the mandatory curriculum as a specific subject. That leads to a 'postcode lottery', where some kids hit the jackpot and learn about saving and investing at school, while others get left behind.[8]

I'm not okay with that. I find it astounding that kids these days still spend more time learning about trigonometry than taxes. Sure, figuring out the angles that make up a triangle improves critical thinking, but so does financial literacy. And, honestly, how many times have the principles of sin, cos and tan helped you in your life to date? I'm guessing rarely, if ever.

Most people leave school ready to face the world with gusto — only to feel like a complete idiot when they fall on their ass at their first financial hurdle. It's like getting something from IKEA that has 74 pieces but no instructions — where do you even start?! Over the years, I've had countless clients tell me they feel like they 'must have missed something' along the way, because everyone appears to be out here 'doing' the money thing, while they feel left behind.

It's not your fault if you didn't learn about money growing up, but don't confuse your lack of formal financial education with your ability to become financially literate as an adult. These are two very different things, and now we're gonna make up for lost time and get you back on track!

Activity: Your financial literacy at school

What did you learn about money at school, if anything? How has it helped, or hindered, you?

If the answer is nothing, you need to remember that when you tell yourself you're 'bad' with money, you aren't—you've just never learned about it! Would you also think you're 'bad' at astrophysics if you had never learned it, or 'bad' at building houses if you had never been taught how to do it?

Next time you catch yourself thinking you're 'bad' with money, or 'not good at this stuff', what's a more helpful way to reframe it?

Stories and stereotype seeding

Mainstream media and pop culture have likely also had a hand in developing and cementing your money beliefs — and this starts earlier than you might expect. Think for a second about the fairytales and films you loved as a child. Chances are, many of them had similar undertones, themes and plot lines, which helped your brain start building beliefs.

For example, fairytale villains are almost always nefarious, morally corrupt, unattractive, unlikeable, 'evil' people — who also generally happen to be filthy rich. Think Cruella de Vil (*One Hundred and One Dalmatians*), Jafar (*Aladdin*), Ursula (*The Little Mermaid*) and Gaston (*Beauty and the Beast*).

Conversely, heroes usually possess many of the qualities we should 'want' to aspire to — including kindness, bravery, loyalty, resilience, strength, beauty (because idealistic beauty standards and ableism starts young!). Most of the time, these heroes were also poor. Think of Cinderella, who lived a life of poverty and servitude, or Robin Hood and his noble acts to take from the greedy rich and give to the poor. Even Jack was a hero — who thought it was clever to sell his mother's only cow to buy magic beans and basically began robbing items from the giant. The giant, meanwhile, died in pursuit of his goods but it was okay, because he was nasty and mean and wealthy — so everyone else lived happily ever after. For some, the tale was one of rags to riches; for others, it was rags to righteousness.

Then we see the characters that portray (and borderline glorify) women as frivolous and fiscally irresponsible — like Carrie Bradshaw. She's great with words but shit at managing her money. Her ultra-glamorous NYC life is somehow funded from a weekly newspaper column and that still left her with enough to wear the latest designer clothes and go to the hottest places in town. (I mean, come on now…) She seems to have it all — except, of course, money. While she has a wardrobe full of clothes — famously noting, 'I like my money right where I can see it. Hanging in my closet' — she has no savings and no assets.

But never fear; she gets *saved*. Oh thank god — a man with a 'Big' fat wallet ensures she isn't destined to live a life of financial instability. I couldn't help but wonder… without him, would she have ended up as the old lady who lived in a (Manolo Blahnik) shoe? A show that was meant to showcase women's empowerment and independence actually ended up reinforcing the very unhelpful and damaging stereotypes they we're trying to break. Of course, that's one (very white and still privileged) example, but there are many, many more.

So many bullshit money narratives are hiding in plain sight all around us. They are small, but important — and, once again, reinforce long-held harmful beliefs. A study from the United Kingdom[9] looked at 600 popular stock images for 'men' and 'women', used in news articles, websites and marketing material, that had the labels 'money', 'banking', 'loans' and 'finance' attached. Now I'm sure if you've been playing along at home, you're able to guess where this is going. But, let me give you the highlights. Firstly, very little diversity at all was represented.

The images of women were portrayed as childlike, immature or unsophisticated. Many are shown handling small amounts of money (such as putting spare change in a piggy bank), in a home, dressed in casual clothes. They are more likely to be alone (suggesting money for women is a private matter). If they were with others, they were more likely to be the person watching on, as a man performed something money related — such as calculating something or paying a bill (because, you know, let's reinforce that women are passive onlookers and not decision makers with money) — or they were getting advice from a man. In most of the images where a woman was holding a bank note, she had a 'comedic' or 'dramatic' expression. Researchers found women were much more likely to look happy in the images studied when they looked at 'women' and 'loan' together — because women fucking love being in debt (don't we, ladies)!

Men, on the other hand, were more likely to be 'more mature', wearing a suit and glasses with wads of notes in their jacket pocket (à la smart, sophisticated and successful), using technology (doing 'serious' money things) and proactively managing their money, or giving expert advice.

Can you imagine what these decades of stories and subliminal messaging do to create and rust-on harmful money beliefs for someone? They're literally everywhere.

Activity: Your subliminal messaging

What stories, films, characters or imagery do you think have helped shape and reinforce your money beliefs? What's the underlying narrative that was fed to you around money?

Consider how you could reframe that belief. Write down what you want to take from those insights moving forward.

Planting insecurities

One of the smartest ways marketing departments and businesses get you to part with cash is to make you feel inadequate. Of course, humans have always had insecurities and self-doubt. But (and this may shock you) we haven't always been bombarded daily with thousands of ads and constant messaging telling us that we're not enough, *yet* (the subtext being... until you've bought this thing, of course).

These messages are served up via our phones from the moment we wake till the moment we go to bed at night. Businesses have clocked onto how to get into our brain grooves and deep, fleshy worries, open them up further and then promise to deliver the elixir that will make it better. Like vultures, they prey on our weaknesses — our insecurities, fears and deepest desires. You are but a purchase away from becoming the person you want to be, so hurry — buy now. Don't miss the chance to be the ultimate version of you, sale ends soon!

Today, more than ever, we are more reachable and trackable. Marketers can now observe user data, browsing history, purchasing patterns and social media interactions to help figure out when you are likely to be at your most vulnerable.[10] They say sex sells, but fear sells better. *Survival-first brain party trick mode enters the chat* When companies sell based on fear, their tactics can cleverly trick your brain into thinking you are in danger. I'm here to remind you that the only thing you are in danger of is spending money and pushing your goals further out of reach.

See, fear grabs our attention, making our brains automatically shift towards it, and we become more alert and aware. Our brain increases its cognitive processing, meaning we are more likely to remember the details about whatever is being marketed to us. Being in a state of fear can make you feel more threatened and vulnerable, and your brain wants to do something as soon as humanly possible to make the feeling go away (like buy now — before you miss out on this exclusive, limited release!). A study from the United States showed that 69 per cent of people made purchases when they were emotional (with stress being the leading cause), in the hope it will cheer them up.[11] Most of them said they felt guilty and remorseful afterwards, and especially those who used debt to fund it.

People used to feel pressure to keep up with their neighbours. But now the 'Joneses' aren't just on your street anymore. They have been lifted off the pavement and transported into our screens. The apps we spend the most time on are designed to keep us comparing ourselves to everyone, every waking hour. We look at our normal, mundane and often messy life and feel inadequate because we assume the highly curated, filtered content we see online is a reflection of other people's real lives. How fucking exhausting.

With the rise of influencer culture (who, by the way, often not only get the stuff for free but are also paid to promote it!), we are seeing trends move at breakneck speed. What was cool yesterday isn't today. The 'must have' product of last week, last month or last year is no longer 'it'. It's a system designed so you can never stay cool — that's the point. You have to keep buying. And it works (well, the constant comparison and buying bit at least).

Dirt bag

One of the biggest culprits of this 'buy now, go broke later' culture is fast fashion, and Australians are some of the highest consumers of new clothing in the world. Collectively, we each buy at least one new item of clothing a week on average. And the cost is so much more than what's on the price tag. If you're one of those consumers, think about how much time you spend looking at trends and scrolling through online stores. Think about the emotional spiral you experience as you consider the kind of person you could be if only you had those items, and the toll that has on you. Think about the time spent purchasing and collecting items (if needed) and the time you have to work to pay for that item. Now think about the cost to your goals, the cost to the planet and the opportunity cost (what that money could have been used for, if it was used differently). Still think those jeans and a nice top were worth it?

The most radical thing you can do is decide you're enough — that you, with your quirks and imperfections, are enough. You can decide that buying the thing that promises to make you cooler, hotter and more attractive is, in fact, more likely to make you poorer, and leave you feeling stressed and guilty. Get out of the cycle of 'Fuck — it didn't work. Maybe this next purchase will do it… okay, maybe this next one… okay, this one will for sure…' Remember: you will be the same you post-purchase, just with less money in the bank and one more thing cluttering up your life.

It's time to understand that making you feel bad about yourself is a sales tactic. You aren't even a person, but an 'avatar' or a 'consumer' — hungry for your next purchase. You are a sales figure. It's a sobering truth. Of course, this is not to say you can never buy *anything* again, or to say that all marketing is evil. But it's about deciding to purchase for the right reasons, with the clarity of mind to know you are still going to be you — with, or without an item.

It's knowing your identity isn't limited to brands, trends or material possessions, and that you are fucking fabulous already. The simple fact you're still here reading this tells me you are.

Activity: Analysing when and why you spend

When do you spend? Is it when you are feeling a particular way? At a particular time of day? (Hello, doomscrolling after an awful day at work.) What are you trying to buy? How does it make you feel afterwards? What about a week later?

Money in the wild: Priya (she/her)

- **Age:** 46.
- **Situationship:** Married.
- **Income:** $104000.
- **Current savings:** $9000.
- **Current relationship with money:** Happy, knowledgeable and always learning.
- **Money monster's name:** I have never given it a name. I am a big saver and almost never give into spending on things I don't need. I do, however, spend on things my kids ask for. However, I have gotten so much better with this. I feel like it's been a long time since I was unhinged with money.

Have you ever had to use your emergency savings, and how did it make you feel?
Twice. The first time I had to use it, I could not get over the guilt. It permeated my life and gave me sleepless nights. Eventually

I outgrew those feelings and I've learned to accept that the money is there for emergencies and that it is fine to use.

Having it has made me feel empowered. It has helped me help my husband to take an international vacation to get his mental health back on track. It has also helped me visit my dying father and then be there for my mother at his funeral. And because I was able to meet the monetary needs of these emergencies, I was stress free and present in the moment.

Do you save or invest?
Currently I am saving towards building my emergency fund and towards spending money for an upcoming holiday. I also regularly invest. Each fortnight, I put aside $250 and once it reaches $1000 it gets invested in ETFs. Once I reach my emergency funds goal, those additional funds of $500 per fortnight will also get invested.

What is a past money decision you're proud of?
Taking charge of my money and learning more about it. Once I learned how to budget with future bills in mind, it just blew my mind as to how I had not seen it before. Previously, I used to dread the months when all the quarterly bills came in—and, somehow, I never had any money leftover. It is no longer like that. I do not worry about any upcoming bill. Most of all I have been teaching my family how budgeting helps you stay calm and confident. I have also sowed the benefits of investing in their minds. So, I have hopefully set my kids up for a better future due to being educated about money.

What's one piece of money advice you wish you knew sooner?
Investing and compounding interest and how they can help you build wealth. I wish I had known this earlier to be able to

save and invest more and 'waste' less. Knowledge is power and it would have pushed me towards making better decisions earlier in life.

What has shaped your relationship with money the most?
The fear of not having money. There was a point in my life when I was the only earning member of the family. My father and brother had both lost their jobs unexpectedly. And I was suddenly overwhelmed by fear—that I had to support the whole family. No-one had asked me to do this, and my family had enough money—but this one even spooked me. It shaped my fearful relationship with money. I didn't check with my parents to see what the impact of the job loss had on them. I just assumed that we would be poor and out on the street. If I had been better educated about money, I would not have been this fearful.

When I got married, I assumed my spouse would take care of the finances. It took me two years to realise that he was terrible with money. This is because his own family was very bad with money. Where my family were savers, his family saw money as something that, when it came, needed to be enjoyed and spent. They would never think about the future or saving for a rainy day. As a result, I got even more fearful about money.

What does 'financial wellbeing' mean to you?
To me, financial wellbeing means not having to worry about money ever. It would give me the ability to take a break when I want and do activities that I like without worrying about how I was going to manage bills or spending.

What's a financial goal you're working towards right now?
Topping up my emergency fund, investing in ETFs and adding additional money into my mortgage.

You win the lotto. What do you do?

I would probably take a holiday. I don't want to buy anything—I am not big on things. I would get an adviser and pay for some advice on how best to invest the money. I would also give a portion of it to some cause close to my heart. And maybe I would pursue a PhD.

Did you have a big 'oh shit' moment that made you realise you had to learn more about money?

It perhaps wasn't a big moment, but when I moved to Australia, I realised that I didn't know much about the money systems here. I also didn't have too many friends here. So I had to learn and teach myself, and this put me on course to learn more about money.

What's one outrageous thing you've spent money on and did you regret it?

I bought myself a diamond ring. I got tired of waiting for my husband to buy me one. So, when it was on sale, I bought it for myself. I did have one moment of disappointment when I realised that the diamond wasn't as big as I thought it was—but, overall, no regrets. I wear it all the time and it brings me immense joy.

Have you ever looked at your bank account and thought, WTF? How did it get this low?

Many years ago before I started budgeting, I would be scared to see my bank account—especially after an evening out with the family. I would then stress about all the upcoming expenses and how to manage them until the next pay day. Once I learned more about money and managed to put my budget together, I was always ahead. I am still amazed by this because the amount I was earning wasn't much different. It just showed me that when the money didn't have a purpose in my account, it just got spent. Now each dollar goes towards something, so there is no opportunity to waste anything.

Treating ourselves like dirt — and digging new pathways

Most people's internal narrative around money is overwhelmingly harmful and self-limiting — and self-fulfilling. You might, for example, be saying things like:

- 'Money is too hard', and then actively running in the opposite direction from learning about it because you have convinced yourself it's too complicated to try.
- 'I can never save', and then spending because you think this tiny amount isn't that big and it doesn't really matter in the grand scheme of things, you can never save anyway.
- 'Investing is too "risky"', and then when share prices move around you think, *See, look at that downturn!*

Your brain wants to confirm your beliefs are correct (hello, confirmation bias) and will look for ways to prove itself right. Often, you need to challenge these beliefs — but how?

Think of your brain like a map, with roads and highways crisscrossing everywhere. When you create a belief or habit, a road is formed in your brain. As you use this 'road' more and more, it morphs into a highway. Your brain gets to know that route well and will want to go down that well-trodden path first. (Who wants to take a longer journey, when you know a tried and tested short cut?). The most amazing thing, however, is that you can build new roads. Your brain just needs to be forced not to automatically take you down the path it wants to go down first.

Of course, in the beginning, forging a new path feels weird and confusing. (*Why the fuck are we doing this when we know there is a 'simpler' route to take?!*). Your brain wants you to be efficient and take the easy road. But, over time, you can make your new belief the 'go-to' highway, and the old one will not be the automatic default. Then, as you start to not use those old routes, they fall away like dead branches as the brain literally starts to prune them.

This process is called *neuroplasticity*. Another way to think of it is that your brain is like playdough — you can shape it however you want. Brains can have the ability to change your thoughts and beliefs throughout your life; but it takes practice and persistence. You are never too old to build new habits. You can choose what to keep and what to let go of. How fucking clever are we?!

Hopefully you can now see that your beautiful brain was, all along, cleverly absorbing so much (often harmful) information in an attempt to keep you safe. By creating all those unhelpful money beliefs and behaviours, it was trying to help you! Now you can see, with fresh eyes, all the ways that external factors, from family and school to pop culture, have played a huge role in shaping what you believe about money. It is important that you pause here and acknowledge that.

Acknowledge that any nasty and unhelpful comments you've made to yourself have served their purpose, but they are no longer required. They aren't going to be the way you talk to yourself anymore. Acknowledge that you would never dream of talking to your best friend like that, so you won't talk to yourself like that anymore either. Instead of shame, guilt and nasty comments, you can be kinder, compassionate and gentler with yourself. From here on in, you can say 'thank you' to your brain when it tries to remind you of those 'hot iron' moments. You can lovingly acknowledge that it is trying to help you, but also that you are choosing a different path now. You see what's going on, and you get it, but you are moving forward another way now.

And if you need anymore convincing that speaking to yourself nicely is so wildly important remember this: evidence has shown that plants grow healthier and faster when they are spoken to nicely (via vibrations). Not only that, but they are also more resilient and immune to pathogen attacks and they change the structures of their cell walls to be more drought tolerant.[12] Good vibes equals better, stronger, healthier plants. I am convinced we are the same, just with slightly more complicated emotions.

Activity: Digging into your beliefs

Building a better internal narrative with money makes you stronger, more resilient and allows you to grow faster. Let's dig.

How does the way you spend (or save) money reaffirm your existing money beliefs? Are those behaviours helpful or harmful? How do you speak to yourself about money? Is it different to how you would speak to a friend if they came to you in the same situation? If so, how would you speak to them instead?

Feeling spendy? Read this

Now that we understand how external factors have a role in shaping our thoughts and beliefs, is it any wonder many of us have no clue how to behave responsibly with money once we're let loose in the world? We are like kids in the candy store of life. Eyes as wide as dish plates looking at all the bright, colourful exciting things that our brains tell us 'must' have. Where once we had an adult saying, 'No darling, you can't have that' to our unreasonable demands of absolutely everything on the shelf that caught our attention, now suddenly we find ourselves alone, unsupervised and *allowed* to buy all the things that we want, without any parental supervision.

But instead of lollies, it's expensive clothes, nice restaurants, and holidays — and no-one is around to stop us! I once heard Tiffany Aliche ('The Budgetnista') talk about this very situation, and that our ability to get those things should be treated in a similar way to how we treat dessert: it comes after you have eaten what your body needs as fuel, and only if you have room.

Thinking about spending in this way is helpful. Just like you know you need to put veggies on your plate, you must do the same for your money — you need to make sure you put money towards your expenses and your goals first. Consider how you would feel if you ate dessert for every meal. Sure, it might feel fun in the beginning, but you know if you don't stop, it's probably going to make you feel sick. And if you keep only eating sweet and sugar-filled meals over and over again, you know over time, your body isn't going to be able to fuel itself properly. It will feel slow and lethargic, and become dependent on the next sugar rush to momentarily perk you back up again. It becomes a nasty, toxic cycle.

A similar process can occur with your money. Those spends create a sweet sugar rush in your brain, releasing dopamine (the 'feel-good' chemical) and making you feel more in control in the moment. Your brain then tricks you into thinking the experience was so good, you need more. Emotional buying then becomes your go-to strategy when you encounter your next *[insert existential emotional crisis of your choosing here]*. Maybe you've had a bad day at work. You had a fight with your partner. You're feeling low, lonely or angry, and now your brain knows what the rush of a purchase feels like, it becomes so easy to give your brain that hit of feel-good endorphins, without even getting off the couch. It's almost too easy.

As this continues over time, your identity can get blurred with buying. You start creating beliefs that you are the clothes you wear or, worse, you want to be known as the person who always has the newest, coolest shit. These beliefs then burrow in deep, setting up camp next to where your worries, doubts and insecurities live. They sniff out all the weak spots and unhealed wounds and feed on them. Not so sweet after all.

Now you have more insight into what's going on, let's unpack what to do when (not if!) you find yourself in that situation again. For example, say you've come home from work, you're tired and you have used every last morsel of energy to scramble dinner together and fold some washing. You flop onto the lounge and start scrolling and come across *[insert your purchasing poison of choice]*, you make a couple of clicks and next thing you know, you're deciding if you want normal or express delivery (because maybe you *must* have this thing you didn't even know about three minutes ago in your life *immediately*).

Here's what to do:

- Take a big fat pause.
- Now take a big breath and close your eyes. (Research has shown closing your eyes leads to an increase in your ability to make better judgement calls.[13])
- Read through the list of easy, free, cup-filling ideas provided in the following activity, noting any that particularly appeal.
- Open your notes section on your phone, or grab a piece of paper, and write down the options that feel right for you. Call this your 'zero bucks given' list.
- Choose one thing from the list.
- Then go and do that thing.
- Celebrate the shit out of yourself for taking yourself down a different path!

Still stuck? If you do the 'thing' and you still feel the item has a hold of you, don't worry — you are prepared for that. Consider a financial goal you have, which is going to deliver you so much more long-lasting joy.

Now, I want you to close your eyes (I know, but as I just said it's science, so stick with me) and imagine exactly what it feels like to achieve that thing. If your goal is being able to go on a safari in Africa, close your eyes and imagine it. Imagine the sounds around you, the animals you will see and the sun beaming down on your face. If your goal is buying your first property, close your eyes and imagine what it will feel like turning the key for the first time knowing it's *yours*. You've done it. You can paint the kitchen a hideous shade of blue and no-one can fucking stop you. You can put nails in all the walls to hang your favourite artwork because they are *your* walls. How does that feel?

My hope is that you now look at that (probably unnecessary, fad-of-the-minute) thing with fresh eyes. You're no longer enamoured by it, and instead look at it with disdain for trying to rob you of your big dream. It was trying to pry it from your hands. Now you can see it for exactly what it is: a distraction that creates distance between you and your goal.

Activity: Building your 'zero bucks given' list

Time to create your extended 'zero bucks given' list. If you started this list in the previous section, add to it now. Or start a new list in the notes section of your phone (for easy finding when you need them), and highlight any that are particularly useful.

Consider the following activities to do at home. If you feel like they will work for you, add them to your list:

▶ Write down three things you're grateful for right now.
▶ Do a five-minute meditation/breathwork exercise.
▶ Grab a journal and a pen and write about how you are feeling, without shame or filtering.

(continued)

- Take a bath—include candles, tea and a book. (Reading in the bath is one of life's greatest joys.)
- Do something creative—draw, colour in, craft, sew or watch a YouTube video and learn a new skill you've wanted to start.
- Put on your favourite playlist and dance around the house wildly.
- Watch your fave TV show.
- Sing loudly in the shower.
- Cuddle your pet (or someone else's if permitted) and/or your partner if you have one.
- Call or message a friend and tell them you're thinking of them.
- Do some stretches or yoga poses in your PJs.
- Set a timer and do one quick life admin task (that can be achieved in less than five minutes).
- Declutter one drawer/shelf/doom pile.
- Water your plants and tell them how much you love them, or go and dig about in the garden (if you have one).
- Make a vision or progress board for your goals.
- Sit in your favourite spot in the house with a cup of tea.
- Make your bed.
- Find a recipe you want to try (that doesn't require the purchase of elaborate or expensive new items).
- Make your lunch for tomorrow and add a cute little note on top saying how amazing you are.
- Turn your phone to do not disturb/sleep mode, or put it in another room for an hour (I know, it can be done) and just be.

- ▶ Write motivational mantras on some sticky notes and put them where you will see them often.
- ▶ Listen to a podcast you love.
- ▶ Put on a face or hair mask.
- ▶ Write out one thing you can do this week as a self-care ritual (such as setting a clear bedtime).

And here are some ideas for outdoor activities:

- ▶ Get some sunshine.
- ▶ Go for a walk (either solo or with a friend) — take a new route or explore somewhere new.
- ▶ Go on a 'no spend adventure' — explore a suburb, museum, art gallery, nature or community event.
- ▶ If you live near water, take a book and hot drink in a flask, find a comfy spot to sit and enjoy.
- ▶ Go for a hike with some friends, with everyone bringing something to share for lunch.
- ▶ Volunteer for a cause that's important to you.
- ▶ Star gaze.
- ▶ Organise to go and visit a friend.

Implementing the 24-hour rule

We all know the drill: 'Only three left!' 'Sale ends midnight!' 'This offer sells out fast'. Urgency is marketing currency in a capitalist society. It activates our FOMO and nudges us to stop scrolling and start buying. So if you find yourself still really wanting the thing, then waiting 24 hours is key (even if they say it'll be sold out).

The 24-hour rule is a great practice to have when buying. You rationally know that tomorrow isn't too long to wait, but it gives you time and space to consider the decision and make sure it is really what you want. You stop trying to wrestle with your brain and instead say, 'Okay, I will just wait till tomorrow to get it then'. You are likely to feel less upset about not getting it now and, more often than not, you're suddenly not as interested in it when tomorrow rocks around.

Activity: Reviewing your spending

If you want to dig deeper into the connection between your emotions and spending behaviour, this exercise is for you.

Identify three items you have bought in one of those dopamine-seeking spendy moments. As best you can, cast your mind back to when you bought it and ask yourself the following:

- How were you feeling when you bought it? (For example, were you feeling angry, stressed, sad, lonely, bored or excited?)
- What did the marketing promise that item would do for your life?
- Has it *actually* done that? If yes, pause and celebrate it. You've spent money on something that is adding meaning and value to your life.
- If not, ask yourself why. Is it that you thought getting the latest hottest clothes for the gym would mean you would go everyday (which hasn't happened)? Did you think the product would make you feel a certain way, and that didn't eventuate? Did you make the purchase under a false hope that buying it would make you the person you want to be, but you found you are still the same you (just with another thing and less money)?

> ▶ What are the lessons from this spend? If you had your time over, would you buy it again? Why? (The idea here is not to pile on the guilt—we are looking for lessons, insights and 'aha' moments).
> ▶ What could that money have been spent on that would have been more meaningful to you in the long run?
> ▶ What is one thing you can commit to doing instead of buying something when you feel like that again? Put this in the notes section on your phone, so it doesn't require brain power when you need it. Also, note down why it will be more meaningful.

I dig you, and you dig money

The best news, and perhaps the whole reason you're here, is this: you can change your thoughts, habits and beliefs if you want to. Remember that 'past performance is not an indicator of future returns' disclaimer at the end of every investing or super ad? Apply it to your money beliefs. How you have behaved in the past doesn't need to be the way you act in the future.

Also, now you know where some of your past beliefs and behaviours have come from, you can use those handy insights to recognise triggers and times when you are most likely to jump back to old habits. Nothing is wasted if you use it to help you grow stronger and sturdier than before.

No matter what's come up for you in this chapter, ultimately, I hope you give yourself a big dose of radical forgiveness and compassion for the way you may, or may not, have thought about and behaved with money in the past. Now you can start to shed them in the next chapter...

Activity: Digging a little deeper

Haven't finished excavating your money stories? Ask yourself the following to dig a little deeper:

▶ What are your biggest insights on money stories and beliefs?
▶ How do they make you feel?
▶ Do you want to mentally forgive anyone to help you move forward?
▶ When you hear a negative thought or idea pop into your mind next, what are you saying to it?
▶ Haven't finished excavating your money stories?

And here are some ways to start changing the story for future generations:

▶ If you have kids in your life, consider what they have already been exposed to about money. How can you have age-appropriate conversations to teach them about money in a positive and proactive way?
▶ How can you show them all elements of managing money and not reinforce traditional gender stereotypes?
▶ How can you build healthy money practices into your home or community that stick?

SHED

Letting go of shame and perfectionism to make space for more helpful money habits

The only person you are destined to become is the person you decide to be.

—Ralph Waldo Emerson

There comes a time in life when you must decide to shed what you have outgrown or that which no longer serves you. The process of letting go and stepping into something new can be hard — but it is essential.

Many examples of this letting go can be seen in nature — such as a snake shedding its skin in order to grow, a deer dropping its antlers every year to save energy and survive the harsh winter, or even a tree dropping leaves in autumn to direct its energy inward to the roots and trunk. Shedding, for us humans, can look similar: we can get rid of something that is stifling our growth, or let go of something to give us more capacity and energy to focus on what's most important to us.

This chapter is all about intention — deciding who you are going to be with money from here on in. It's about building habits and understanding the parts of your life that are holding you back. And it's about being deliberate about what you're letting go of and what you're replacing it with. Because winging it with money very rarely works out well. Sure, you might have moments of luck and good fortune, but you'll also (and mostly) have stress, juggling and hoping like hell it will all pan out.

You've already done the hard (and potentially painful) work to dig up the past and unpack why you think and behave in certain ways with money. Now you get to start building the future. And so, we must shed.

Self-care (beyond bubble baths)

The concept of looking after ourselves isn't a new one. Way back in ancient Greek times, philosopher Socrates advised, 'My friend ... care for your psyche ... know thyself, for once we know ourselves, we may learn how to care for ourselves'. But somewhere along the way this whole 'care' thing got co-opted by capitalists.

When you think about self-care, what immediately comes to mind? For me, it's a lady with a face mask on, lying in a bubble bath, surrounded by candles. Okay, that sounds nice, but it's a bit narrow. You can be marketed a million things a minute under the guise of 'self-care' but if you really want to get great at managing money (and I'm pretty sure you do!), you need a wholesale redefinition of what 'self-care' looks like, and this definition has to include your finances.

Much like tending to a garden is not all 'smelling the roses', true self-care is much harder than slipping into a bubble bath and hoping all your worries and troubles melt away. Self-care is also showing up for yourself, even when it feels hard — because you know it will benefit you in the long run. It's doing the hard thing when you want easy.

Meaningful self-care takes discipline, boundaries, persistence, reflection, connection and compassion. Self-care is taking care of you, *all of you.*

Financial self-care means actively working to reduce stress and uncertainty, and seeding and growing the building blocks so you can flourish. From practical routines such as checking your bank account or setting up automatic savings plans, to setting a budget or saying no to spending when it doesn't align with your values or goals, financial self-care is about making sure you are safe, protected and informed, and prioritising what really matters to you.

For me, this is the kind of self-care that we actually need to be doing more of. Because who benefits from us staying stuck in the mud and sucking on self-care from over-sized sippy cups instead of getting our hands dirty? It sure as shit ain't you. Or me.

Does that mean you can't 'treat yo'self'? This is the question most people want to ask. And the answer is — it depends. Put it this way: financial self-care is not doing things to temporarily soothe or numb yourself. So if that's what's motivating your 'little treats' fix, then, yes, they're probably more self-sabotage than self-care and they might have to go. The truth is these little things add up and could actually be doing the very opposite to what you're aiming for, stealing your time (and money) and stopping your progress.

Activity: Your first shed

Which money habits of yours need to go? Which ones need to grow? What are you doing to bury your head in the proverbial sand (be curious, not shameful here)? What would you like to start shedding first? What kind of gardener do you want to become?

Money in the wild: Steph (she/her)

- **Age:** 38.
- **Situationship:** Single.
- **Income:** $105000.
- **Current savings:** $8500.
- **Current relationship with money:** Frustrated, annoyed, grateful.
- **Money monster's name:** 'Mad Mandy'. She shows up when I'm really stressed or when everything else in my life is not under control, but spending is something I can do. (See later in this chapter for more on naming your money monster.)

Have you ever had to use your emergency savings and how did it make you feel?

Yes. I was relieved I had them to use, but worried that it reduced my security buffer. I'm now working towards a $20000 buffer.

What does life look like right now?

Okay. I have a decent job, live alone with two pets and can save each month, but don't have too much 'fun money' unless I am really careful. I'm building up savings again after purchasing my first home and dealing with unplanned medical costs.

What is a past money decision you're proud of?

Getting out of a personal debt cycle (I had $12000 of personal debt) and saving up to buy my first home. It got me better with money and proved I could be good with money and set up my future.

What has shaped your relationship with money the most?
Money was a taboo topic growing up and I never had a safe place to learn or ask questions.

What does 'financial wellbeing' mean to you?
Understanding money and being able to make informed decisions about it. Getting secure with managing money and how to use it for wealth building.

Did you have a big 'oh shit' moment that made you realise you had to learn more about money?
Not a single moment, just a regular feeling of being behind others and not in control.

Have you ever looked at your bank account and thought, WTF? How did it get this low?
This was my entire 20s! Yes, I eventually stopped the cycle once I had learned there were ways of managing my money and ways to reduce the debt. I wish there were more financial lessons earlier in life; not having a safe place to share my struggle was hard and lonely.

The shed where shame lives

Undoubtedly, one of the biggest areas many people need to shed with money is shame. Shame is a dark, quiet prison. It loves to keep you stuck in a space that's isolated, small and silent — because it thrives there. It emerges in that nasty voice that tells you you're behind, broken and a failure. What does shame give you that's helpful? Honestly, absolutely nothing.

Shame tells you you're 'bad' or 'unworthy' of getting this shit sorted because of who you are. It's quite different to guilt, which is normally an internal alarm bell that you have done something that wasn't aligned to your values. Instead, shame is telling yourself that *you* are bad, rather than you *did* something bad. See the difference?

No matter what that nasty little voice in your head has been telling you all these years, I'm here to tell you that you are not 'bad' with money. You're not. But (you knew a 'but' was coming), you may have made some financial decisions that weren't so good. Your first step here is to separate yourself from your actions.

Of course, the reason shame can fester, swell and grow for so long is because openly talking about money is one of the last societal taboos. Intentionally turning towards your financial situation and talking about it (even if it's only with yourself to begin with) not only confronts shame but also releases its hold on you. No more living in a shame shed. It's time to free yourself from that dank, dark place and step into the light. The following table highlights some ways to do so — through embracing all the things that shame hates.

Understanding how shame works

Shame loves	Shame hates
Silence	Sharing
Comparison	Self-compassion
Secrecy	Vulnerability
Isolation	Community
Criticism	Support
Perfectionism	Empathy
Judgement	Courage
Mistakes	Curiosity

Confront your money monster

When I was little, we had a shed in the back garden that my dad convinced me to stay well away from — by telling me a dragon lived there. Terrified I might be gobbled up by a fire-breathing beast,

I stayed well away from it (unlike my prior hot iron incident from the previous chapter — *#growth*). Turns out, the shed was just full of tools and equipment he didn't want me to touch.

Much like what I imagined to be lurking in that shed, I believe we all have a deep, dark place inside of us where a 'money monster' lurks — untamed and often threatening to derail us or block the path to progress. Part of your shedding process is to meet your money monster head on, and then slay it. So how the hell do you do that?

The exercise I'm about to share may sound ridiculous and honestly too simple to work, but let me assure you, it has helped hundreds of people I've worked with. You need to create a persona for your money monster — that little (often nasty) voice inside your head. The monster who reinforces any unhelpful money beliefs or whispers to your brain things like, 'You're just shit with money; you will never get it'. The inner saboteur that tries to convince you to 'treat yourself; you deserve it'. Literally, before you go any further, give that beast a name and describe how they have caused havoc for you. Because naming your monster not only makes it easier to recognise it when it pops up but also creates distance between you and your thoughts — so the 'monster' is less tied up with your own money beliefs and identities.

My money monster's called 'Stacey the Staller' — because she's always trying to distract me from doing the thing I know I *need* to do. Instead of acting, she gets me to stall on making big decisions (because maybe it's not the 'right' time, I don't have enough information or the moon isn't in the right phase). When I heard about Parkinson's law — the idea that work (or life admin decisions) expands to fill the time available for its completion — I realised Stacey had helped me swell some simple 'work' by giving me too much time to make a decision on it.

She has 'helped' me waste time, energy, money and opportunities. Ultimately, she's linked to my 'money memoir' (your monster probably is too!). (Refer to the previous chapter for more on writing your money memoir.) Let's meet your monster.

Activity: Name it to tame it

Here's how you can get to know — and tame — your money monster:

‣ Give your money monster a name — and the funnier or more ridiculous, the better. Also, give them a job title, like 'the staller', 'the impulse buyer' or 'the dawdler'.

‣ Identify when they usually show up — for example, when you're overwhelmed, emotional, wanting a distraction, finished work or on the bus to work.

‣ Rate how often they're currently in control of your money decisions, from 0 = never to 10 = all the freaking time.

‣ Work out what you're going to say to your Money Monster when you next notice it. (Swearing is not essential, but strongly encouraged in my expert opinion.)

The money monster cast list

To help you come up with your own money monster, here are some examples from the community I work with, and the kinds of mischief they get up to!

Anxious Annie

Signature move: Overthinking every purchase.
Catchphrase: 'But what if...?'
Where she lurks: Online shopping carts and sleepless nights.
Why she's dangerous: Stops you buying things that would actually save time and energy.

Impulsive Isla

Signature move: Copycat spending when everyone else is doing it.
Catchphrase: 'I'll have what she's having!'
Where she lurks: Restaurants, group trips and nights out.
Why she's dangerous: Leaves you paying for other people's choices and regretting it later.

Scarcity Sue

Signature move: Fear of not having enough, even when there is.
Catchphrase: 'Better not, just in case...'
Where she lurks: At the checkout and during investment decisions.
Why she's dangerous: Keeps you stuck, afraid to spend or grow your money.

But you deserve it Diana

Signature move: Turning every whim into a self-care essential.
Catchphrase: 'You deserve this.'
Where she lurks: During stressful weeks, sales or bad days.
Why she's dangerous: Blurs the line between needs and wants, eating into long-term savings.

Mad Max

Signature move: Spending to reclaim control when life feels chaotic.
Catchphrase: 'At least I can buy this.'
Where he lurks: Stressful work weeks, family drama and burnout seasons.
Why he's dangerous: Creates comfort in the moment but compounds stress later.

F*ck-It Frankie

Signature move: Throwing caution and the budget to the wind.
Catchphrase: 'YOLO!'
Where they lurk: Midnight sales, discount bookings and post-payday binges.
Why they're dangerous: Leaves future you footing the bill, often with interest.

Treat yourself Tracy

Signature move: Buying 'little rewards' when stressed or sad.
Catchphrase: 'Go on, treat yourself.'
Where she lurks: Cafes, checkout lines and online shops after long days.
Why she's dangerous: Small splurges snowball and undermine your bigger goals.

Shedding the perfectionist

As you decide who you want to become with money and start working towards that, I want to be super clear: you are going to fuck things up. You're a human being. You're not going to get it 100 per cent right, 100 per cent of the time. You just aren't. That can be both confronting and infuriating. Listen, I get it — I'm the kid who didn't want *any* mistakes on my homework in *kindergarten*. (Skip back to chapter 1 for a refresh on that story.)

So rather than pretending that you're never going to make a mistake, my advice is to instead build out a plan for when it happens.

Within this plan, the first point to remember is that progress is much better than perfection when it comes to your money. Think about trying to move a boulder — it's hard to get it moving, but once it does it's much easier to gather pace and keep rolling. Your financial momentum is the same. If you're stopping and starting all the time so you can do it 'perfectly', it's going to feel much harder and heavier to keep moving forward.

Ask yourself what doing something 85 per cent well looks like — and aim for that. This will feel hard if, like me, you tell yourself that's not good enough. But I'm sure that if you, too, suffer from unrealistic perfectionism tendencies, you're also guilty of having plenty of good things that never got to see the light of day, because they weren't 'perfect' enough. Good is good enough in a lot of instances with your money. (Hell — done is better than good if you need that reassurance also.) Start with good and you can always come back and tweak it later.

And as you make mistakes, learn from them. These are your seedlings for the future. Keeping a journal of these financial fuck-ups and money mishaps can be helpful, and gives you an opportunity to not only go back and reference, but also create the reframe your brain needs to keep you moving forward.

Activity: Your money mishaps

Here's what to note down when recording your financial fuck-ups and money mishaps:

▸ What happened and why did it happen? For example, 'I dipped into my emergency savings because my car broke down and I hadn't budgeted for repairs'.

▸ What have you learned from it? For example, 'That unexpected things always pop up, and it's less stressful when I plan for them'.

▸ What are the good things that will happen as a result of this? For example, 'I've started a fund for car expenses, so next time it won't throw me off track'.

Starting scared

When you're shedding, it's pretty common for fear to rear its nasty little head. I used to think bravery was doing something without fear. But bravery isn't the absence of fear; it's moving forward in spite of it. It's perfectly normal to feel scared when you start implementing certain financial strategies into your life. You don't need to wait till you feel like some heroic, brazen, fearless version of yourself — start *now*, exactly as you are.

Think about the last time you said yes to something that pushed you out of your comfort zone — something that you didn't feel ready for. Perhaps it was a new project at work, a new job or tagging along to a line-dancing class only to discover everyone there had been learning the routine for months. How did it feel in the beginning? And how does it feel now?

You've survived all of the things that have scared the shit out of you to this point. Sure, you may have experienced some tough moments and made some emergency panic calls to a bestie. But in some weird, fucked up way, you're probably a stronger, more capable person because of these experiences. So it's okay to feel terrified, sweaty-palmed and teary — and still take a step forward.

Building new money habits can feel daunting. Confronting your debt or spending can feel terrifying. Investing for the first time, buying a property or setting up a will and being confronted with your own mortality can all be scary. But the scarier thing is what happens if you don't make changes. Staying where you are right now is the 'scary' no-one seems to talk about. Yet, it's also the thing that keeps most people up at night. Don't be scared of doing something for the first time or the next time — be scared of what happens if you don't.

Activity: Feeling the fear—and doing it anyway

When fear* stops you in your tracks, ask yourself the following:

▸ What's one area with money where fear is holding you back? This could be unpacking your money beliefs, investing, checking your super or completing a cash flow plan.

▸ How is this linked to your money monster (for example, 'Stacey the Staller') or money memoir (that is, what you believe about money)?

▸ What exactly is worrying you?

▸ What happens if you never take action on it?

▸ What is one *teeny tiny* thing you could do to take some form of action now?

▸ How would you feel if you did the thing and it worked?

*You may find something other than fear is holding you back—such as control, perfectionism, shame, worry or analysis paralysis. You can still use the preceding questions, but amend each one to fit whatever mental block you're currently experiencing.

Is your glass half full, or half empty?

In my 20s, I was lucky enough to attend a talk by a Stanford professor. I can't remember his name, but I'll never forget his main argument. You might have heard something similar before, but essentially it was: 'No matter if you believe the glass is half full, or half empty, you are correct'.

He didn't drop the mic, but he could have. Basically, he said whichever side of the optimist/pessimist fence you sit on is an active and conscious decision. From that position, you'll hunt down things that prove yourself right. And each time you do, you're reinforcing your existing belief and making opening yourself up to changing harder.

This was the first time I'd heard about confirmation bias and the idea that we are capable of choosing how we respond or react in any given situation. It blew my mind. I left thinking, *Holy fuck! Does he mean I can just decide how I want to think/respond/react/behave, and it can work?!*

As an experiment, every day for the next 12 months I wrote down at least one good thing that had happened that day. I kept a jar by my bed to store each observation, and I soon realised I was subconsciously looking for moments that could go in the jar. Once I started looking, I found them everywhere. I wasn't suddenly having whole new experiences, but I was actively acknowledging them and being more aware when they happened. That's when I started to become curious about how I could apply the same logic to money and financial advice.

You may need to go through a similar process when it comes to your mindset, beliefs, habits, behaviours and actions with money. If you need to, get a jar and do what I did, adding a daily little win each night. Alternatively, put the win in the notes section of your phone. When you are feeling stuck or stressed, or facing a setback, read through your wins. We live in a culture that celebrates outcomes rather than effort and so this process is important—because our brains feed off progress.

Research into this whole idea of motivation and changing your mindset, led by psychologist and researcher Dr Carol Dweck, reinforces this.[1] Looking into how people's brains behaved when they made a mistake, Dweck identified two distinct 'mindsets': fixed and growth. Here are the typical attributes of each:

- *Fixed mindset:* People with this mindset don't want to engage with errors; instead, they want to avoid or check out from the discomfort of it all. This is correlated to lower levels of brain activity, which means these people are less likely to learn from the mistake to improve for the future. Basically, their process is avoid, ignore, repeat. A fixed mindset assumes abilities and circumstances are set in stone — 'I'm just bad with money', for example, 'I'll never earn more' or 'I wasn't raised wealthy, so I'll always struggle'. This thinking is static, limiting and often rooted in shame or comparison.
- *Growth mindset:* People with this mindset do the opposite and try to learn from mistakes. This means they have much more brain activity when errors occur. They lean into them and pay attention so they can correct similar mistakes in the future. Their process is assess, learn, adapt, improve. In the financial context, a growth mindset sees money skills and circumstances as things that can be learned, practiced and improved over time. It doesn't mean everything is 'easy peasy lemon squeezy' but these people are able to frame challenges as opportunities to build financial confidence and resilience.

If you identified more with having a 'fixed mindset', then thank yourself for your honesty — and then ask yourself if that's who you want to be moving forward. If it's not, you can take advantage of a simple way to start improving your mindset right now — and it starts with a three-letter word that can change your brain: yet. It's wild to think that a word so small and seemingly insignificant can help you cultivate a growth mindset.

How does it work? Well, according to Dweck, the word 'yet' equals hope in the human brain. 'Yet' creates possibility, permission to change, and space for growth and learning. And is that not exactly what you're trying to do here? You are showing up and doing the work to shift your unhelpful money beliefs and behaviours, and replace them with better ones that are more aligned with where you want to go. So, next time you tell yourself something negative or some BS you know you need to bust, add 'yet' to the end and see how it creates space for things to change moving forward. The following table provides some examples.

Using 'yet' to move from a fixed to a growth mindset

From this (fixed mindset, can't change)...	...to this (growth mindset, space for change)
'I'm not good with money.'	'I'm not good with money... *yet.*'
'I haven't found a way to save.'	'I haven't found a way to save... *yet.*'
'I don't know how to invest.'	'I don't know how to invest... *yet.*'
'I don't feel confident with money.'	'I don't feel confident with money... *yet.*'

Avoiding the backslide

People slip back into their old habits, which are as well-worn as my old pink bathrobe, for lots of reasons. Next time you catch yourself on the slide, ask yourself these questions:

- What is at stake if you don't shed your unhelpful money beliefs and behaviours?
- How would it feel if you were more clear, calm and intentional with your money?
- What would be possible if you felt more confident and considered?
- What if you had a plan and felt able and supported to stick to it?

The best part about changing your thinking is you can actually just decide to do it differently and then, like, do that! Often we focus only on the outcomes we want to achieve and hope (*fingers crossed emoji*), it'll become a reality. But the crucial missing step here is you.

As James Clear, author of *Atomic Habits*, explains, changing your beliefs involves two simple steps. First, you need to 'decide the type of person you want to be'. Secondly, 'prove it to yourself with small wins'.[2] Basically, Clear argues that where people trip up when it comes to goal setting is by starting with the goal itself. Instead, you need to start with who you want to be and then show yourself the 'proof' that you are becoming the person who can *actually* do it. For example, rather than starting with the goal of buying a house, you start with shifting your identity to a 'saver' and celebrating every $1000 you put into your savings account.

Before you panic, fear not — you already know how to do this. You already have many examples in your life where you act in an intentional and considered way — such as getting a specific train, knowing it will get you to work bang on time. Or packing a particular item for a trip away, because it literally goes with everything and doesn't need to be ironed (hurrah!). Some people consider and plan many aspects of their lives with meticulous detail and care, from weddings to meal prep. So believe me when I say, you already have the skills. Now let's supercharge them.

Holy-shit, Batman! Creating your money alter ego

This is the (hopefully even more?!) fun bit, where you get to create a persona of *who you want to be* with money. It's time to shed the habits of the past and create the identity of your new money alter ego. You don't need a cape or a superhero costume (although, obviously, I won't stop you), but it is time to build the person you want to be with money.

Why have I suggested Batman? Because research shows that when children were doing a task as 'themselves' (as opposed to someone else), they had very different outcomes — and I think the findings can help you become the (super)hero in your own life. The study divided participants into three groups, with one group being told to take a first-person perspective ('I'), one a third-person perspective ('Jessica' or 'she') and the last told to impersonate an 'exemplar other' (i.e. a character such as Batman). Children in each group were then asked to be a 'good helper' by completing a boring task for 10 minutes while resisting the temptation of taking a break or using an iPad. (And let's be honest — while these were kids, this sounds a lot like us adults who would often rather do almost anything other than financial admin!) The kids who were doing the task as 'themselves' gave up the fastest, followed by those who took a third-person perspective. But those who were told to act like 'Batman' spent the *most* time on the task.[3]

Why does it work? By embodying an alter ego, the kids started to take on the characteristics they would expect Batman to have — and he ain't scrolling when the world needs saving! In turn, they improved their self-control and their ability to withstand discomfort in the face of challenges. And they performed better. By creating self-distance, their perspective on the task shifted from 'what should I do?' to 'what would Batman do?' (WWBD), which turns down the inner critic and boosts confidence and executive function.

This can be a really simple way to help you start behaving differently with money. Over time, as you act like your alter ego (who doesn't wait to feel motivated or in the 'mood'), your brain starts connecting with this new identity and, soon enough, that version becomes *your* default. (Remember those neural 'highways' from the previous chapter, and how your brain prefers them?) You literally become your own version of your money superhero. (If that isn't the coolest thing you've read in a money book, I don't know what is!)

Activity: Transforming into your money superhero/alter ego

Here's how to become your own money superhero:

▶ Give your money alter ego a name (maybe it's more 'Sasha Fierce' than Bruce Wayne with his undies on the outside).

▶ Define your alter ego's traits (for example, confident, curious, action-oriented, efficient, focused and/or brave enough to start something).

▶ Decide how you want to feel when you are 'being' your superhero (for example, powerful, bold, empowered, decisive and/or clear).

▶ Think about what your alter ego would say or do in hard moments. Give yourself a few powerful lines that can be part of your internal script when you need them.

▶ To test and see if this works, identify one easy task your alter ego could help you tackle in the next 24 hours—and then action it. How did you perform it differently to how you might have if you were doing it as 'yourself'?

Showing up for future you

Without thinking too hard, you can probably already see a whole bunch of ways that you're showing up for future you in some way, shape or form. Maybe you make your bed every morning—because it feels great when you can get into a made bed at night! Or you wash up and clean the kitchen before you go to sleep—because tomorrow you will appreciate it. So how can you show up for future you with your finances too?

Basically, you want to create appreciation internally for doing things you know are going to help you down the track. Every time you put money towards something you know will help future you, acknowledge it and celebrate it.

You want to connect with a future version of yourself who you know will be grateful for your efforts and actions. But you don't want to wait years to get that positive feedback loop — so start by thanking yourself now and seeing that it does make a difference in the long run.

Activity: Appreciating future you

What are you already doing with your money now that is looking after future you? For example, are you gradually paying down your debt so that future you has less interest to pay? Or are you paying bills on time so you don't get slugged with late fees? Or maybe you're making extra contributions to your super so future you has more choice?

Write down three things you're already doing to look after future you, and a few ideas on what you could start doing now to build a better future with your money.

Companion planting: Finding your cheerleaders

When you are shedding, changing and growing your money habits, you may find your efforts aren't always met with the celebration or accolades they deserve. You might even find they're met with resistance, hostility or attempts to derail you. Some people watch those seedlings start to grow and, instead of encouraging them, want to trample on them.

Who you have in your patch matters. You want to surround yourself with people who will not only scream and high-kick, cheerleader-style, words of encouragement but also help propagate your success. You want people with you who are also on a journey of shedding and growing; those who will motivate and inspire you to keep trying and learning.

Any good gardener will tell you that companion planting (that is, growing certain plants together for mutual benefit) increases growth, offers protection from nasties and increases pollination, which can lead to a bigger, more bountiful harvest. You can apply the same strategy to your finances.

Telling the people in your corner the journey you are on is important. By sharing with them what you are working on with your money, who you want to become and why it's important to you, you're making sure they know how to best support you. If you tell your friends you aren't going to be able to spend like you have in the past because you're saving to buy a house or paying off your HECS debt, they can then hold you accountable so you don't hurtle back into old habits.

Life is too short to spend your time with people who don't want the absolute and very best for you. You want the people who share insights generously, who cheer when you win and catch you when you fall. They tell you how they asked for a pay rise or started investing, and what they wish they knew sooner. They don't gatekeep and they don't judge. They will let you cry on their shoulder as you let out loud snotty sobs. But they will also tell you when you need to get up, dust yourself off and get on with life. If you don't have these kinds of people around you yet, find them — I promise you they are out there.

Money in the wild: Callum (he/him)

- **Age:** 32.
- **Situationship:** Single.
- **Income:** $145000.
- **Current savings:** $2000.
- **Current relationship with money:** Under control, stable and curious.
- **Money monster's name:** 'Alex'. They love to impulse buy something if it's new and shiny. I now try to sleep on it overnight or google when a good sale is going to happen. It's helped me stop impulsive buying.

Have you ever had to use your emergency savings, and how did it make you feel?

Yes. I recently had to move because the landlord wanted to sell, and I needed to dip into it for some things.

What does life look like right now?

Looking to get a promotion within six months with a pay rise. This will help put money towards a home deposit. Home ownership is looking like it's going to be very difficult and at least five years away. Rent is only going up. I would like to travel more but I'm also trying to balance saving for a deposit and some down time so I don't burn out at work. A 5 per cent deposit would put me in so much debt and I'd have to stay in Sydney, which is where I feel safe and comfortable as a gay man.

Do you save or invest?

Yes. I have a portion allocated to investing each month—$100 plus I round up on my spending using an app, so approximately

$130 per month. I also save each month. I split this into top-up emergency savings, holiday account and house deposit account.

What is a past money decision you're proud of?
Organising my cash flow. I have a spreadsheet that I adjust and automate all of my money using the Greenhouse waterfall methodology. I have a master account and from this automate money into all my other accounts. I pay myself weekly and this helps me stick to my savings goals.

What's one piece of money advice you wish you knew sooner?
How to organise a cash flow. I really stuck my head in the sand and didn't look into where my money was going and how to budget. It isn't something that's ever taught so if you don't try to learn it seems very overwhelming.

What was your biggest 'ouch' money moment, and what came from it?
Credit card interest. That hit me hard and I was stuck for a long time with a huge bill that didn't seem to go away. I had to use an agency to pay off my huge debt and set up a payment plan with them, which was also costly but I didn't know what else to do.

What has shaped your relationship with money the most?
Family for sure. I had two different views on money so it was very jarring to try and look at what was 'right' or 'wrong'. We never spoke about money or strategies. I moved to Sydney when I was 21 and everything was so expensive. I got caught up in the Sydney lifestyle and I wanted to be seen to be going out and living the life rather than putting my hand up saying I was struggling.

What does 'financial wellbeing' mean to you?

Being stress-free and not having to worry about how much your weekly groceries are going to cost and how that will eat into your weekly budget. Freedom to have choices in your life. Having money you can use to invest and plan for your future rather than just paying rent and surviving.

Did you have a big 'oh shit' moment that made you realise you had to learn more about money?

The realisation that I might be renting forever without owning a house and I'd be fucked when I retire because the pension doesn't take into consideration you might not own a place. They assume you do.

What's one outrageous thing you've spent money on and did you regret it?

Laser facials at $450 each. Yes, because I don't know if they did a lot :(

5

PLOT

How to set money goals that matter and make decisions on what to grow

> Beautiful days do not come to you. You must walk towards them.
>
> *—Rumi*

If you want to use your money to build the life you want, you gotta have goals. Plotting out where you want to go and how you are going to get there is how you intentionally build the roadmap for your life. So before you go any further, I want you to ask yourself: what big ideas or plans do you *really* want to make a reality? What would make you look back and think, *I'm so fucking happy I made that happen*? Be it starting to invest, shaking up your career or getting the credit card cleared, you need to work out what you're working towards. To plot is to create the future you want.

Most people flirt with goal setting, usually around the start of a new year, only to dump those goals and return to life as usual a few short weeks later. The days then start to get filled with 'if onlys'. (*If only I started investing years ago...If only I took that trip when my health was good...If only I added a bit extra into my retirement savings...If only I got on top of my money stuff sooner...*)

Another way to look at goal setting is to consider what you would look back on and regret *not* doing. One of the most common regrets of the dying is that they gave up on a dream they once had. Taking your last breath with your goals still stuck inside? Never doing the big, hard, scary, potentially bold moves needed to make your dreams happen? Not on my watch.

Langston Hughes' famous poem *Harlem* speaks to the idea of a 'dream deferred'. (Look it up if you don't already know it.) His words pull at the soul strings — because what *does* happen to them? Do they change? Do they simply wither away — not because they weren't worthy, but because they weren't nurtured? Do they stay and swell inside us like a brewing storm, or do they come and go like the tides?

I'm sure at some point you, too, have experienced 'goals remorse' — that anger and frustration for not achieving the thing you said you wanted to. But what if you could set goals that make you feel light and excited? Ones that you want to stick with? What if you didn't wait for a new day, week, month or year to build out your money roadmap? What if you started from exactly where you find yourself right now (yes, with your current job, income and savings balance)? How can you make sure you don't leave this world lamenting 'if only'?

In this chapter, I outline a science-based system for setting and achieving goals. I have used this same system myself and with hundreds of people I've worked with, including many who've never set goals before and felt nauseous at the thought of it!

A garden of one's own

Think of plotting financial goals as being much like how a seasoned 'green thumb' plans out their garden. Okay — let me explain. Garden plots are where things grow *intentionally*. They're well thought out, and take into consideration *what* goes into the ground *when*, and *why*.

Each of your goals is like a precious seed that needs to be planted and nurtured, waiting for the right conditions to burst to life. The quality of the 'soil' (your beliefs and mindset) matters, but it's not the only thing that determines success. And of course, your goals will always have the weather to contend with (that is, external forces that you have little control over — share market falls or tariffs, anyone?).

Just like plants, your goals need ongoing support and care. You've got to be prepared to get your hands dirty. And while planting seeds alone *might* yield some success, regularly tending to them ensures they are given the best shot of thriving. You also need to be careful about putting too much in your plot — because overcrowding means each seed, or goal, doesn't get the sunshine and space it needs to thrive.

Okay, so I know I've stretched this gardening analogy *almost* as far as it'll go, but I'm nothing if not determined to squeeze a little more out of it. Because, as you start to plot out your plan, you'll likely be tempted to want to take a peek over the back fence to check out the neighbour's thriving veggie garden, and ponder how they've managed to achieve so much in such a small space. But here's the thing: each plot is unique. What gets planted, and how it grows, is based on what's important to you, what season of life you're in, the environmental conditions you face, and the amount of work you put in — not the goals and conditions of your neighbours.

I know it can be inspiring (and envy-inducing) to see the literal fruits of someone's labour — but therein lies the point. Their success has taken work. It's taken patience, care, time, effort and energy. Chances are they didn't plant their seeds yesterday and wake up today to a bountiful harvest. But the reality is you don't actually know. You don't know when they planted them, how much they watered them, or how many hours they've spent tending to them (or tearing their hair out). All too often, we look at someone's achievements and think, *I want that*—but we (conveniently) forget the years and maybe the tears they've spent tending to them. It's easy to gaze at the sea of fragrant flowers. But you must not forget the fortitude it's likely taken to bring those flowers to bloom.

They say that comparison is the thief of joy, but it's also the thief of satisfaction and pride when you achieve something you really set your mind (and your money) to. So if you really want to achieve your goals, you need to accept that it's going to take planning, practice, persistence and patience. But I'm here to tell you that it's worth it, in every way.

Acknowledging the lottery of life—and plotting anyway

It's also important to acknowledge that a fair amount of privilege comes with setting big, ambitious goals. Not everyone has the same starting place, opportunities and support to make them happen. And it can be painful and frustrating when you feel like others are getting a leg-up—perhaps through support from one of the country's biggest unofficial lenders (aka the 'Bank of Mum and Dad'), while you're struggling not to slip below the poverty line and eating packet noodles for the tenth day straight.

Goals are as diverse as we are. For some, they are big and audacious, such as retiring early or having a portfolio of investment properties. Others are more humble but no less important, such as being able to keep a roof over your head or keeping the kids fed and clothed. Recognising that it's not a level playing field is important. And while many excellent people are working hard to make the financial world more fair and equitable, you can only start from wherever you are and with whatever you have.

One of the words we talk a lot about when it comes to building wealth is 'freedom'. Ah, that blissful idea that you can do what you want, when you want. How and where you spend your time would be totally up to you. Honestly, ask most people what they want to achieve as a result of getting their financial shit sorted, and 'freedom' is the answer.

But 'freedom' the way it's often conceptualised — having enough passive income from investments to bankroll you forevermore — is somewhat of a unicorn. It's a rare, mythical and romanticised beast. Setting a goal to have total and complete financial freedom, from your current vantage point, might seem impossible, even farcical. And it might well be. Once that realisation hits, it can hit hard. Like after discovering that magnificent unicorn horn was actually a bloody narwhal tusk all along (seriously, look it up), suddenly the world feels slightly less magical. You feel like you've been duped.

But what if freedom, however you define it, wasn't a lofty and unattainable ideal but something actually within your grasp?

In *The Handmaid's Tale*, Margaret Atwood famously explores the difference between 'freedom from' (violence and harm) and 'freedom to' (make choices about how you live your life). This is a brilliant way to redefine financial freedom, taking it from hugely aspirational to far more achievable. If you sense your chest tightening at the idea of setting big goals right now, framing them instead in terms of what you want to be free *from* and what you want to have the freedom *to do* can help.

Maybe your goal is freedom *from* being stuck in a job you hate, so you decide you want to have enough saved up to cover six months of expenses. This gives you the freedom *to* quit and find something else. Maybe you'd love freedom *from* the stress of having to check your bank account before doing groceries, so you make a plan to build a healthy buffer that will give you freedom *to* shop with more confidence.

Perhaps you'd like the freedom to have one extra leave day a month to focus on recharging your batteries, or freedom to have a longer parental leave period. Maybe it's the freedom to leave a partner you know isn't right for you, while having enough funds so you don't need to couch surf or sleep in your car.

Your seeds, or your goals, not having the ideal conditions to grow can feel really hard. Going through periods when you feel like you're being pummelled with so many lemons you can't even begin to make lemonade is common. And, again, it's okay if other people's goals are different (and maybe feel way out of your league right now). It's okay to remind yourself that the lottery of life can be, and often is, wildly unfair. Your plot is yours.

Don't let your money monster (hello, Stacey the Staller, my old friend) talk you out of trying. Don't let it convince you to give up on starting, or tell yourself it's pointless — because it's not. This is *your* life we are talking about. You are the point! You're the main character, and your goals are worth trying for. And you are wildly fucking capable of doing hard things.

Good. Glad we got that sorted. Now, wanting your goals alone doesn't automatically breathe them into existence (how annoying!), but I can offer some clever ways to help you make them happen. Let's dig into some super cool science (not words 15-year-old Jess would have ever thought she'd say).

Science-backed goal superchargers

Have you ever walked through scrub so thick that every step feels treacherous and you keep getting smacked in the face with branches? It's exhausting, disorientating and almost impossible to keep your bearings. That's how life can feel when you haven't got a clear direction on where you're heading.

I've been on my own personal journey with goals over the years, having spent many moons leaving my dreams in the hands of the Goals Fairy. (Who, by the way, never once left a fulfilled goal under my pillow in my sleep!) Now I approach goals entirely differently. No more waiting for them to magically manifest under the mattress. I don't wait to be in the mood, or be less busy. I *make* time for them.

Every Monday at 5 pm you'll find me working through my life goal to-do list with my coach. Regular accountability has been a game changer for me. Carving out time for my goals forces me to step out of the weeds of daily life (more on that in the next chapter) and gives me a view of the treetops, so I can realign my actions with my goals every week. I track my progress, plan my time and am kept accountable to my commitments. Work is done without good hair or fanfare, and it's not always rosy. I have sick days and disappointments, as well as the odd health or family crisis (joy!). I have moments of lying on the floor, deep breathing (which apparently is good to ground you when you feel like the world is spinning too fast). What matters is making sure I always get up and back on the horse — because I have seen just how far she can take me.

Back in 2022, after selling my share of the financial advice business I co-founded, I plonked myself on a Greek island for two weeks, where I inhaled books, research papers and an obscene amount of podcasts on brain function, neuroscience and goal attainment. It became an obsession (or, as I now realise, #hyperfixation). I felt like I was unlocking the secrets to the universe as I learned how to hack the brain for success. I wanted to know *everything*. What follows are my takeaways from all the ferocious notes I took — which you can now take advantage of as you plot your financial goals.

Create goals that tip the scales in your favour

Did you know that writing clear goals makes you 42 per cent more likely to achieve them?[1] Without writing them down, it's difficult to know how to allocate your income correctly, which investments are going to work best, how much risk you should (or shouldn't be taking), or if you're on-track. Without clear goals, you have no track at all — just thick, dense forest that feels impenetrable.

Clear goal setting can help reduce that constant tension and confusion about what to do or where to focus your attention. It also means you can figure out how much money needs to go towards each goal, which investments might be the right fit, and what tiny tasks and habits you need to do regularly to see them into existence.

Take advantage of the brain's filtration system

Have you ever considered buying a new model of car, only to suddenly start noticing that car *everywhere*? Perhaps it's a sign from the universe that you should absolutely and most definitely get the car? *Maybe.* More likely it's because of a very clever filtering system inside your brain that you probably didn't even realise you had.

The reticular activating system (RAS) is essentially your brain's filtration system. It takes the millions of pieces of information (sounds, sights, smells, sensations and thoughts) your brain is bombarded with daily and decides what's important enough to be let through the filter. In other words, this system decides what makes it into your conscious awareness, and what needs to be filtered out as background noise. By getting clear with yourself on what you want, the RAS will quietly start looking around for things aligned with your goals and bring them into your consciousness.[2]

I'm sometimes asked if I believe manifesting works. My honest answer is that I think what's actually going on is your RAS is suddenly making you feel like the opportunities you're 'manifesting' are appearing more frequently. So feed it your goals!

Use visualisation and rehearsal

Visualisation is your brain's version of a dress rehearsal before the big show. While the idea of visualising something into reality might sound cute (or a tad 'woo-woo'), the concept of 'faking it till you make it' when it comes to achieving a goal is actually heavily steeped in science. In fact, our brains are quite shite at differentiating between real and vividly imagined experiences, which we can use to our advantage! Brain imagery has shown that when we imagine ourselves taking action, it uses similar neural circuits to the ones used for *actually* executing that action.[3] Visualising helps you rehearse, plan for obstacles and refine tasks, making you likely to perform better when you do it for real.

Interestingly, thinking about failing is also an incredible way to anticipate obstacles and motivate yourself to take action. Your brain doesn't like negative experiences, so by focusing on how shit it would be if you didn't reach your goal (like never getting out of debt, never taking that holiday or never getting on the property ladder), your brain will get fired up to help you avoid the pain of not achieving it and be motivated to get to work.

You can visualise the outcome you want by creating a vision board or writing out daily motivational sticky notes. (Creating a new note each day often means your brain won't get used to the same one and will continue to engage with your desired outcome and not let it fade into the background.) Put your visual cue somewhere you can see it every day. I have my goals as the screensaver on my computer and printed out on my office wall. I also write notes like, 'You can do it!' or 'Don't give up now—the magic is just starting. Let's go'. and plonk them all over my house when I need a good pep talk. You can also practise affirmations like, 'I am capable of achieving great things' or, 'Money flows freely and easily to me'. Then when you see signs of these affirmations coming true (like that $5 you find under the lounge), use them as signals to your brain to reinforce the belief. It sounds simple (and it is), but it works. Try it and you'll see.

Win over your brain with effort, action and outcome

While your teenage years may be long behind you, the brain can still hang on to some of that moody behaviour. As you create goals, it often petulantly crosses its (metaphorical) arms and huffs, 'But *whyyyyyy*?' If you've ever tried to win over a teen and turn them into an enthusiastic participant, you'll know it's no mean feat. It can be the same with your brain. But here's the secret: it wants to know two key things before it says yes to playing ball. The first is *why*, the second is *how*.

Firstly, it's trying to figure out whether this thing is really worth doing. Basically, your brain is trying to test if you value this goal *enough*. If the answer is no, your brain is probably shutting the door in your face. If it's still playing along, then it next wants to understand what actions need to be taken and whether they're worth the effort. If your brain doesn't think the outcome is worth it, it gives it a hard pass. So, make sure you really connect with why it's worth the mud, sweat and tears, and you'll have a better chance of getting it on board.

Make your goals... just right

Remember the curious golden-haired porridge thief who wanted the perfect midpoint between hot and cold? Setting goals is much the same. I call it the 'get Goldilocks goals' method or 'GGG'. When you're setting goals, if they're too easy your brain won't engage with them enough. But if they're too hard, your brain is likely to think they're unattainable and give up. You get where I'm going with this, right? You want your goals to be in the Goldilocks 'just right' sweet spot. Make them just enough of a stretch that you know, if you put your mind to it, you could achieve them.

Break big goals down into bite-sized pieces

How do you eat an elephant? Apparently, one bite at a time. It is the same with goals. Microtask the shit out of your to-do list, and break each goal into the teeniest tasks or 'chunks'. Instead of 'sort out finances', for example, try:

- Log in to online banking.
- Download last month's statement.
- Highlight all Uber Eats expenses.
- Set a limit for takeaway food next month.
- Set a calendar reminder to check in again next month.

Yes, 'wasting' time writing out all the small, tiny little steps in each goal, which you know you need to do, can feel silly — until you get to the point where you can start ticking things off your list. (Honestly, I don't know if anything is more satisfying than ticking off items on a to-do list!) Every tick gives you a dopamine hit, which actually starts to rewire your brain to seek out more progress.

Mark the milestones

Now you know your brain gets a boost from progress, you can use that to your advantage. The trick is to make your progress visible. Create a milestone tracker for each money goal — perhaps for debt reduction, savings increases and/or investment parcels — and update it every pay cycle. For example:

- *Debt reduction:* Draw a simple thermometer or bar with your starting balance at the top and zero at the bottom. For every repayment you make, colour in the next slice down.

- *Savings goals:* Write your target at the end of the bar and add markers for specific increments as you move towards it — perhaps $500 or $1000 increments. Each time you top up your savings, colour in the bar up to the new level.

If you're a stationery lover, break out the highlighters and textas. I'm always less likely to want to dip into savings or use debt to buy something if I know doing so will muck up my progress bar (no? just me?!). Otherwise, set up a tracker in a spreadsheet or even just the notes app on your phone with checkboxes. I also like to include a date for each milestone, so I can look back and see all the times I did something for future me. (There is something really lovely about timestamping all the dates you showed up for yourself.)

Celebrate the wins

You don't need to publicly broadcast every milestone you reach. But you should find a way to meaningfully acknowledge and celebrate every win along the way (without spending!). Our brains need to not just look forward and see where we are going (important), but also identify how much of the track we have already walked down (just as important). So when you get to certain milestones, pausing and recognising that is a must!

We are often scared of promoting our progress for fear of being labelled a 'try-hard' (so cringe) — which is honestly hilarious, because we *should* celebrate the shit out of people who get up and try hard to make it happen. 'Tall poppy syndrome', especially in Australia, has taken down too many of us. Fight against this and find the people who will celebrate your attempts and achievements. Or join a dedicated community where people want to celebrate your wins with you. You're going to work hard at your goals. You deserve to celebrate the milestones along the way.

Money in the wild: Ayan (he/him)

- **Age:** 43.
- **Situationship:** Single.
- **Income:** $159000.
- **Current savings:** $20000.
- **Current relationship with money:** Work in progress.
- **Money monster's name:** Ayan—it's me, I'm the problem.

Have you ever had to use your emergency savings, and how did it make you feel?

Not yet, but recently I had an unexpected bill that related to my car and made me feel uncomfortable when factoring other large expenses coming up in the next couple of months. I want to save up to six months' worth of expenses and I'm not there yet.

What debts do you currently have?
Mortgage.

Do you save or invest?
At the moment not really, on account of adjusting to new house expenses, working on an updated cash flow plan to adjust budgets where needed and freeing up funds to both save and invest.

What's one piece of money advice you wish you knew sooner?
I wish I'd been taught financial literacy and discipline in high school as part of life skills before going out into the world and not treating money with purpose. Money lessons are ongoing; your

relationship with money is ongoing and requires maintenance and effort. Don't lose track of hindsight, learn from it.

What is your biggest 'ouch' money moment?
Taking out a mortgage and suddenly having a large drop in savings. I know it is an investment and worth it, but I felt very vulnerable at the time.

You win the lotto. What do you do?
Have the freedom to not stress about money, travel annually, reduce work hours, and support my family.

Have you ever looked at your bank account and thought, WTF? How did it get this low?
Yes and yes. I realised I needed help, advice and support if I ever wanted to make a difference, so I invested in a financial adviser.[4]

Connecting your values with your goals

Now you know the science behind goal setting, your next step is figuring out what drives you — before you plot specific financial goals. That means working out your *values*. Your values are like your personal North Star, or a guiding light in the fog of life. These are the things that, at your core, are most important to you — and they're what cause you to feel friction or frustration when they aren't being met. Sure, they can change over time but, in my experience, they often stay the same.

Knowing what drives you is important in a world with so much choice and 'shoulding'. Sure, it's great to be inspired and motivated by others, but knowing what really lights *you* up helps you filter out what's good for *them* and focus on what's good for *you*.

By linking your financial goals to your values, you create a bridge that connects them together, giving you clarity, focus and determination. I've watched many people achieve things in their life they thought they *should* want or be happy with, only to feel a strange hollowness when they get them. That's what happens when a goal isn't truly aligned to any of the values that drive you. If a goal doesn't connect to your values, then ask yourself: why are you doing it?

I've also watched plenty of people have lightbulb moments when they realise one of the reasons they haven't made progress on their financial goals is because they weren't aligned with their values. People, for example, who struggled to set (and achieve) savings goals because they told themselves they weren't overly 'motivated by money'. But it's not about building money for money's sake. Once they can see what money can give them — such as the freedom to go on a European adventure for a milestone birthday, or the freedom from a mortgage or credit card debt — their eyes light up and they shift into gear. You don't have to love money, but most goals cost something, so you do need to connect them to something you value. It feels powerful to say 'hell, yes!' to the things that light you up — and, even more importantly, 'no, thank you' to things that won't. So do some work now to identify what is most important to you.

Activity: Identify your core values

Think about the values that drive and motivate you, and keep you showing up (not the ones you wish you had). The following table provides some common values, or you can add your own. Select your top ten values:

Achievement	Adventure	Authenticity
Balance	Certainty	Challenge
Comfort	Connection/community	Contribution
Control	Creativity	Curiosity
Discipline	Freedom/flexibility	Fun
Generosity	Gratitude	Gratitude
Growth	Happiness	Independence
Integrity	Joy	Justice
Knowledge/learning	Leadership	Legacy
Love	Peace	Purpose
Recognition	Resilience	Safety
Security/stability	Service	Simplicity
Structure/organisation	Tradition	Wellbeing

From your top ten values, now select your top five. These will then become your core values. (Selecting only five can be hard, but it is important!). Without filtering, judging or curating, for each of your five core values, ask yourself:

▶ Is this value really yours, or one you've been told you 'should' value?

▶ Why is this value so important to you? How does it drive you?

> ▸ How are you currently embodying this value?
> ▸ Where are you not?
> ▸ How does this value show up in your money or financial decisions?

Assessing your current values alignment

If you were living a life in full alignment with your core values, what would be different to how you are living right now? This question was often the most emotionally triggering of all the questions I asked my financial advice clients. So I want to acknowledge that it might have just brought up some really uncomfortable realisations for you too.

You may have just had the proverbial penny drop hard on your head that lots of areas of your life need adjusting. Maybe you now realise you've been chasing something that doesn't align with what drives you. Perhaps you've gotten clarity on areas that need more focus or change in the future. Or, maybe you've realised, 'I'm actually living pretty aligned with what I value' — which, if that's the case, I genuinely love that for you!

Most people feel happier and more motivated when they are living in line with their values, so if you've identified any areas that need to shift, that's the starting point for plotting out your financial goals.

Getting on the same page with a partner

If you are in a relationship, I cannot emphasise enough how important it is to explore your goals and values together. Values shape so much of our financial decision making, including what goals to focus on, and how to spend, save, invest and donate your money. Knowing what makes you both tick is crucial to building a strong foundation.

Complete each step of the core values exercise individually, and then come together and share your insights. As each of you is sharing, the other person's role is to actively listen — not to judge or criticise. It's not about telling each other whether their values are 'correct' or not. And a perfect match isn't necessarily the goal either. This exercise is primarily about awareness.

Many couples I've worked with had what appeared to be opposing or clashing values. One person was driven by security, for example, while the other was driven by freedom. Without clear conversations and spending systems in place, this either left one person feeling stifled and suffocated, or the other feeling stressed and anxious.

You don't need to have exactly the same values for your relationship to work. But you do need to be able to have open and honest conversations, as well as money systems set up to track what goes where, plus regular check-ins so you both stay aligned and accountable.

Tackling goals as a couple: An interview with Nicole Haddow

Nicole is the author of *Couple Goals: Building a strong financial future and an even better relationship*. So I thought who better to gain insights from on how you can negotiate money with your partner? Here's some of the knowledge she shared with me.

What do you think is best practice when it comes to couples setting goals together?
It's essential that the goals are authentic and true to you as a couple and as individuals, because that's how you'll achieve them. If you're setting

goals based on external or societal factors, your heart might not truly be in it. You need to believe in what you're trying to achieve and be motivated to keep going. In my experience, the goals are easier to work towards when they're in alignment with values and lifestyle objectives.

It's rarely about the money in isolation; it's about the life you aspire to live. It's also important to recognise that not every goal will be shared. Perhaps early in the relationship, when there's a big goal such as saving for a house, you'll throw everything you've got at it as a team. But there are still two people in the relationship and at times one person might have a financial goal that is important to them. Compromise will be required at times, and the goal posts often move, so you need to be prepared to shift your priorities as life changes.

What to do when you and your partner have misaligned values, priorities, ideas and goals?

I suggest removing the goal itself from the conversation and talk about how you want life to look in 5, 10 or 20 years from now. If one person wants to take an international holiday and the other wants to pay off a car loan first, can you look at the long-term implications of each decision? Can you say, 'How about we pay off the car first and then save for the trip?' There will always be compromise in relationships and, when it comes to goals, it's worth looking at which immediate goals will provide a better foundation for the future.

How do you keep each other accountable and on-track, without creating conflict?

Something my husband and I do regularly is ask each other if we're giving our best. It removes the money from the conversation and encourages us to focus on our dedication to shared objectives. Sometimes conflict is inevitable—and it's often better than bottling things up, provided you know how to listen and talk through the issue at hand. If you're able to explain your frustration and really feel heard, that's a step in the right direction. Hopefully, if one person is not keeping up their end of the bargain, they'll take on the feedback and make meaningful changes.

What if one person is really interested in goal setting and the other isn't? Is it a sign the relationship is doomed? How can you get them on board and excited by it?

It's extremely common for couples to have different levels of financial motivation. Is the person who's less motivated prepared to grow? Behavioural changes with money can take time, but if there's a willingness this can absolutely happen. Rather than focusing on the goal itself, it can be wise to look at long-term lifestyle. For example, saying, 'If we invest a certain amount for this many years, we can reduce our workloads or take more frequent holidays' moves the focus to the value and the lifestyle outcome. One person mightn't be motivated by the work required to get there, but visualising the outcome certainly helps.

Who you partner with can profoundly impact your financial outcomes. I'm not arguing you need to find a stonkingly rich partner. But finding someone who wants to work with you to build the life you both want requires both of you in the arena. Both of you need to show up for yourselves and each other. You both need to communicate, listen, compromise and care. It's about supporting each other, sharing the load and being on the same team. If they can't play along, maybe you need a new teammate (or want to look into single sports!).

Time to get plotting — the GROW method

Now that you know your values, and have all the science-backed insights you need to supercharge your goals, it's time to plot out your plan. But where do you start? And how will you make sure that your goals are nurtured and have what they need to grow?

One of my all-time favourite frameworks for setting (and actually achieving) goals is the GROW framework, and not just because its name aligns *sahhhh* nicely with this whole garden metaphor I've got going on here! The GROW framework is based on Sir John Whitmore's coaching model, which I've adapted over the years to help thousands of people achieve big financial life goals. Let's go through the key elements of the GROW framework one by one, as well as the questions to ask yourself and the actions to complete, so you come out the other side with a clear map of your goals. Then, in the following chapters, I help you figure out how to help those goals grow and flourish. So let's get into it.

Here's how the elements in the GROW method work together:

- *G* = *goals:* Do they align with your aspirations, hopes and dreams?
- *R* = *reality:* Is it realistic, or a fantasy?
- *O* = *options:* How could you make it happen?
- *W* = *will:* How are you actually going to make it happen?

And here's what you'll need to really get stuck in:

- your new money alter ego (your version of your Batman persona — refer to the previous chapter)
- a quiet space with little to no distractions (a sign on the door that says, 'Do not interrupt, currently planning my future' is optional)
- paper and a pen (you can complete this on a computer, but typing engages fewer neural circuits, meaning your brain isn't engaged in the same way as when you get oldschool with paper and pen)

- highlighters, textas or coloured pens and pencils
- your favourite playlist and headphones (if this helps with creativity and focus)
- drinks and snacks (surely no explanation needed)
- a friend or partner (if you work better with an accountability buddy or using body doubling).

A note for my ADHD friends: I am particularly sensitive to sounds, light and interruptions when I am hyperfocusing (or hoping to hyperfocus!). You'll know what works best for you, but get yourself in the right space to support yourself for this task. For me, it's meds, no bright lights, shoes on, fave playlist on, phone to 'do not disturb', timers set so I don't fall down a rabbit hole and large rolls of brown paper because small pieces of paper make me feel hemmed in.

G is for goals

You're the main character of your life, so you get to curate your plot line. You probably won't have it all figured out yet (no-one does!), and it's okay if things change down the track, but do this exercise based on the best info you've currently got — that is, what you know to be true today for your situation.

The 'G' in the GROW method has five distinct steps to it, and each builds on the one before it. It sounds like a lot so let's break it down.

Step 1: Think big and identify your time lines

So you can see the path before you step foot on it, you are going to arrange your goals into different time horizons. Divide a piece of paper into three sections with the following headings:

- One year
- One to five years
- Five+ years

Here is how I think of each of these time frames:

- *Short term (one year) = bamboo:* This is for fast-growing, easy-to-see progress goals that you can feel excited about and which can regrow season after season. Think smaller savings goals that require a few thousand dollars, such as an annual holiday fund, buying a new winter coat, replacing the laptop or adopting a pet. These are all great — but you don't want bamboo to take over your entire space. It can, and will, if you let it! You need to leave some space (and money) for other things to grow.
- *Medium term (one to five years) = fruit trees:* These goals take a few years to mature, meaning you've got to love and care for them, even though they don't bear juicy goodness straight away. But, you know, after just a few seasons of care and consistency, you'll get to enjoy the fruits of your hard work. Goals in this category might include getting the bathroom renovated, saving for a house deposit, paying off credit card debts, taking parental leave or upgrading the car.
- *Long term (five+ years) = oak tree:* Oak trees are slow (like, real slow) growing but they are strong, providing shade, shelter and stability for decades (even centuries) into the future. They don't grow upwards until they've built a deep root system, just like your money when it's compounding — it can feel like nothing much is happening until you finally start seeing growth. These goals provide you with long-term security and can even (potentially) benefit generations to come. Factoring in the growth time, generally, the sooner you plant them, the better. Goals in this category include having a home you live in debt-free, starting or adding to an investment portfolio, buying an investment property, paying for your kid's or grandkid's education, having a sabbatical or retiring early.

Step 2: Fill in the details

Based on your time horizon (when you want to achieve them), list out each of your goals and remember to be as descriptive as possible. The following provides one example for each time frame, but you will likely have more for each category.

Plotting goals by time frame

	One year (bamboo)	One to five years (fruit trees)	Five+ years (oak trees)
Goal	Travel to New Zealand for three weeks next winter to ski with my family.	Pay off student debt so I have additional cash flow and borrowing capacity.	Pay off my mortgage ten years earlier than scheduled so I can direct more of my money to building a legacy for my family.
Target $	$6000	$24420	$550000

Step 3: Identify how your values align with these goals

Write next to each goal which of your core values it most aligns with. Some may align to multiple values, so you can list more than one if needed.

Aligning goals with core values

	One year (bamboo)	One to five years (fruit trees)	Five+ years (oak trees)
Goal	Travel to New Zealand for three weeks next winter to ski with my family.	Pay off student debt so I have additional cash flow and borrowing capacity.	Pay off my mortgage ten years earlier than scheduled so I can direct more of my money to building a legacy for my family.
Target $	$6000	$24420	$550000
Core value alignment	Connection	Flexibility	Security

Step 4: Narrow down what's most important to you

Choose one 'must have' goal from each of the three time horizons (one year, one to five years, and five+ years) and circle it. That will give you three priority goals to start with.

Given these are 'must haves', now is the time to commit to doing all you can to make them happen. This is a promise to your future self, with love from current you. I'm probably a complete odd-ball, but I like to close my eyes here, put my hand on my heart and tell myself exactly what I am committing to. Maybe you want to try it too?

Step 5: Visualise your success

For each of your three 'must have' goals, grab a fresh page and write a paragraph from the perspective of having already achieved it. (This helps your brain get more connected to it.)

What did you need to do to make it happen? What obstacles did you have to overcome to achieve it? What does life feel like and how's it different, now you've reached that goal? Link your answers back to your core values if you can.

Maybe you can travel and go on adventures without draining all your savings, or take a few months off to volunteer at a local charity and not worry about not earning an income for that period. The more you can connect with your goal, the more likely you are going to fight for it when it matters. (Remember the science about visualisations and rehearsing for success from earlier in this chapter?)

R is for reality

Okay, not to be the fun police, but now you need to do a reality check. Based on what you're currently doing, can you achieve the goals you've just listed out? Go back and assess each of your goals based on the following traffic light system:

- *Green:* Goals are likely to be achieved based on your current progress.

- *Orange:* You could *potentially* achieve these goals based on current progress.
- *Red:* You're *not* likely to achieve these goals based on current progress.

What did you notice? Are all of your goals one particular colour? All red helps you see that if you really want to achieve these goals, you need to take serious and potentially drastic action to make them happen. If they are all green, are they too safe or easy? Do you need to get a bit more Goldilocks with your goals?

Are you likely to achieve your short-term goals, but not your longer term ones? That's common, because humans are much better at thinking and planning for what's immediately in front of us, than for our longer term needs. This tendency is something most of us need to consciously work hard at overriding, because, annoyingly, our long-term goals often need years to grow and compound (like the oak tree).

What colour are your three 'must have' goals? How do you feel about that?

Realising you might need to prune some of your goals right about now is common. Perhaps you simply have too many and not enough resources to practically make them all a reality. This can be a frustrating and genuinely painful step. But pruning does give space for your most important goals to thrive. Numbering your goals from highest to lowest in terms of importance across all time frames is the easiest way to do this.

You may only have capacity to work on one financial goal right now, or one might be particularly urgent (such as building an emergency savings account). It's okay to put your focus and effort there for now. When you've achieved that goal, you can pick up the other two 'must have' goals.

O is for options

If you really want to achieve these goals, now's the time to get creative about how you can make them happen. Put all the options on the table (even the weird and wonderful ones!), and then sift through them to see which ones are the most feasible or available to you.

For example, say your goal is to save $80 000 for a house deposit in the next five years. Here's a bunch of ways you could kickstart this goal:

- have a no-spend day, week or month
- start a dedicated bank account with monthly savings automation
- move in with friends or family
- take up pet sitting or house sitting
- start investing
- sell your old clothes or items
- get HR to salary sacrifice some of your income to your Australian super fund (to then use as a deposit within the First Home Super Saver Scheme)
- negotiate a pay rise
- move to a cheaper area
- swap take-out for home-cooked an extra night a week
- cancel any subscriptions you could live without
- don't go on that trip you were considering
- buy secondhand
- do paid surveys
- take public transport instead of a taxi or ride-share
- downgrade the car.

Once you have some options, consider:

- What's worked for you in the past?
- What would your alter ego do to make it happen?
- What are the advantages of each option?
- Which are the easiest to start on and which are the ones that are slower and harder? (Rank options from easiest to hardest.)

W is for will

You've got your goals, your time frames and your reality check. You also know how the goals align with your values, and you have options for how to make them happen. So this is where you bring all the pieces together and decide what you *will* do to make your goals a reality.

This element of the GROW framework might just be the success secret sauce — or the super-nutritious fertiliser, if we're keeping this garden analogy going (which, frankly I low-key have to at this point). This is when you make a commitment to both your goals and yourself to make those dreams happen.

Because you can have the most exciting values-aligned goals ever, but no-one can force you to show up for them. No-one can pry things out of your online shopping cart, and no-one's going to stand over you and force you to cook dinner instead of buying takeaways. It's on you. No-one is coming to rescue you — not even Batman.

To lock in your focus, write down answers to each of the following for your top three goals:

- *What* goal are you committing to exactly? For example, this could be saving $80 000 for a house deposit to buy your first home.
- *How* are you going to do it? For example, saving $1800 a month, plus any future pay rises or additional income you receive. Or you could move to a cheaper rental when your lease is up, or go on a low-budget hiking or camping holiday.

- *When* are you going to achieve this by? For example, in one to five years.
- *Where* will this money go? For example, in a specific high-interest savings account, in an offset account or in an envelope under the bed (please don't do this last one!).
- *Who* is going to keep me accountable? For example, your partner, bestie or financial adviser. (It could even be me and your fellow Get Growing alumni — but more on that later.)
- Do you need to stage the goal, so you don't get overwhelmed? What could that look like?

By now you should feel a sense of clarity on what you're focusing on, why you're committed to it and how you are going to make it happen. It should feel really exciting right about now. If you aren't feeling that, a block exists somewhere. Go back through the GROW process and find the issue so you can work through it.

Okay, sunshine — let's do this

Remember — you're capable of achieving big things in your life. You're smart. You can do tough stuff. You can shake up your beliefs, habits and anything else that needs changing to make your goals a reality. You can be abso-fucking-lutely terrified and still keep going. You can. I know you can.

Yes, I realise the path won't all be peaches and cream. You'll have days when rain tries to wash all your good work away. But then, the sun will come out again. You will grab those garden gloves and get back to your plot and nurture your dreams. Because I'm pretty damn sure you do want to achieve them. You want to look back on your life with immense pride having made your dreams happen. And you will.

The next chapters will help you with this too — starting with good ol' weeding, then by sorting out your cash flow, so your goals have the water they need to thrive.

6

WEED

Ditching bad debts and patrolling the doubts that are slowing your growing (creepers, crowders and resource suckers)

Lost time is never found again.

—Benjamin Franklin

You want to achieve your goals, right? Then you've got to give them space, time, money and a whole lotta love. You also have to get rid of anything that's getting in the way and stealing vital nutrients from your goals — and that means it's time to weed.

Weeds are the financial and non-financial things that quietly creep into your life and grow quickly. Over the years, I've seen way too many goals squeezed out by the weeds of life. Mostly, these are the bog-standard, common household weeds that take a stronghold and strangle our goals out of existence — everyday use of debt or credit cards to pay for essentials, for example, or the burden of how tasks are divided in a household. On their own, they may be small and innocuous, but they gradually take over. Then there are the more insidious and hard-to-dig-up types of weeds, from wasteful spending and systemic discrimination (aka the 'dirt' covered in chapter 2), to unhelpful money stories (we did the digging on that one in chapter 3).

The problem is, in many cases, you don't actually realise the weeds are a problem until they've completely overgrown your garden. Or you might assume your goals can grow around them. But let me tell you: by weeding them out you will have a much, much better shot at making your goals a reality, and I have a sneaking suspicion that's why you're here.

Recognising garden-variety weeds

Some common household weeds include:

- *Lifestyle creep:* Your expenses increase with each pay rise.
- *Shiny object syndrome:* Impulse or convenience purchases that may offer short-term gratification but don't retain their value in the long run.
- *'Spendy' habits:* A 'treat yo'self' mentality that robs future you by frittering $10 here, $100 there.
- *Decision fatigue:* By the time you've made a hundred other decisions in a day, you say 'screw it' and order takeaway again when you've already bought groceries.
- *Going into debt for something that doesn't grow in value:* This could be a new car or household items such as a couch or new TV.
- *Buy now pay (regret) later schemes:* These schemes normalise a culture of 'if you want it, you should have it — now', no matter the true cost.
- *FOMO or saying, 'Fuck it, why not?':* Even when you know you could be saying, 'No — that's not a priority for me right now'.
- *People in your life who encourage you to spend:* Even when they know you're trying to save.

- *Having too much on your plate:* You don't have any time or energy left to give to your financial priorities.
- *Perfectionism and analysis paralysis:* The idea that if you can't do something 'perfectly', you shouldn't start at all. Or you put things off until you've 'got your shit together'. (*Spoiler:* That day rarely comes!)
- *Social media influencers and 'comparisonitis':* Seeing other people's seemingly perfect holiday, house or wardrobe causes you to subconsciously spend to 'keep up', or buy something to emulate or imitate someone else.
- *Chasing 'get-rich quick' schemes or passive income pipe dreams:* Even when you don't have a clear plan to make them happen.
- *Crossing all your fingers and toes:* Putting your trust in the universe, the moon, the stars, Taylor Swift — that working hard alone will mean it all works out!

How many of these weeds do you need to nip in the bud so your financial goals can grow? Which are the easiest to eradicate now and which will take a bit more effort or change to weed out completely? What practical steps do you need to take to make it happen? And what would getting rid of those weeds give you — more time, more money, more capacity or more confidence in your capabilities to achieve your goals?

And, trust me: just like actual weeds, even when you think you've plucked those money-suckers out, they often come back when you're not watching. This means weeding needs to be a regular part of your plan. No-one likes a creep, and you certainly don't want them to quietly return uninvited, settle in once more and wreak havoc on your goals. As Shakespeare's Hamlet advises, 'And do not spread the compost on the weeds'.

Figuring out your net ~~worth~~ wealth position

One of the best ways to assess where you're at is by getting a bird's-eye view of your current financial position. You're looking at the big picture here: how much you have in assets versus what you owe in liabilities. Taking stock in this way can give you insights and clues on the areas you just might need to give some love and attention to.

In the money world, you often hear this called a 'net worth position', but let's just pause right there for a second — because your worth as a person has fuck all to do with what this number is. I hate the terminology so much, due to its clear implication that your worth is directly linked to your wealth. It isn't. It never was. That's why I like to call it your 'net *wealth* position' instead. (See, much better!)

What is a net wealth position? It is a number that shows the difference between your current assets (something you own that increases in value, such as a house), minus your current liabilities (any money you owe, such as a mortgage).

Activity: Getting started on your net wealth position

If this is your first time ever doing this, welcome! I'm so glad you're taking the time to do this vital step, which so many people skip over. This exercise gives you a bird's-eye view of your current overall financial situation. It's helpful as both a starting point and a snapshot of how your financial situation might have changed over time. At a minimum, I recommend you do this once every six months (or more regularly if big financial changes occur in your world).

So assets minus liabilities equal your net wealth position. Your assets may include things such as savings, superannuation, investment portfolio, your home, other properties, and some collectible or rare items. They don't include things that go down in value, such as household items and clothes.

Your liabilities are things such as credit cards, personal loans, car loans, money owed to buy now pay later (BNPL) schemes (for example, Afterpay, Klarna and Zip), mortgages, investment, business or student debt.

Here's how to calculate your net wealth position:

1. List out all your assets and their approximate current value. (If you own a percentage of an asset, add the value based on the percentage you own.)
2. Add up your current total assets. This is now your total asset position.
3. List out all your current liabilities. (Again, if you share any debts, put down the percentage you are responsible for.)
4. Add up your current total liabilities.
5. From your total assets, minus your total liabilities. The number you are left with is your current net wealth position! This number can either be positive or negative, depending on your current situation.
6. Add a date to your calculations, so when you do them next, you can compare your position.
7. Put a note in your diary six months from now to do this exercise again.

You can access my simple Net Wealth Calculator Template via the QR code at the back of the book.

The following tables run through some examples of calculating the net wealth position in various scenarios.

Example 1: You want to clear debt and start investing

Assets	Value	Liabilities	Amount owed
Emergency savings	$3010	Credit card	$4200
Cash buffer	$0	BNPL	$827
Holiday fund	$1700	Personal loan	$18864
Retirement (super) savings	$45000	Student debt	$32000
Total assets	$49710	*Total liabilities*	$55891
Total assets ($49710) – total liabilities ($55891) = net wealth position			**–$6181**

In this example, you can see that, because the total assets add up to less than the current liabilities, the net wealth position is a negative figure. If you're in a similar situation, this can seem daunting, but keep your eye on the prize. If a big chunk of your liabilities is student debt (as in this example), you're likely already paying this off based on your income. So now consider what your plan could be with the other liabilities. Which could you focus on clearing or reducing down first?

Example 2: You purchased a property by yourself

Assets	Value	Liabilities	Amount owed
Emergency savings	$25000	Credit card	$850
Cash buffer	$1000	Student debt	$15000
Home	$950000	Home loan	$620000
Investment portfolio	$16000		
Retirement (super) savings	$111000		
Total assets	$1103000	*Total liabilities*	$635850
Total assets ($1103000) – total liabilities ($635850) = net wealth position			**$467150**

In this example, you can see that the net wealth position is a positive figure. If you're in a similar situation, you still have some debts to clear, but you're taking action in lots of areas to grow your wealth, from investing to retirement savings (such as through super) and buying a property, while also having some cash on hand if a financial storm hits.

Example 3: You purchased a property 50/50 with a partner

Assets	Value	Liabilities	Amount owed
Emergency savings	$25000	Credit card	$850
Cash buffer	$1000	Student debt	$15000
Home value ($950000) @ 50% ownership	$475000	Home loan ($620000) – 50%	$310000
Investment portfolio	$16000		
Retirement (super) savings	$111000		
Total assets	$628000	*Total liabilities*	$325850
Total assets ($628000) – total liabilities ($325850) = net wealth position			**$302150**

The preceding example also has a positive net wealth position, but shows how to calculate your position if you own a property 50/50 with a partner.

If you're in a similar situation, remember — even if you and your partner have each agreed to be responsible for half of the debt, most mortgages are taken out as 'jointly and severally liable' — meaning the lender can chase *either* one of you for the whole amount if repayments aren't made.

If you do this exercise every six months, over time, you'll gain useful insights into how your situation is (or isn't) changing. Sometimes your situation will change due to reasons out of your control — for example, share markets can go up or down, which impacts your asset value. But regularly checking your net wealth position can also show if you need to put more focus into a particular area. For example, maybe your goal is to increase your savings, but the number hasn't budged. Or perhaps you want to reduce a chunk of debt, but the amount isn't being reduced as much as you'd planned. This exercise will show you how you're tracking in a broad sense and clue you in to where you might want to make subtle (or significant) adjustments to improve your position.

Recognising your most valuable asset

When I ask people what they think their most valuable asset is, I get a flurry of responses — from their house to their savings, to their car, or even a piece of art or their grandmother's jewellery collection. *Spoiler:* It's none of those things. It's time. Time is your most precious, non-renewable asset. Once you spend it, you never get it back. And the kicker is you never know how much of it you have.

To survive in a capitalist system, most of us have to literally 'spend' our precious time to earn money. You clock into work and swap your time in exchange for a pay packet, which you then use to buy the stuff you need to survive. You then get to spend the rest of your time on the other things you actually want to do. It's a catch 22 — you need money to survive, but working is costing you precious time you can't get back. This isn't to say you should quit your job tomorrow and have all the time in the world to do as you please, because, annoyingly, you normally need money to keep yourself afloat. However, it might help you see exactly how much time you are exchanging to afford your life — especially in a world constantly trying to persuade you to purchase *everything*, all the fucking time.

Realising you traded your *literal* life for material things that grabbed your attention for mere moments can help you become more selective and intentional about how you spend both your time and money in the future. Because while these weeds have pretty flowers and perhaps even an alluring fragrance, they can be toxic and seriously affect your health and happiness over time.

If you look around your home, could you tell me how much each item cost you? How long did you have to work to get them? Was it hours, days, weeks or even months? That's a *lot* of life to give up, isn't it? Maybe some things are worth it, but you can probably spot others that absolutely aren't worth trading your precious time for, just so they can gather dust in the corner or be worn once.

I highly recommend you figure out your 'life-swap' hourly figure. This is based on the concept of 'life-energy spend' created by Vicki Robin and Joe Dominguez in their book *Your Money or Your Life*. By doing some quick sums on your time cost, you'll become much more confident in your spending decisions. You might choose to redirect the money to important goals. Or you might choose to reduce your spending so your life isn't as expensive and you can work less. This can give you some time back to spend on things that bring you joy.

Activity: Unearth your life-swap hourly rate

This exercise helps you understand how many precious, never-getting-back hours you're swapping for items you spend money on.

To figure out how much time your purchases cost you, you first need to identify how much total time you spend earning, and how much you earn. Then you can work out your life-swap hourly rate.

(continued)

The following steps run through this in more detail.

Step 1: Calculate the amount of time you spend on 'earning money' activities, on average per week.

This could include:

▸ the hours you spend working
▸ any unpaid overtime you do
▸ the time it takes to get ready for, and decompress from, work
▸ work travel time
▸ lunch breaks.

Combine these to arrive at your total money-earning hours per week.

Step 2: Calculate how many hours you spend on work annually.

Next, you need to take your total money-earning hours per week and multiply this number by 48. (This assumes you take four weeks of leave per year. Reduce this number if you take more leave.)

The number you arrive at is your total annual hours spent earning income.

Step 3: Calculate the amount of after-tax income you receive per year.

If you're not sure, check your previous tax return to confirm this amount or use an online pay calculator to determine your after-tax income. For example, your annual net income might equal $80 000.

Step 4: Work out your life-swap hourly rate.

Now you can simply divide your net (after-tax) income by your total annual money-earning hours.

For example, let's say you earn a take-home (after-tax) annual salary of $80000, and you've worked out you spend, on average, 50 hours a week on income-related activities.

50 × 48 = 2400. (That's the total amount of hours you spend per year on earning money related activities.)

$80000 ÷ 2400 = $33 per hour.

That means your life-swap hourly rate is $33.

The following table highlights how far that gets you in terms of some common expenses.

Item	Dollar cost	Hours spent working to buy item (cost divided by hourly rate)
New pair of jeans	$120	3.6 hours
Coffee and a croissant at a cafe	$11	20 mins
New fridge	$1500	45.4 hours
Dinner out and drinks	$200	6 hours
Weekend away	$800	24.3 hours
Lunch at work	$15	27 minutes

Don't get stuck in the weeds

Plenty of people tell me the reason they haven't sorted out their money (yet) is because they don't have time. They are 'too busy'. And it's often true.

The 2024 National Working Families survey[1] found that 74 per cent of Australian women (in hetero relationships) feel stressed trying to balance work and home life. And a 2020 Families in Australia survey found 41 per cent of household tasks are always or usually done by the woman, with only 9 per cent always, or usually, done by the man.[2] There needs to be a better balance.

Frankly, the world needs more women to have the time and space necessary to invest in their financial literacy, learn how to grow wealth and have time to do the actions needed — because it benefits not just them, but also their families, communities and societies as a whole. Numerous studies show that an increase in women's wealth and financial independence improves children's health, nutrition, education, and even children's survival rates in some parts of the world. For too long, women have been relegated to the washing up, with no time to spend on wealth-building activities. It's time to change that.

If you know you're shouldering the lion's share of the (likely unpaid) work at home, lightening your load is priority numero uno. It's all well and good to have a clean and tidy house, but not at the expense of your money world feeling like chaos. And I'm not just talking about chores, either. Also think about all the things that need to happen to have your household run smoothly — such as booking appointments, planning meals or travel, and making the Book Week costume. I'm talking about the mental load, the life admin burdens, and being CEO of Home Life. It can be a lot, and almost all of it is unpaid, under-appreciated, and unseen. If you're carrying too much of this load, it's time to bring it into the light and renegotiate your terms just as you would in any job.

To help you carve out more time to spend on your finances, start by creating a list of everything that needs to get done to make your house function. Write this up on a whiteboard or shared note system. Awareness of what you're doing is the first step. Next, split up the tasks with your partner. You both need to proactively add to the list and take from it. Some partners will deliberately 'forget', do a task poorly, or say that it isn't something they've done in the past because you're just 'better at it' or 'you always take care of it'. Beware: 'weaponised incompetence' (that is, when someone pretends they are incapable of doing something so they don't have to do it!) is real and often gendered.

You didn't study how to stack the dishwasher or fold clothes; you just worked it out. *Your partner can work it out too.* Do not rush to save or correct them. You don't have time for that, and it will reinforce their beliefs that you're just better at it and thus you should do it. Sure, it might mean it doesn't get done the way you like it or would have done it, but I think you can live with it if you know it's saving you time to work on other much-more-important-in-the-long-run things.

As author, podcast host and lawyer Mel Robbins says, *let them.* Let them do it differently to you. Let them eat soggy spag bol, have no clean socks to wear, or have the milk run out because they were meant to get it and forgot. Let them see you aren't going to swoop in and fix it. You could, but you won't.

Your future needs you to *have* time to work on your future goals, so you *must* make time. Let go of what you can, so you have space and time to build for your *future.*

Weed patrol

Along with not having enough time, the other main reason people cite for not getting their finances sorted is money itself. What they mean by this is that they don't have 'enough' of it to save or invest or put towards their goals.

But thinking you don't earn 'enough' to start setting something aside is one of the quickest ways to ensure that you don't *actually* have enough. Remember ol' mate the Stanford professor from chapter 4: 'No matter if you believe the glass is half full or half empty, you are correct'. So let's put this idea of not having enough money to the test with a little spending audit — and see if we can't find a few dollars buried in the garden.

One of the members of my Greenhouse Money Growing Program[3] had convinced herself that, because she didn't earn a huge income and she was in her 60s, it wasn't possible to save. So she spent — not on big or outrageous things, but on little things that she didn't believe would matter much in the long run. But, boy oh boy, did these 'little treats' add up. Using the following exercise as a catalyst, she *radically* changed her view. And by the time she'd completed the 10-week program, she'd changed not only her mindset but also her spending behaviours. For eight weeks, she decided not to spend on *anything* non-essential, and saved more money than she *ever* thought possible. She used to get pleasure from those little spends; now she gets it from seeing her bank account and willpower rise. She inspired many within our community, and proved it's *never* too late to start.

Activity: Your spending audit

Provided here are some different options to do a check-in with your spending. Choose the activity level that feels best for you right now.

Level 1 (beginner, should take about five minutes)

Write down the last three things you bought that might be considered 'non-essential'. Perhaps that cute necktie for your dog, yet another houseplant or that daily takeaway coffee (even though you might think caffeine is essential).

Next to each item, rate how much value you got from those discretionary spends, and whether you'd prefer to redirect that money to your goals in the future. You can rate from zero to ten, or use a simple traffic light colour next to them — green if it was a great use of your money, orange if it was 'okay-ish' and red if you didn't get any value and wouldn't spend the money if you had your time again.

What's one takeaway from your audit that you can use for the upcoming week?

Now tell your partner or text your bestie what you're committing to, and ask them to keep you accountable.

Level 2 (intermediate, about a 30-minute task)

Download from your online banking or list out your expenses from the last month.

Use a scale of zero to ten to rate each discretionary spend (aka not a bill or essential item) based on how well it aligned with your core values, with zero being not aligned at all and ten being impeccable alignment. For example, say you spent over $84 on Uber rides because you were running late. You might decide to give this spend a 3/10 rating for value alignment, because while they were convenient, they don't align to any of your core values. On the other hand, you may have spent $300 on a two-hour snorkel with seals experience for a friend's birthday, and decide this was 10/10 for alignment with your core values of adventure and experiences.

If you have a partner and joint accounts, you can complete this task in a shared document or spreadsheet. (They can do all expenses for the first 15 days, for example, and you the remaining days in the month.)

Once you have your items reviewed and rated, look for clues, patterns and insights. What categories or items are rated the lowest? Which are the highest?

(continued)

Total how much you spent over the last month on everything rated a five or below.

Write down key insights and set yourself a weekly challenge based on your findings—for example, 'For the next week, I am going to bring in my lunch every day or only take public transport'. You can mix up your challenge every week. (This keeps it fresh and your brain engaged, while not overwhelming you by trying to change too much at once).

Tell someone what you're committing to—or, better yet, find an accountability buddy who will do it *with* you. Share your progress, including your wins and lessons, and ask for support if you need it.

Level 3 (advanced, about an hour or two—but worth it!)

Build out a full list of all your annual expenses, not just from the last month. Don't forget 'one-offs' that actually happen annually, such as doctor and dentist visits, weekends away, gifts, car maintenance and registration, and pet vaccinations. What says your numbers? Have you got enough income coming in to cover all your costs? Is a surplus available to put towards your goals?

If you aren't sure how much things cost, such as annual electricity bills or fuel, use an average from the last 12 months and then add a buffer on top for inflation. It amazes me how many of my Greenhouse members do this exercise, only to realise they actually don't earn enough to support their current spending habits.

Now you've worked out your full annual costs, you can clearly see where all your money is going. What costs can be immediately cut? Which area or expenses can be reduced?

What weeds do you want to get rid of first and where can you whack that cash instead? You might even consider doing a 'weed week' where you allocate time daily to research and get better deals, cancel subscriptions not used, or look for ways to bring your expenses down.

Let's talk about debt (baby)

Debt. Now, this little word can stir up all sorts of emotions and actually be a real silent B. It's not as simple as saying 'all debt is bad' but debt, used irresponsibly, can destroy dreams. It can feel like it's free — 'Hey, here, have some money you don't have to buy that thing you want'. But borrowing money comes with a price tag: interest rates. Repayments chew up cash that could, instead, be used to fund your goals.

Think of the interest you pay on debt as a 'thank you for lending me some dosh' penalty fee. The longer you stay in debt, the more penalty fees you pay on what you still owe — and, therefore, the more the lender pockets. And just like with other fees, you don't get any of the money you paid in interest (fees) back. And this is why being able to afford the repayments on your debt is only part of the equation. Another part is what economists call the 'opportunity cost' of that money, especially when you take interest fees into account. How could that money have been used to *earn* you money, not *take* it from you?

Our society has completely normalised debt. We don't blink an eye when someone buys a car with a car loan, uses a credit card to pay for dinner or buys a new outfit on their buy now pay later account. But we should. Too often, banks will let you borrow bucketloads of cash, enough to feel like you're drowning. Why? Because they make *a lot* of money from it.

If you step back and think about what people use debt for, in many instances it isn't to buy assets that go up in value or produce an income. It's often for things that go down in value and don't provide an income. Let's just pause and think about that for a moment: we borrow money (which, over time, costs us a lot more than the price tag) for things that ultimately reduce in value. The math ain't mathing, is it? I once had a client come to me with $100 000 in debt (a lethal combo of credit cards, personal loans and store cards), and she was having to come up with over $18 000 every year just to meet the interest repayments.

Weeding out 'bad' debt that isn't growing your wealth, and then keeping it at bay, is a hugely important part of the money-growing equation. If you know you've spent too long in debt cycles, now is the time to commit to changing that. That means you're going to need to find money in your cash flow plan. You'll also need to tell your nearest and dearest that you're embarking on a debt-busting journey, because you want their support and encouragement every step of the way (and not to be invited to tempting, expensive outings during this time).

So let's look at different types of debt and how to weed out the ones that have a stronghold of your wallet.

Good debt and mortgages

'Good debt' is considered to be debt you've borrowed for an asset you believe is going to go up in value over time, or provide you with an income. This type of debt includes a mortgage for your home, an investment property, an investment loan and even student debt (assuming it leads to income opportunities). This debt can help you grow your assets and significantly increase your wealth position.

Don't be scared of this debt, but do make sure you have sufficient cash flow to be able to cope with any interest rate changes you may encounter in the future. As your asset grows and your debt reduces, you build what's called *equity* (how much of the asset you own) and, depending on your position, you may be able to borrow against this equity to buy additional assets.

A mortgage is a debt you take on for a property, but unlike a regular loan, it comes with a catch: the property itself is used as security (also called *collateral*). That means if you can't keep up with your repayments, the lender has the legal right to take possession of the property and sell it to recover the money you still owe.

The word itself comes from très vintage Français, meaning death (mort) and pledge (gage). Essentially, once you've paid it back, the pledge becomes void (or dead). (As house prices have soared in more recent times, it could also be taken to mean 'a debt till death'.) With the average first-home buyer in Australia now being 36 years old, taking out a 30-year term and likely to upgrade further down the track, you can see how an increasing number of people are worried about being in debt until they, well, drop.

You generally have a few mortgage product options to choose from. I always recommend using a trusted mortgage broker to help you. They generally have access to a wide range of lenders and will be able to help you decide which may be best for you. Generally, they won't charge you for their services, because they're paid directly by whichever lender you choose.

Once you decide on a lender, the main options you have are a fixed-rate loan, a variable-rate loan, or a hybrid of the two.

Fixed-rate loan

These types of loans have a fixed interest rate for a set period of time (for example, 5.5 per cent for two years). Fixing your rate offers certainty, because you know exactly what your repayments are going to be for that amount of time. If interest rates go up over that period, you will be locked in at your existing rate. But, similarly, if they go down, you'll continue to pay the rate you originally agreed to.

If you're considering a fixed rate and think you'll have additional money to put towards your mortgage, check if additional repayments are allowed. Some fixed-rate loans have caps on how much you can add annually without being penalised. You also may have a 'break fee' if you want to get out of the product before the agreed time period is up.

Variable-rate loan

Unlike a fixed rate loan, the interest rate you pay with a variable-rate loan will vary — meaning it could go up or down. This could benefit you if rates are reduced, but you will see your monthly mortgage repayment go up if rates do.

Variable-rate loans (generally) offer more flexibility and allow you to make additional repayments.

Split loan

To borrow the wise words of Old El Paso, '¿por qué no los dos?' — why not both? You can choose to split your loan between the two options, with a portion fixed and the rest variable. Some people want to fix a portion for certainty or because they think rates might rise soon, but keep some at a variable rate so they can pay extra off it and hedge their bets in case rates do go down.

Making additional mortgage repayments

If one of your goals is to be debt-free before the scheduled time frame of your mortgage, adding small amounts of additional money can really add up! You can either pay these amounts directly off the debt (if your mortgage product allows you to), or add them to your offset or redraw facility. An offset account is kind of like a savings account linked to your mortgage, with the money sitting in it helping to reduce the interest you're charged. And a redraw facility lets you make extra repayments on your loan but then pull that money back out later if you need it, almost like an emergency fund built into your mortgage.

Example: How weeding could see you mortgage-free faster

Let's say you want to buy a $1 million property (so basically a shoe-box apartment in Sydney). And let's assume you have a 20 per cent deposit (normally the minimum banks require you to have to avoid paying lenders mortgage insurance or LMI).

So with a 20 per cent deposit ($200 000), you would need to borrow $800 000 in order to buy a property worth $1 million. Here are the basic details for the loan:

▸ *Debt:* $800 000.
▸ *Interest rate:* 5.5 per cent.
▸ *Loan length:* 30 years.
▸ *Monthly repayment:* $4542.

The following table outlines how regular additional payments can reduce both the length of the loan and total interest paid.

Effect of regular additional mortgage repayments[4]

	Regular amount	Regular amount, plus $200 per month	Regular amount, plus $400 per month
Monthly repayment	$4542	$4742	$4942
Time taken to pay mortgage off	30 years	27 years, 1 month	24 years, 9 months
Total amount paid	$1 635 232	$1 538 711	$1 463 908
How much time saved on loan length	0 years	2 years, 9 months	5 years, 3 months
Interest saved	$0	$96 521	$171 324

(continued)

> *Note:* You can still get into the property market even if you don't have a 20 per cent deposit. For example, you may be able to take advantage of the 5% Deposit Scheme[5], or other federal or state-based first-home buyers grants and exemptions, depending on the area you're buying in and your price point. These calculations also don't take into account purchasing costs, the biggest of which is usually stamp duty. Again, as a first-home buyer, you may qualify for an exemption of stamp duty. If you don't qualify, you will also need to take this expense into account.

Bad debt

In the finance world, we usually refer to 'bad debt' as borrowing money for things that generally don't grow in value, don't earn you income, and usually lose their worth over time. They normally attract a higher interest rate, and include personal loans, car loans, credit cards and buy now pay later schemes.

An example of bad debt is borrowing money to buy a car. Sure, it may be essential in your life, but cars (almost always) go down in value. So you're stuck paying off a debt based on what you originally borrowed to buy the car (not its current value) plus interest (the penalty fee), all while the car continues to reduce in value. Meaning, in the end, you'll have paid off way more than the car is worth. That's not good debt. As the 'Barefoot Investor', Scott Pape, aptly advises, 'Buy the cheapest car your ego can afford'.

Toxic debt

Toxic debt is what I call the debt that comes from the serotonin-secreting, sugar-rush-style spending of money you don't have. It's dopamine-fuelled debt, driven by the quick hit of buying something now and dealing with the consequences later. This mainly happens through buy now pay later arrangements, some interest-free financing, and potentially also credit cards or borrowing money from friends and family. Hopefully the work you've already done to name and tame your money monster will help you understand why you may have done this in the past, and you now know what your go-to strategy is moving forward.

Dealing with multiple debts

If you currently have multiple debts, it's important to list them all out and then create a prioritisation plan to get things under control and reduce the total balance (and interest). Strategies to consider include debt consolidation and/or refinancing. Maybe you can roll them all into one loan, for example, or pay off the most expensive one first. Or, as a very first step, grab some scissors and cut up that credit card once and for all.

When you're listing your debts out, be sure to include how much you owe, what interest rate you're being charged, the debt category (good, bad or toxic), and if any are tax-deductible — which I get to next. (Jump to the section 'Clearing debt: Snowball versus avalanche method', later in this chapter, for much more help in this area.)

Clearing debt: Snowball versus avalanche method

If you have multiple bad debts, chances are it's taking up way more of your energy and creating a lot more subconscious worry than you realise. I'm here to tell you that it is absolutely possible to be bad debt-free. I've watched so many people conquer debts they once felt were insurmountable. It wasn't always easy, and they certainly had trips and slips along the way, but nothing beats celebrating them being done and dusted!

I once had a client bring both his credit card and two celebratory pottles of yoghurt to a meeting and we held a little 'cut up the card' ceremony. We snacked and celebrated the shit out of all his hard work getting his credit cards completely cleared and closed. He then redirected all the money he was putting towards clearing debt to starting a property deposit fund. What a win! And you can get there too.

Once you've decided to get out those gardening gloves and get to work on creating your debt-free life, you'll need to decide *how* to do it. There are two common debt-repayment methods: the avalanche or the snowball method.

The avalanche method

This strategy is called the 'avalanche method' because it's like you're starting at the top of the mountain and pushing your money downhill, allowing it to gather momentum and make a huge impact. How to do it:

1. List your debts based on how much the interest rate is, from highest to lowest.
2. Pay the minimums on all the debt balances each month.
3. Put any extra money to the debt with the highest interest rate first.
4. Once that debt is cleared, move on to the one with the next highest interest rate. Repeat until they're all cleared.

The avalanche method often works best from a purely financial perspective and saves you the most money over time, since you're tackling the most expensive debt first (that is, the one that's costing you the most in interest). It can take longer to feel like you're making progress but if you can stick to the strategy and stay consistent, this method can seriously reduce the total amount you repay.

The snowball method

The 'snowball method' is about starting small and rolling your money into something bigger. How to do it:

1. List your debts based on the balance remaining, from smallest to largest.
2. Pay the minimums on all the debt balances each month.
3. Put any extra money to the debt with the smallest balance first.
4. Once that debt is cleared, move to the one with the next smallest balance. Repeat until they're all cleared.

This method is all about building momentum and motivation. While it might not be the most efficient on paper, it can feel really exciting to clear an entire debt and gain confidence as you prove to yourself you can do it. This is the one I have seen most people have the most success using. Clearing and closing small-balance debts gives people a big boost to keep at it.

Once you decide which option you're using, set up automatic repayments, and close the accounts once they're paid off. And be sure to celebrate every repayment and milestone. (Just don't do so by buying more stuff! Remember your 'zero bucks given' list from chapter 3!)

Deductible versus non-deductible debt

By now you know that not all debt is created equal; however, it's not just your friendly red-haired money expert telling you this — the Australian Tax Office (ATO) sees it much the same. The ATO categorises costs associated with debts as deductible (because the debt is linked to income-generating activities) and non-deductible (because the debt is for purely personal reasons). In terms of your finance strategy, any tax-deductible costs you have are likely to be those associated with a loan for an investment property or share portfolio. The biggest of these costs is likely to be the interest on the loan.

Generally speaking, if you have a mix of both deductible and non-deductible debt, beyond making your minimum repayments, tax-deductible debts should be paid down last. So if you have spare cash to deploy, it usually makes sense to pay off debts that aren't giving you any tax benefits (check with your accountant if needed).

The following table provides some examples of different types of debt and whether the costs are deductible.

Example types of debt

Debt provider	Amount owing	Interest rate	Debt type	Costs deductible?
Credit card, Bank A	$2300	18%	Bad debt	No
Home loan, Bank A	$550000	5.5%	Good debt	No
Investment property, Bank A	$400000	6%	Good debt	Yes
Car loan, Bank B	$20000	6%	Bad debt	No
Buy now pay later account	$740	Late fees apply	Toxic debt	No

How minimum payments keep you trapped in debt

Let's use the example of the $2300 credit card balance from the preceding table to demonstrate how making only minimum payments keeps you in debt.

Here's what you end up paying, even without *ever* using the credit card again:

- *Debt:* $2300.
- *Interest rate:* 18 per cent.

- *Monthly repayment:* $46 first month, decreasing based on outstanding balance owing.
- *Time to repay:* 21 years and 8 months.
- *Total amount paid:* +$7000.[6]

Yes, you read that right. It could take you 21 years and 8 months to pay it off and cost you over three times more than the amount you borrowed. That's more than *two decades*. Think about how old you'll be then. Do you really want this debt hanging over you in your 40s, 50s, 60s, or after you retire? Not only that, but remember the opportunity cost here. This money could have been used to make you money! If you took the $4700 you paid in interest (which benefited the bank) and invested it instead, after 20 years at an average 8 per cent return per year, you'd have about $22 000 (not including any tax payable).

My advice? Don't feed the weeds. Get rid of the bad and toxic debt ASAP and instead use your money to grow your goals.

Keeping on top of your debt plan

Like most things with money, paying your debt off is more marathon than sprint. The aim is steady progress at a consistent pace. One common mistake I see is going too hard, too fast. Once someone has decided it's (finally) time to kick their bad debts to the curb, a fire lights within them. You can see in their eyes they mean business. They are so committed to getting their debt cleared that, as soon as they get paid, they put a giant amount of their income into paying it down. While this feels good, they soon realise they haven't left themselves enough to live off, and so have to use the credit card until the next pay day — which doesn't feel good.

Instead, take it slow and steady. Allocate an amount to debt repayments that won't see you needing to dip back into it. Don't try to sprint the distance of a marathon.

Finally, some banks will offer to take on your debt with a low-, or no-, interest period via a balance transfer (that is, when you switch the balance from one credit card to a new one). Sounds good, right? It can be, but often little wee devils are hiding in the details. Banks aren't charities; they aren't offering you this because they know you're a really great person. They do it because research shows you're not likely to prioritise the debt or pay it off before the low interest period ends — in fact, according to ASIC, nearly one in three people who took on such debt increased their debt by more than 10 per cent during the promotional period, and just over 15 per cent increased their debt by more than 50 per cent.[7] Once the honeymoon period of low rates is up, you go back to normal (or even higher) interest rates. So make sure you do your sums and always check the fine print. For example, sometimes any new purchases attract a standard interest rate from day one. Also understand how balance transfers (that is, when you switch the balance from one credit card to a new one) show up on your credit history — check with your bank if you're not sure.

So if you're going to do a balance transfer, make sure you've got a plan in place to clear the debt before the honeymoon ends — just like your money-savvy alter ego would. You know the one: confident, clear-headed and refusing to get caught in the debt spiral again.

Time to pull the weeds out

You now can see how the BS weeds of life compete with (and completely fuck over) your goals for how you ideally want to spend your time, energy and money. Everyone thinks that weeds are just a regular part of life, but they don't have to be. Regular weeding can help you conserve precious resources and give you additional capacity to focus on what really matters to you.

Based on everything in this chapter, here's a list of activities for you to work through while you're weeding:

- *Unleash your money alter ego:* How would your money alter ego tackle any weeds you have right now? How much time would they allocate weekly or monthly to weeding-related tasks? When would they squeeze this time into your diary? Would they do it when the calendar reminder came up, or would they ignore it? What would they focus on first? What habits would they do differently? List these habits out from easiest to hardest and start with the easiest first. What mantras would they say to themselves (for example, 'I am one step closer to being debt free', 'I am okay with the household tasks being done differently, because now I have more time to focus on my financials', 'I am making progress and it feels so fucking good'). Okay — so why don't you do that?

- *Calculate your 'life-swap' hourly rate:* What have you recently spent money on and how many hours' worth of your life does that equal?

- *Household split:* Do you need to assign tasks differently in your house to give you more breathing space? What conversations need to happen, or choices need to be made?

- *Assess your debt position:* Figure out what your current debt position is and what types of debt you have. Are these good, bad or toxic?

- *Choose your debt-busting method:* If you have multiple bad debts, are you going to use the snowball or avalanche method?

- *Track (and celebrate) progress:* How will you track your progress? For example, will you create a chart or visual to track milestones? When will you next do your net wealth position calculations so you can see what progress you're making?

- *Rally your crew:* Who do you need to tell about your debt-free plans? How can they help you stay motivated and not derail you? Tell them how they can best support you and why it matters.

- *Scan the garden:* Can you spot other money areas that need to be weeded out to give you more capacity to put towards your goals?

A note for my fellow ADHDers

In my experience, the ADHD tax is real! If you know having access to bad or toxic debt is likely to see you impulsively spend, do everything you can to clear them and then close them. Make sure your debt repayments are set up as automations, so you don't have to remember to make them on time. (You don't want to get any late fees.) If I know I have to do something that feels hard and heavy, I either do it with someone else (body doubling), or I turn up the tunes and set a timer, telling myself, 'I only need to do this for five minutes'. When the timer goes off, I'm usually in the flow and can keep going. Or I say, 'this for that' — if I do this task I'm dreading, I can dedicate some time to reading, going for a walk with the dog, or having a little (often needed) nap. My brain needs to know what great reward I'm getting for my effort.

I am also not good at doing tasks around the house — I'm much better at doing my work that I love (and that brings in money). So rather than being overwhelmed with tasks my brain doesn't engage with, I buy time by paying for a cleaner every week. While this may seem counterintuitive, it's a good use of my money because the house is clean (which my brain likes but doesn't like making happen) and I can focus on the things I'm good at and which bring in money for my goals.

Lastly, if you're anything like me, time might not be a concept you understand well. For me, this can easily lead to additional costs as I find myself running late so choose an Uber instead of public transport. Or I forget my lunch, so have to buy it. Or I leave behind my phone charger every single time I travel somewhere new (why?!). I've tried to build lists and rituals to help me manage these aspects, without incurring additional costs — and it works (mostly). I hate that I hate routine, but I also need it. The more routine you can bring into your money world, the easier it gets — trust me!

Money in the wild: Sienna (she/her)

- **Age:** 33.
- **Situationship:** In a relationship; live together.
- **Income:** $190000.
- **Current savings:** $10000.
- **Current relationship with money:** Improving, hesitant, average.
- **Money monster's name:** 'Treat yourself Tracy'. Comes out when I'm highly stressed (which happens quite a bit with my job) and emotional or down.

Have you ever had to use your emergency savings, and how did it make you feel?

Yes. I had some unexpected hospital and medical expenses recently. It was actually a little hard to dip into it because I like having that set amount in there but had to tell myself this is what the emergency fund is for. It was great to know I have a back-up for emergencies outside of my main savings account. I think it needs to be a bit higher though given my expenses and lifestyle.

What does life look like right now?

High-responsibility/high-stress career. Living in a three-bedroom apartment so both my partner and I can have at-home offices but rent is high. We both earn about the same amount of money, but keep separate accounts. I'm working towards buying an investment property and investing and my partner is working on continuing to build his own company/side hustle, so we have different goals we are putting our own money towards.

Do you save or invest?
Save but very keen to get into investing; still a bit nervous about making that leap.

What's one piece of money advice you wish you knew sooner?
Track your expenses and build a budget.

What has shaped your relationship with money the most?
Mum was a very savvy saver. She only spent on important things (house, education, life experiences) rather than material possessions. As a child, I didn't understand why and then as a young adult once I had my own money, I very much wanted to buy myself all the nice material things. It's taken me a long time to break this habit and think about my long-term goals. I really wish I had learned about money a lot earlier in life and even in school.

What does 'financial wellbeing' mean to you?
Not feeling stuck in any situation, and having the funds to make change when needed. Having a plan and goals to work towards.

What's a financial goal you're working towards right now?
Buying an investment property on my own.

You win the lotto. What do you do?
Fly first class around the world for a year and visit as many countries as possible. Buy an investment property (or multiple).

What's one outrageous thing you've spent money on, and did you regret it?
Getting porcelain veneers ($23 000 in total). Not one bit—except the pain was terrible! The money was hard to part with initially but

it changed my life and confidence after being self-conscious about my teeth my entire life and not smiling in photos.

Have you ever looked at your bank account and thought, WTF? How did it get this low?

More so when I racked up quite a bit of credit card debt (around $5000). I was always good at paying my credit card off if I needed to use it. (It used to be my emergency fund before I had a cash emergency fund.) I had to look at my monthly spend and cut out some 'nice to haves' to pay off the credit card.

7

SEED

Building a conscious cashflow plan that feeds your goals and seeds your future

> So never lose an opportunity of urging a practical beginning, however small, for it is wonderful how often in such matters the mustard-seed germinates and roots itself.
>
> —*Florence Nightingale*

Now you've got a plan to rid your life of those pesky (and persistent) weeds, it's time to build a system that's going to channel your income into funding your life and seeding your future. Think of what you're building as the self-fulfilling ecosystem that manages your moolah, even when you're not watching. Without a clear plan on where your income goes and why, any system you create will still require a bucketload of manual intervention — and you don't have time for that! Instead, use your precious time to take the next step towards achieving your goals — not just moving money from one bank account to another. Setting up your financial framework can feel tricky at first, and you might feel a little out of your depth in the beginning, but don't give up on it! Tweak and change as needed. And remember: your goals don't happen by accident. Like seeds, you must plant and water them so they grow.

One of the quickest ways I could tell whether my clients were going to achieve their goals or not was how well they embraced (and stuck to) their cash flow plan. It's often one of the most overlooked tools in your money-growing toolshed. To nail it, you need to get excited by the idea of making changes to how you currently do things. You might need to change how many accounts you have and how you divvy up your dosh. You might even need to break up with the bank or super fund you've (accidentally) been in a committed relationship with since your very first job. My ask of you is that you approach the ideas in this chapter with an open mind, try your darnedest to get giddy about gamifying your spending and be open to shifting any strong-held attachments you've got to how you currently do things if a better way is possible. I know, all of that is easier said than done.

Most people I've helped over the years didn't have a goals-based system for their income. Some felt stressed and unsure about whether they'd set themselves up correctly. Many felt like they were working simply to exist. Money in and then — boom! — money out again. This chapter can help you figure out what you need to do to stop the rot.

Time to take the plunge and sort your money out

Have you ever watched a doco or clips on baby barnacle geese? (Just my algorithm?) Born on steep cliffs, they must catapult themselves off the ledge to avoid starvation. And when they take the plunge, it's not a graceful descent. First they freefall from the equivalent of a skyscraper, which perhaps feels a little like being a teenager — the world at your feet and the wind beneath your wings. Then, with a brutal thud, they smack into the rocky world below, which leaves many stunned and bewildered.

That is how I felt when I entered the 'real world' my parents had warned me of. Even with their warnings, I flew the coop totally unprepared. Managing my income and bills felt hard and really unfun. Honestly, why hadn't Disney made *that* coming-of-age story to prepare me for what really lay ahead? This would have been far more valuable than one where if I accepted a monstrous beast (with a fucking brilliant library), I would be serenaded by a candlestick, served soup de jour and never need to cook or clean, ever.

At 19, I attempted the ultimate 'I've moved out and am now a highly successful and independent lady, here is proof' move. My friend and I drank a bottle of red wine and spent an entire evening trying to build an IKEA bookcase. Instead of being a strong and sturdy home for newfound adult knowledge, it precariously wobbled and swayed like a drunken sailor for its entire existence. If a piece of furniture could symbolise me before I got my financial shit sorted, that was it. At any moment, she could have come crashing down.

I was working hard, but I had no clear plan for my money. No system set up to support my goals, or to make life easier for me. My savings sloshed together — which made it tricky for me to track how much was allocated to what. I spent hours moving money from one account to the other to pay bills. It was stressful and frustrating.

At 22, I got a job at an investment bank that paid me monthly. When pay day arrived, everyone flocked to the cafe below our office and splashed cash like it was confetti. It was a stark contrast to the days leading up to payday, when the cafe would be empty. The office fruit box and biscuit supplies were usually snapped up by midmorning. And based on the notable absence of apples right before the 15th of every month, I wasn't the only one who didn't have a handle on my cash flow. It was feast and famine, literally, for some.

Then one day, seemingly out of nowhere, as I was folding laundry in my bedroom in the share house I lived in, I realised I needed to make a change. It was like a bolt of lightning struck me. I can still remember where I was standing when it happened. First, I needed to figure out where my money was going. Then I could look at how the hell I was going to set it up to work for me. I have now used that system for over a decade, and it has also helped thousands of people gain control of their spending and achieve their goals. But it does require a shift in perspective.

Everyone who knows me would say I'm a loud and proud frugal person. I spend on things that align with my values and I'm ruthless with the things that don't. Being frugal isn't something to be ashamed of; instead, it's a hyper-awareness that, in the cost-of-living-dumpster-fire world we live in, every dollar you spend on something 'meh' is an invisible trade-off with something that could have been a 'yeah'. Frugality is about considering what purchases are a better use of your money and time. It's about being economical, intentional and conscious about where you spend your money and what you spend it on.

The latest clothes and things 'everyone' is buying — for me, that's 'meh'. Being able to travel solo around Europe and Morocco for four months — yeah. Eating out whenever I want, buying lunch or drinking barista-made coffees every day — meh. Saving up to be able to go to some of the world's top restaurants — yeah. Upgrading my phone every time a newer model is released — meh. Surprising my NZ-based Nana with a trip to see her at Easter — yeah.

You don't have to want to spend in the same frugal way as I do, but the point is you want to be able to say, 'hell, yeah!' to the things that matter and 'absolutely not' to the things that don't. If you want to financially flourish, you need to be more considered and creative in your spending, and conscious of how it impacts your goals. Honestly, it can be quite fun. My hope is you, too, become a proud and fiercely loyal member of the frugal community. (I'm sure we should have pins or badges or something — but, of course, we wouldn't use our money on them.)

So my frugal (or soon-to-be frugal/intentional/conscious) friend, what must you know and do to get your income set up in a way that can support your current and future life? In the following sections, I bust some common money myths, and then show you how to set up your system for seeding success.

Just, like, stop being poor

I'll tell you this much for free: you can't budget your way out of poverty. Too often, people on minimum wage, single parents on an average income or people who receive government payments are told that if they just managed money 'better', their financial woes would be solved. 'You just aren't doing it right', people say. 'Perhaps if you just decided to stop being poor, things would be easier for you.' Let me call bullshit on this. No-one is better at being across their costs, or making money stretch as far as possible, than someone who has very little of it to go round. Most people in this situation are being told to cut fat when they are already down to the bone. It's ignorant (and steeped in privilege).

Here are some examples of the kind of advice you may have heard before:

- 'If you stopped buying smaller quantities and bought in bulk, you'd save.'
- 'Maybe if you stopped buying cheap crappy shoes that broke every year and instead bought one good pair that lasts years like I do, you'd save.'
- 'If you just pay your insurance annually, you'll get a discount and have more money.'

See, fixed it for you. Easy.

The problem? You need to have surplus money to buy in bulk, buy quality items or have enough stashed away for annual bills. Being poor is expensive — and there is no denying it. It costs more and it's mentally exhausting. So as we go through how to set up your money plan, if you know you are already doing all you can to manage expenses, know that I know you would win a gold medal at the budgeting Olympics if we had one.

By now, you've met your money monster and are starting to get a handle on what might be behind any dopamine-fuelled impulse buys. And I delve further into discretionary spending and even adjusting fixed costs later in this chapter. But if you're already running pretty lean, I'm not going to pretend you can budget your way out of your current financial state. Instead, I'll be clear: the best way you're going to be able to get yourself ahead is by bringing in more income (while we also work to dismantle inequitable systems).

Earn more

To make sure you have enough money to cover your life costs and goals simultaneously, you generally have two options: spend less or earn more. Actually you have three — you could do both. It's that simple. But simple doesn't mean easy, so let's consider how you might put a plan together to bring in more money.

You might have already identified ways you can bring in some extra cash straightaway when looking at the 'O is for options' section in the GROW method back in chapter 5. If you still have some items from that list to action, they could be a good place to start bringing more money in right now.

Thinking more long term, most people want to get maximum return on investment (ROI) for their time, and sometimes that means getting more money from the work they are *already* doing. So let's talk about how you should approach getting a raise.

Top tips for earning more

Sadly, bursting into your boss's office and demanding more pay so you can afford your bills rarely works out well. Here's what to do instead:

- *Keep a file with all your achievements, and positive customer or stakeholder feedback:* I call this your FIGJAM folder (which stands for 'fuck I'm good just ask me' — yep, own it). Keeping a record of how fabulous you are might feel awkward, but you need clear examples to use as evidence.
- *Show the value you're bringing to the table:* Businesses need to understand how valuable you are to them, and the easiest way to do this is with numbers. What did you do that reduced expenses or increased the bottom line? Quantify your achievements as best you can. If you created training manuals or built new processes that save time, list them. If you had an idea that got implemented, what has that led to?
- *Do your research:* Look at what competitors are offering for someone with similar skills and experience to you.
- *Book a meeting:* Many people never bring up money because they're hoping their boss will notice how hard they work and look after them. Don't do that! Advocate for yourself. Be proactive. When other team members are chirping for more and you're staying quiet, you might find you'll get fed last. Know when remuneration conversations happen in your organisation, book a meeting well ahead of time and be really specific on what it's for — for example, 'I would like to discuss my performance with you and my remuneration package ahead of our annual review'.
- *Practise what you're going to say:* Grab a friend, partner or mentor to give you feedback on your approach. It feels awful,

but do you know what feels more awful? Fucking it up in the meeting because you didn't practise.

- *Leave your emotions at home:* I know this is easier said than done, but this is also where having your FIGJAM folder, cost savings or profit increase estimates, and market-reviewed data can help you stay calm and composed. Your boss is unlikely to be able to say yay, or nay, in the meeting. Instead, it's the time for them to hear why you believe you are ready for career progression or an increase in wage. Be clear on what amount you are looking for.

- *Keep a record in writing:* If they say to you that if you achieve *x*, *y* or *z* you should be on track to have a certain outcome, send them a thank you email for their time and confirm in writing your understanding of what they said. Doing so doesn't guarantee you'll get what they said, but it will help you if any confusion emerges, or if a new leader takes over in the future who isn't across what was discussed. If your boss flat out says no to your request, ask them what you'd need to do beyond what you're currently doing to achieve your request. Put their response in writing and send this back to your boss.

- *If they can't meet your number, have a back-up plan:* Perhaps your boss can give you additional training, extra paid annual leave or other non-monetary benefits (just remember these won't pay your bills).

- *Don't make threats:* Threatening to leave unless you get what you want is never the path to go down, unless you are prepared to actually leave.

- *Go for the promotion you're not ready for:* Listen, if you meet 100 per cent of the criteria for a more senior role, you should already be doing it. Many people wait until they feel like they have all the necessary skills and experience before putting their hand up. Every single person has had to fumble a little at first and then figure it out.

- *Be sure to negotiate your salary:* This goes for when you get a new role or switch organisations.
- *Consider a role or career change:* If you know you have capped out your income because of strict salary bands (as in some public sector or government roles), you may need to consider your broader prospects.

Taking advantage of the 'rule of five'

For a long time in my corporate career I sucked at advocating for myself. I simply thought my performance would speak for itself. It wasn't until I got a new boss who asked why I hadn't booked in a time to pitch for a promotion that I realised I was missing something. Apparently I was the only one in my team who hadn't. I was horrified that everyone was playing a game I didn't even know existed. By not doing this (or having a FIGJAM folder at the ready), I left money and opportunity on the table. So I made a rule for myself moving forward. I call this the 'rule of five', and here's how it works:

- *Spend five hours a month actively improving your career:* This could be putting your hand up for small work projects that get you in front of other managers, joining industry association committees and attending monthly meetings, or going to work-related networking events. I usually used one hour to plan for the months ahead and the remaining four hours were spent doing one hour a week on the activities.
- *Spend up to 5 per cent of your income on education:* This might be books, attending events and conferences, programs — or anything you can do that will keep you learning, growing and improving. You may not be able to spend that amount, but having some money allocated for this is likely to pay dividends in the long run — especially in a world where many jobs are likely to change in the coming decades.

- *Book in five coffees a month:* You have to network. I booked in five coffees a month with experts and potential mentors inside and outside my organisation. This meant I had at least one meet-up each week. (I assumed at least one would reschedule, so this meant I had one extra in the bag.) People often said they couldn't believe how big my network was. Let me tell you — it didn't happen by accident. As a secret introvert, I would much rather have sat at home reading than be out having coffees with people I barely knew. But the amount of advice, opportunities and introductions I got from these meetings was huge. People want to help you, so let them!

Money in the wild: Tahlia (she/her)

- **Age:** 23.
- **Situationship:** Single.
- **Income:** $100000.
- **Current savings:** <$1000.
- **Current relationship with money:** Toxic, emotional, lost.
- **Money monster's name:** 'Issy influence'.

Have you ever had to use your emergency savings, and how did it make you feel?

I've never had an emergency savings buffer, but now I am building it up with $100 per fortnight and I am excited to feel more secure.

What does life look like right now?

I have just started a new career and I love it. It has given me the opportunity to move to my dream place to live, which I will be doing soon. Money-wise I overspend a lot. I pay my bills and don't use credit or buy now pay later schemes, but I still struggle not to spend my savings.

What's a past money decision you're proud of?
I closed all my credit cards and buy now pay later accounts.

What's one piece of money advice you wish you knew sooner?
That you don't need the newest clothes and the fanciest car.

What has shaped your relationship with money the most?
My family—when they had money, they would spend, spend, spend.

What does 'financial wellbeing' mean to you?
Freedom and safety.

Did you have a big 'oh shit' moment that made you realise you had to learn more about money?
When I was taking money out of savings and spending thousands of dollars on gym clothes to keep up with influencers.

Cash flowing in all directions

Now, let's get into the down-in-the-dirt details of how and where your money is currently being spent, so you can ensure money is allotted to those precious seeds that are going to grow and help you achieve your goals.

In the following sections, I run through the different spending and saving categories, along with some aspects to consider for each.

Emergency savings—money set aside for the big 'oh shit' moments

This one is non-negotiable. No matter how much your other goals spark joy and are aligned with your values, if you don't have this sorted, it should become your number one priority. Ideally, aim for enough funds in this account to cover between three and six months of living costs. If you can't get income protection insurance (more on this in chapter 9) or you're self-employed, you might want a larger buffer amount. This must be in an account only you can access. (I don't care how much they love you, keep it separate!) This is money you'll hopefully never need to use, but if you find yourself needing to leave a relationship, being made redundant, needing emergency surgery or in any other genuinely sticky situation, this money is here to save your ass.

Cash buffer — money for your whoopsies

This category is different from your emergency savings. Instead, it's your petty-cash moneybox for non-petty life situations. Think, a 'whoops' not an 'oh shit' situation. This fund could be used to cover a bill that comes in higher than expected or if your car needs new brakes that you didn't budget for. It's money you need, but it's not for an emergency situation. How much? You do you, but I normally recommend at least $1000.

Fixed expenses — money for ze bills, bills, bills

Your fixed expenses are those you need to pay regularly. These are usually known costs, such as rent, mortgage repayments, insurances, strata, car payments, electricity and subscriptions. You may look at these and think you can't reduce them — they just are what they are. But often we pay the 'loyalty tax' on fixed expenses.

Businesses bank on you setting and forgetting (because you have no time to look for better deals, remember?). If it's been a while since you've given your fixed expenses a good look over, it could be costing you thousands of dollars per year. Haven't had your mortgage rate reviewed in years? Call a mortgage broker and ask them to find you a better deal. Cancel any unnecessary subscriptions or that gym membership you no longer use. (If you aren't sure if you could survive without them, cancel them for a month and see if you miss them.) Do a quick search to see what competitors are offering for similar services, and then call your provider and ask them to match it.

Activity: Have the hard conversation with your providers

If you're unsure about how to talk to services providers about a better deal, try the following script:

> Hi, I am an existing customer and have been with you for x years. I wanted to check if I'm on the best deal. Do you have any promotions, discounts or plans that would give me a better rate? Can you review my account and let me know if I'm paying more than I should be?

If you've noticed they offer a better deal to new customers, try the following:

> I've noticed that you are now offering new customers *(provide details of the deal)*. I would like to stay with you, but won't if I am unable to access the same benefits as people who are just signing up. Can you match this offer?

And if your research identifies a better offer from a competitor, ask your current provider to match it:

> I have just seen that x competitor is offering y. I want to stay with you, but I need the deal to be more competitive. Do you price match?

Remember — you don't need to be nasty or rude. Be polite, but firm on what you're asking for. And always consider the implications of moving. Any new life insurance policy, for example, will normally consider your updated health situation, so if your health has changed considerably, you might find that moving means you will not be able to get the same terms or benefits.

I once had a Greenhouse member find $2000 in annual subscriptions she didn't even remember she still had. Another was able to negotiate $800 in annual savings from her internet, electricity and home insurance provider. And perhaps the most impressive (or terrifying) of them all was someone who realised her bank was taking a huge loyalty tax from her mortgage, which hadn't been reviewed in years. She ended up saving over $8000 a year by moving to another bank. This is money that can be used to supercharge your goals, without any lifestyle or income changes!

Discretionary expenses — food, fashion and frivolity

Discretionary expenses are the costs that we (mostly) have control over. These are the little (and sometimes not so little) expenses that can quietly derail our finances, and include groceries, eating out, clothes, beauty, gifts, homewares and hobbies. You do need to eat, but do you need to eat exclusively from the artisanal aisle at the fanciest grocery store in town? Probably not.

The key here isn't about cutting all the joy — it's about being conscious of where your money's going. Are you spending on things that genuinely light you up, or are you just filling space, time or boredom? Look for patterns, set some boundaries, and remember: every 'just this once' adds up. You don't have to become a minimalist monk, but you do get to decide if you'd rather keep splashing cash like it's free-flowing rosé, or start using it to build the life you actually want.

174

How much of your income goes on discretionary expenses? Have your salary increases been absorbed by lifestyle creep? Could you cut some out without feeling a big impact?

Joy money — for now, soon and later

A big part of seeding your financial goals is figuring out where your money actually goes — and making sure it reflects what matters to you. And that includes Joy.

Joyful spending is part of a healthy money ecosystem — but like everything else, it works best when it's intentional rather than accidental. That's why I almost think of Joy like a person — for me, it's that mix between your cool aunty and that person in your office who's been there the longest, knows all the rules and takes care of everybody. We all need a little more Joy in our lives, right? But we need to make space for her on purpose and then give her three jobs (because she's a multi-tasking queen):

- *Now Joy:* Everyday fun and feel-good spending.
- *Soon Joy:* Short-term goals and purchases.
- *Later Joy:* Long-term goals and future plans.

The Joy we know (and love) isn't going to let you only have fun in the here and now; she'll also make sure you have it all the way through. She knows too much Joy now, means less Joy later. As you create your cash flow plan, ask yourself, 'What would Joy do?'

Activity: Bringing Joy to your (money) world

The idea here is simple: instead of leaving Joy as an afterthought, you're going to make intentional decisions about what she wants, when she wants it, and how to get there — all while staying true to your broader financial goals.

(continued)

Now Joy

How much Joy money do you need to allocate to yourself on a weekly basis? A weekly allocation means you don't have to reconcile every cent you spend. Instead, figure out your existing life costs and how much you need to allocate for your goals, and then allocate some weekly money just for Joy. What I love about doing this is you get freedom within boundaries. You can spend this money on whatever you want—but once it runs out, it's gone until you get next week's Joy money. Them's the rules. I like to gamify it, so I get maximum Joy from my weekly allocation.

I now pay Joy every Wednesday. You do you, but I've found that if I have a spendy weekend, surviving Monday and Tuesday with a total of $8 in my account is tight but doable. I've got clarity on where I am at all times and I know if I stick to my allocation, I'm not going to screw over my goals.

What amount could you trial putting into your weekly Joy account? Will it include money for food and fuel, or will it have an account of its own?

Trial this amount for a month and see if you need to change the number. In the beginning, leave any leftover money in there for any spendy weeks you have. However, if you're sure after a month you've allocated too much every week, change your weekly transfer amount (and move the excess to go towards a different goal—yes!).

Soon Joy

Your Soon Joy funds are for shorter term goals—perhaps an upcoming holiday, some upgrades to the house, an item you've really wanted for a while. You can use your one-year (bamboo) goals from chapter 5 here. Look for ways to save, or cut back and redistribute any leftover funds if you want this Joy sooner (but don't rob from your Later Joy funds!).

What bigger expenses or plans do you have in the next 12 months, and how much do you need for these? Divide that amount by how many pay packets you have between now and then. Automate the payment to go into a separate account specifically for this.

Later Joy

This covers how much you need to commit to giving Joy for your long-term goals. She must be treated like every other fixed expense and automatically allocated as soon as you get paid—be it directly into your offset account or investment portfolio, towards paying down debt, or into your retirement (super) savings. Usually these funds are for goals that require you not to keep the money in cash, because it needs to work hard and get a better return than the interest rate you'll get in the bank.

Where do your long-term goals need you to direct money to?

Get your cash flowing correctly

Listen, I think the word 'budget' should be *banned* (as should the word 'diet'). Just no. Our brain immediately thinks ~~fun and happiness~~ restriction and deprivation. Never have I wanted chocolate cake *more* than during the times I (stupidly) attempted some ridiculous diet. It's the same with budgets. Thinking about all the things you can't spend your money on is almost automatic when you're on a 'budget'. And just like trying to survive solely on cabbage soup, or a *miracle* tea cleanse, too many budgets are unsustainable and unhealthy. You want something that's going to last.

Just when you thought we might be done with the nature metaphors, here comes another one. I want you to think of your income like water — because it's where that cashola flows that matters. Without a clear system for your money, it can easily wash away, leaving your goals without the precious resources needed to make them grow.

Instead, you want to create a system that allows your money to easily flow to where you want it. Build dams to pool your savings, and fix any holes in your spending buckets where money may be leaking out without you even noticing. And, just like water, one 'droplet' of money isn't a big deal — but when each drop gets pooled together, it can be powerful!

Activity: Review your current money system

Use this activity to do a quick check of how much is leaking in your money system. The following questions help you see where you already have things flowing well in your current money system, and which areas might need a patch-up. Ask yourself:

▶ How well is your current money system working for you? Rate it between zero and ten, with zero = shite, not working at all, and ten = perfect, love it.

▶ Do you have different accounts for different areas of your life? For this rating, zero = no, it's all in one account, and ten = I have different accounts for specific purposes.

▶ Do you run out of money before you reach payday? Rate this between zero = welp, yes, every damn pay, and ten = I never run out of money before I get paid.

▸ Do you have all your payments and transfers automated? Between zero = no, I do all my transfers and payments manually, and ten = everything is automated.

▸ Is debt chewing up most of your income? Between zero = yes, it's bleeding me dry, and ten = no, it's manageable.

▸ Are you across where you're spending money (beyond bills)? Between zero = not sure where it goes and ten = every dollar is accounted for.

Mostly zeros = 'Dear Liza, there are holes in my bucket': You don't yet have a system either set up or working properly for you (yet).

Somewhere in the middle = Floating, just: You've got some parts of your money system sorted, but it's either missing some parts, or it isn't set up to work as efficiently as it could.

Mostly tens = River boat queen: You have a clear money system that requires little intervention and (hopefully) you have money already allocated to seed your goals.

Understanding how a money ecosystem can help

Most people assume that having awesome goals is enough to stay motivated to somehow make them happen. As James Clear (of *Atomic Habits* fame) reminds us, however, it actually works in the opposite way. Clear argues, 'You do not rise to the level of your goals. You fall to the level of your systems'. Ain't that the truth.

By building a system that automatically directs money to different spending categories every time you get paid, you're allowing your system to do the cash flowing for you. I call this system a 'conscious cash flow plan' — and in the following sections, I outline why you'll love it and how to do it.

It's future-focused

Many people spend a lot of time looking at what they have already spent. Although this can be helpful to find leaky holes, reconciling past spending doesn't always help you plan ahead and ensure you'll have enough money for your upcoming expenses and goals. Instead, a conscious cash flow plan anticipates upcoming costs — such as that interstate wedding you're attending, the removalist costs for when your lease is up in eight months and you want to move, or the replacement tyres you're probably going to need in the next year.

Action: Make a list of any additional items and expected costs you think you need to have funds at the ready for over the next year or so.

You allocate every dollar

Just because I don't like the word budget, doesn't mean I don't want you to know where your money is spent. Every dollar in your conscious cash flow plan has a job and gets put to work. List out all your current expenses for one year (sorry if you thought you were getting out of that one!). In the previous chapter, I included a spending audit activity. If you completed the level 3 'advanced' section of this activity, you've already got this. If you didn't, now is the time to do so. Once you have your annual expenses, add an inflation buffer (I generally recommend at least 3 per cent).

Action: List out your expenses (review the section 'Cash flowing in all directions', earlier in this chapter, to ensure you include everything), and then add inflation. Diarise a day to review and update your expenses annually (because take-home income and expenses are likely to change). If any changes to your income or expenses occur that could drastically change your plan, update it straightaway. The following table provides example items in the fixed expenses category.

Example fixed expenses: Bills, bills, bills

Expense item	Current cost (per month)	With 3% inflation added
Rent	$3567	$3674
Utilities	$317	$326
Internet	$89	$91
Private health cover	$166	$170
Income protection	$230	$236

By adding some additional funds to account for inflation, you will have already allocated funds to be able to cover any increases or bill shock if (when) your costs increase.

Money is allocated to your goals

Planting seeds is pointless if you don't give them what they need to grow, just like having beautiful goals is pointless if you aren't going to give them any money to make them happen. Once you know your goals, you then need to build them into your cash flow plan — so money flows to them. By giving every dollar a purpose, you can be sure that any money allocated to goals won't leave you short in another category. Or, if you see that your expenses aren't leaving you any money to put towards your goals, you know you have to find a way to earn more or spend less.

The following table outlines how funds can be allocated according to goals.

Allocating money towards your goals

Goal	Target date	Amount to be allocated each pay cycle (assumed monthly)
Trip to New Zealand costing $6000	Six months away	$1000
Home deposit savings of $80000	Four years	$800 for the first six months, and then $1800 when back from New Zealand.
Building a $1000 cash buffer	Within the next 12 months (currently at $0)	$83

Action: Now you have a full list of your expenses (and an inflation buffer included), how much can you put toward each of your goals every pay? Calculate if you will need to amend your goal target amount or time frame.

You create separate bank accounts called 'buckets'

You need to have different bank accounts (buckets) set up for different purposes and priorities. In the next section, I provide more detail on how many accounts you may want to have.

Action: List out all your current bank accounts (and credit cards if you still use them for spending), and draw how money moves into and out of each and for what purpose. Identify any accounts that have a mixed spending or saving purpose.

You can automate how much gets allocated to each account or goal

In this system, you set your money up to automatically flow to each of your buckets, based on how much you've anticipated each needs.

In other words, you get out of your own way. Once the system is set up (through your banking app), you get peace of mind that the right amount is going to the right place, minus the mental load.

Action: Work out where you're manually moving money from your accounts, perhaps to increase savings or pay regular bills. You can use this list once your new bucketing account structure is up and running to identify what needs to be automated.

You have instant visibility and clarity

By naming each of your accounts based on their purpose, you have instant certainty over how much money's currently available for each of your priorities. Get invited to dinner, but only have $3 in your Now Joy account? Maybe next time. Similarly, your 'soon joy' account will show you exactly how much you have for your one-year goals.

Action: Do you want your spending accounts to be with the same bank as your savings accounts (or will this create too much temptation)? You might want all your Soon Joy and Later Joy funds in offset accounts if you have a mortgage. If so, ask the bank if they can hide any accounts from your view when you log in (if you don't want the temptation of spending these funds every time you log in).

You get freedom within boundaries

This system isn't about forcing you to tally up how much you spent each week. Instead, it's about setting your income to flow and building out a plan that is clear and intentional. This plan is about looking forward and flowing out your money for the future (not only based on what you spent in the past).

Action: Decide what day of the week you want to make your weekly Joy payday.

Setting up your conscious cash flow plan

Let the good times flow! You just need to decide what accounts you have, what additional ones you need, what their specific purpose is and how much gets allocated to each. The following figure provides an example plan.

An example conscious cash flow plan

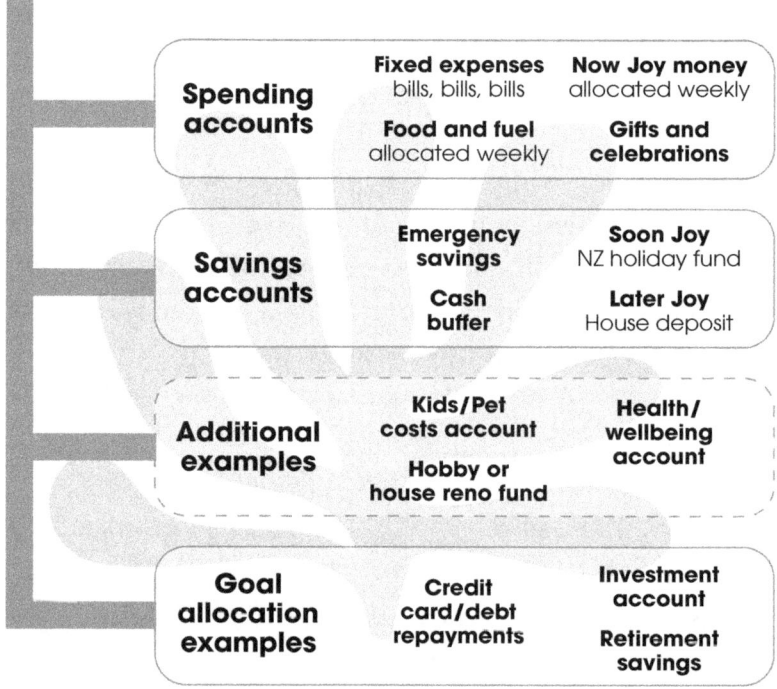

Master income account
Receives income and flows it to other accounts/goals

Spending accounts	Fixed expenses bills, bills, bills	Now Joy money allocated weekly
	Food and fuel allocated weekly	Gifts and celebrations

Savings accounts	Emergency savings	Soon Joy NZ holiday fund
	Cash buffer	Later Joy House deposit

Additional examples	Kids/Pet costs account	Health/ wellbeing account
	Hobby or house reno fund	

Goal allocation examples	Credit card/debt repayments	Investment account
		Retirement savings

You might have noticed that, in the preceding figure, I've included a Later Joy bank account. *What?!* You might be thinking, *I thought you weren't meant to put that in a bank account.* For this example, I've continued the earlier example goal of a house deposit within four years. Given this time frame, you might prefer to keep the savings as cash in the bank rather than invest them.

No magic rule exists for how many accounts you 'must have'. You can tailor your system based on what is going to work best for you. I've had members set up specific accounts for buying clothes, monthly bougie dining experiences, pet and/or kid costs, or hobbies that are important to them. The idea is you can log in to your online banking at any time and see exactly how much you have allocated to each important category in your life.

However, whatever your number of accounts, I would say bucketing and automating are the two golden cash flow rules. Here's the system I use and recommend:

- *Master income account:* This is the top of the waterfall. This account only has two jobs: receiving income and dispersing it to other accounts.
- *Fixed expenses account:* Payment of all fixed and regular bills comes from here. Be sure to add allocations every pay for annual expenses (such as car registration, insurances and annual memberships).
- *Emergency savings:* This is a personal account for proper emergency situations. No-one else should be able to access this account, ever.
- *Cash buffer:* This account holds funds for when any wiggle room is needed due to unexpected bills or costs that aren't an emergency.
- *Food and fuel account:* This can be wrapped into your Now Joy account, if you're confident you can have it all together without causing confusion. Otherwise, split it out and have money allocated for these weekly expenses.

- *Gifts and celebrations account:* This can be used for expenses during the festive season, and for weddings, birthdays, baby showers and 'your business turned five' celebrations. Add an amount every pay cycle.
- *Now Joy account:* Allocate a weekly amount to this account to spend on joyous activities — including eating out, buying coffee, going out, purchasing clothes or anything else you want. Drip-feed funds to this account from your master income account weekly (irrespective of your pay cycle).
- *Soon Joy account:* This account is for your shorter term goals, and can be named accordingly. If funds in this account will be used for a holiday, for example, use the destination as the account name so you don't get tempted to rob from it. Generally, use this account for the goal you want to achieve within the next 12 months. Add to it every pay cycle.

Some other points to consider in setting up your accounts:

- *Fees:* Look for accounts that charge low, or no, monthly account fees.
- *Name:* Title your accounts according to their specific purpose, so it's clear what each is for.
- *Automation:* When you are setting up automations, give some thought to the timing of your bills. If you only add one transfer into your fixed expenses bucket, for example, and you have a bunch of bills coming out the next day, you may find you don't have enough to cover them all. In situations like this, if you can, 'borrow' money from your cash buffer (be sure to pay it back when you can).
- *Joy day:* Choose a day of the week for your Now Joy money to be allocated. It's your personal payday, so pick whichever day you please.

- *Offset usage:* If you have a mortgage with an offset functionality, you may want to use it. Every day money sits in your offset accounts, it reduces the amount of interest you pay. This means more of your repayment goes to paying off the principal (the amount you borrowed from the bank). Most banks let you have multiple offset accounts. If you think this account type could work for you and you don't already have this set up, call your bank or broker to see what they can do. Also ask about any additional costs or fees involved in setting this up.

- *Turning taps off:* If you use your phone or any other devices to pay for things, make sure only the appropriate accounts are linked (such as your 'food and fuel' and Now Joy accounts). Set up your fixed expenses as direct debits out of a dedicated account, so you don't need to access this account for other transactions and everyday spending.

- *Credit cards:* Should you use credit cards? Probably not. Research shows that we tend to spend more when using credit cards, because we can — our brain's reward system gets activated when spending on credit (not ideal!).[1] So, I generally recommend avoiding them if you can.

Conscious cash flow planning for two

I am a big fan of a split system if you're in a relationship. Why? It's likely you'll have shared costs and shared goals, so having a joint account for them makes sense. But you're also individuals. Having some solo accounts creates more safety and generally less conflict. In saying that, if one of you earns considerably more than the other, how are you dealing with that? If one of you goes on parental leave, how will you fund your costs? Have the chats needed to answer these kinds of questions (and the sooner, the better!).

Here is a structure you could use when setting up a joint conscious cash flow plan:

- *Master income account:* You could have both of your incomes go into this account, or a set amount of each of your incomes. If one of you doesn't earn an income, this should be a joint account. You should never receive an 'allowance' from your partner, with no direct access to accounts. That's a red flag, my friend.

- *Joint fixed expenses account:* Some couples choose to split their fixed expenses and have only joint expenses coming from this account. They then have a separate fixed expense account for personal regular bills. Others have all fixed expenses coming from the same account.

- *Joint Soon Joy account:* This account is normally used for things like holidays, renovations or other shorter term goals you're both committed to. Having this as a joint account makes sense, because it's going to take a team effort to achieve them. You may also want your gifts and celebrations account to be a joint account.

- *Joint spending:* I encourage you to have a joint account for your food and fuel expenses (if that works for you), and for your Now Joy spending on things you do together or as a family. However, each of you should still have a personal Now Joy account and weekly allocation. This then means you jointly contribute to money for things done together, but you each also still have full control over how you spend your personal Now Joy account. This gives you both a sense of security (you both know if you stick to the agreed amounts, your goals and bills are sorted) but also freedom (you don't need to justify why you decided to spend on a particular thing because the money has come from your personal spending account).

Importantly, working out this plan requires you both to sit down together and figure out, or test, your system and see what's going to work best for you both. If it needs adjusting, adjust it!

For all joint accounts, make sure you have joint signatories attached to them, so that one person cannot withdraw over a certain amount without the other's approval. What matters is you communicate and create a plan that works for you both. One person shouldn't have full control, access or responsibility. (I cover ways to protect yourself within a relationship in much more detail in chapter 9.)

A note for my ADHD friends

If you haven't previously had any structure with how you manage your accounts, I suggest one of the following:

- *Start small:* Perhaps just focus on splitting out your emergency savings and Now Joy weekly allocation, and continue to build out over time.
- *Grab a friend and settle in for a 'do it dinner':* Pizza + drink of choice + cash flow planning = much more fun than doing it alone.

Beyond automations, set up reminders for any bills and add notifications onto your banking app so you can see when money has been debited. This can help you avoid accidentally going over your balance — and being charged additional fees. Move your savings account to another bank, or see if you can remove the online view if you don't want the temptation of seeing the balance when you log in. Or perhaps move your Now Joy and 'food and fuel' accounts to a separate bank. You'll know what might tempt you to spend, so plan for that and set up your accounts in a way that will support your goals.

If you're like me, you'll need to really believe this is going to help you to get it all set up. What could you reward yourself with once it's done? Perhaps a long walk in nature, a sleep in or a re-watch of your favourite show? Not having any money left in your Now Joy account for impulse purchases might also feel frustrating, but that's the point. I cried a few times when I was getting used to it. But it really did help me have freedom within boundaries. So know that, like me all those years ago, you might not enjoy all of it all the time — but you will enjoy the results!

A note for parents and carers

Teaching your kids about spending and saving is one of the best ways to get them learning and engaged with finances from a young age. You may choose to adopt a save/spend/give strategy with them. You might offer to dollar-match (up to a certain level), for example, or give them bonus interest on any money they choose to add to their savings or giving fund. They can decide what they are saving for, or you might help them figure that out if you think they would benefit from some guidance (most kids don't want it, but need it).

Depending on their age, they may want to decide how and where they would like to give money, which helps them understand that they can use their money to not only assist themselves, but also make a difference to the world.

Always be on the lookout for moments to include them in money conversations in an age-appropriate way. Get a large bill? Tell them what that means and how reducing it as a family means more money to do other things (such as a trip to the zoo, or a picnic with their favourite snacks). Don't be surprised when small children want to spend all of their money instantly and then want to know why it's all gone — it can take a while for them to grasp the concept. A useful strategy is to take out cash when they are going to buy something, and hand it to them so they can give it to the person at the shop (if you aren't buying it online). Let them experience what handing over cash feels like and you might just find the 'must have' item isn't actually where they want to spend their money anymore. Teach them the things you wish someone had shown you when you were a child, with patience, curiosity and grace when they make a mistake.

If you've completed the activities provided through this chapter, you'll have built out your system and plan for your cash to flow into the important areas of your life (well done, you!). If you thought you would read it all first and then go back later and do it, welcome to later. Now's the time to complete (or, at the very least, put it in the diary to do) any outstanding elements discussed in this chapter. Yes, you might have a fair few things to tick off. But this is what's going to make sure you can seed your goals, and not give up on joy in the process. And that's so absolutely worth it.

8

SPROUT

What to know before you grow: the risks and rewards of investing

With opportunity the world is very interesting.

—Beatrix Potter

You've weeded and you've seeded. Now it's time to get your money sprouting! If you've never dived into investing before (welcome!), a bunch of aspects will be new for you in this chapter. Even if you've been at this investment caper for a little while, hopefully you'll learn something new too. And because investing concepts were created by people who clearly didn't want non-finance people to be able to understand them, I do have to warn you: you might have a bit of jargon to get your head around. If you feel a bit like a fish out of water (or should it be tomato among the tulips?), remember that this is because the system was designed to be unnecessarily complicated. (I am convinced that's the case.) So it's not you; it's them. But you're wildly capable, remember? And you're not going to let anyone gatekeep your ticket to freedom.

Growing anything—a plant, a new skill and even your hair after a bad haircut—takes time. Investing is the same. In fact, it requires a lot of patience. Greek philosopher Epicurus once said, 'The greatest fruit of self-sufficiency is freedom'. Now I'm not sure he was talking about having a thriving investment portfolio when he said it. But if he was, he's a genius! Growing your wealth through investing can allow you to financially sustain your life and achieve a level of freedom that is so hard to attain otherwise.

In this chapter, I run through some investment basics so your hard-earned money can start sprouting some returns. I cover the different stages of wealth and where you might be up to, and answer any lingering questions you might still have. Then I take you through the most common investing options (including the pros and cons of each) and what to look out for as you start building out your plan.

I've focused on the 'must-knows' to help you start (and stay) invested. Come back and reread this chapter as many times as you need to. Make notes, highlight the bits you need to and talk about it with your friends. Are you ready to become a savvy and strategic investor? Hell yes, you are!

Different stages of wealth

They say 'Rome wasn't built in a day'; well, neither is financial freedom. Most of us take years, if not decades, to build wealth. Even that 'overnight success story' or 'instant millionaire' likely poured plenty of hours into growing their money, but we're only seeing the highlight reel. So what are the different stages of wealth, and how can you build towards the next one?

I've broken the stages of wealth into the four main ones, shown in the following figure.

The four stages of wealth

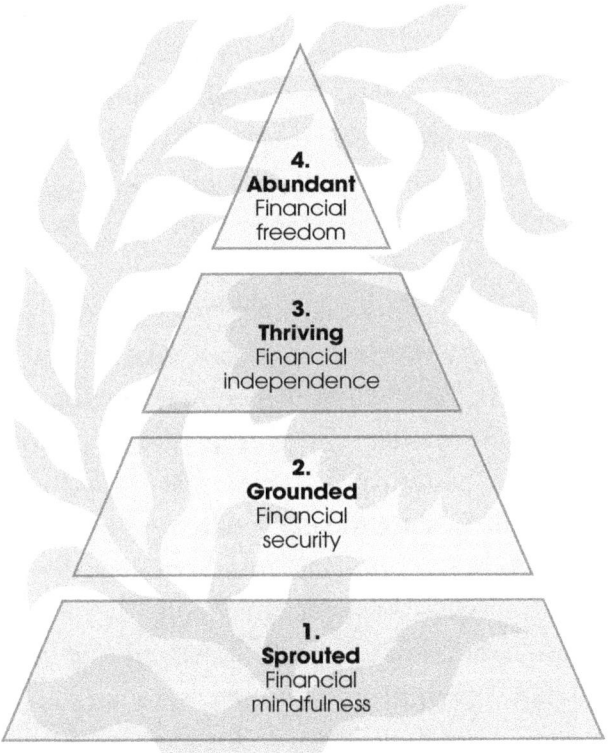

Let's take a closer look at each of these stages:

- *Stage 1: Sprouted —financial mindfulness:* You're just getting started and are already doing some good work with your money. Your income covers your everyday needs and money is allocated to your goals. You're beginning to see growth — in your knowledge, habits, savings and overall financial position. But if you stopped working for a long period, you don't yet have enough assets to be able to support yourself for more than a few months (without going into debt or needing to sell an asset). This is the stage that most people spend a lot of time in, and that's because it can take a while for everything to get sprouting. Stick with it!

- *Stage 2: Grounded —financial security:* After you've been tending to your money for a while, you'll start feeling like your hard work is paying off (literally). Your debts are reducing and your assets are growing. You feel grounded, secure and better able to weather life's storms. You can't give up work or completely bankroll yourself (yet), but you're happy knowing you've got some financial wiggle room and your goals are on track.

- *Stage 3: Thriving —financial independence:* You'll know when you arrive at this level because you'll have cleared your debt and your assets will be at a point where they give you a passive income (money you get from returns or dividends) equivalent to your current lifestyle costs. Your financial ecosystem can sustain the life you live today.

- *Stage 4: Abundant —financial freedom:* Okay, this is the unicorn level I discussed back in chapter 4. This level is often talked about, but rarely seen. Those who do get here have investments growing for them such that their passive income can fund their dream lifestyle. I don't necessarily mean private jets and huge trunks full of rare jewels, but *your* dream lifestyle. This level of wealth provides full control over how to spend your time and the capacity to financially support future generations, without impacting your goals or lifestyle.

Feel like you haven't even reached stage 1 yet? That's okay. That's why you're here. If you follow everything from the previous chapters and combine it with what you learn in this and the following chapter, you'll be well on your way to climbing the pyramid!

Can I achieve financial freedom without investing?

Chances are you're reading this chapter (or have skipped ahead straight to it) because you've heard that investing is the only way to achieve financial freedom — aka enough wealth so you can work because you want to, not because you have to. (Unless, of course, you win the lotto, inherit a bajillion dollars or move completely off-grid and live off the land with no real expenses — which in the current state of the world actually sounds like quite an attractive option.) But for the rest of us, investing is the best way to grow true wealth and freedom.

You can eliminate debt, save, cut your spending, build an emergency buffer and put it all in the bank to grow very slowly — if at all. But the way money works is that inflation can outpace any interest rate you might earn on your savings, meaning your money is technically losing value over time, and you're going backwards even though it feels like you have a good amount.

Wait a minute, what? I know; it's hard to get your head around. But inflation, also known as the 'cost of living' (or my favourite love-to-hate term, 'cozzie livs', which sounds like something you wear to the beach), in simple terms means how far your money stretches. As costs go up, the value of our money — or how far it goes — reduces. In Australia, inflation is tracked by the Consumer Price Index (CPI).

Remember how many lollies you could buy in primary school with $1? Loads. Today? A lot less (boo!). Don't even start me on 'shrinkflation' (when product sizes shrink, but prices don't). Have you seen how skinny poor Freddo is these days? The once delightfully rotund little frog now looks like he's been kept away from, ahem, chocolate for some time. Honestly, justice for Freddo!

Investing regularly is what helps your money really grow. Without it, building wealth is harder (not impossible, but a *lot* harder). If you're not investing it, your money isn't working for you — it's just sitting there. That's why I call your investment portfolio a 'freedom fund'. It's not any specific 'fund' per se, but the total pot of investments you've built (generally outside of superannuation) to do what you want in life before you're able to access your retirement savings. Depending on your age and goals, you may choose to build your freedom fund in your personal name. Most people who have a goal to retire as early as possible choose this option, over focusing on their retirement fund or super fund. One reason for this is that, in Australia, strict rules cover when you can access your superannuation balance. (I cover this in more detail in chapter 9.) A personal freedom fund gives you options, so you feel less stuck on the work, or life, hamster wheel.

Do you know why hamsters use those spinning things in the first place? Because they're *stuck* in a cage (for our benefit), needing exercise and enjoyment, but here's the thing: when they've had enough, they jump off. Many people have told me they feel like they're in a similar situation and going round in circles. But, crucially, they feel unable to escape the system. They can't just jump off, take a break or nap whenever they like. They've gotta keep running — hard. They feel like they've been going round and round for years, and will for decades more — until they 'retire'. I don't know about you, but that sounds kinda shit to me.

It's okay to want to work, to run hard and build something for yourself, because you *want* to be there. But no-one wants to work and feel they can't escape it. Some may say capitalism as a system is carefully designed to keep the masses perpetually busy and exhausted, working to benefit the people at the top — because who's going to do all the work and make the billionaires more billions if we're all wealthy enough to do whatever the hell we want with our time? That's not wrong. Oh, the irony that this chapter is teaching you how to benefit from that system. Yes, I'm aware.

Dismantling the system aside, the most effective way to achieve financial freedom is to act like less of a hamster, and more like a squirrel. You have to spend less than you earn and the leftover cash needs to be squirreled somewhere it can grow. Put your money to work *making* you money. Then put those monies to work to make you more money. This is the concept of 'compounding' — described (and not by Einstein) as the 'eighth wonder of the world'. It is never too early (or late!) to start investing, and the best news? You don't need a huge amount to begin. But starting can be the hardest part.

Growing pains

The main reason people don't invest is fear. Some are so scared they are going to muck it up entirely that they delay, delay, delay — and then never get around to it. Or, when they do bravely begin, analysis paralysis sets in and they freeze. This is also called the 'paradox of choice' (coined by psychologist and author Barry Schwartz). At first, having so many options can feel exciting. (*I can invest in all these different ways and different companies — this is amazing!*) But soon all those options become overwhelming. A bit like that iconic early 2000s TV ad where the lady at the local corner store rattles off all the different types of milk they sell and the man at the counter stands stunned and says, 'I just want milk that tastes like real milk'. The stress of making the perfect decision is enough to put us off making a decision at all. Cue regret and a lifetime of 'what ifs'.

Now I don't think many people are sat at home lamenting their milk selection; however, many people *do* dwell on the financial decisions they both did and didn't make. After decades in the finance industry, the way I see it is that not doing anything is normally the worst decision of them all.

I get it — maybe your parents or communities have never invested their money, so you've never been taught about it. Maybe you've been told it's like gambling (it's not!) and too risky. If you're a woman, perhaps you've been told that you're not likely to be any good at it. (Rubbish — women make excellent investors!) Whatever you've been told, or whatever you've told yourself in the past was the reason you couldn't or shouldn't invest your money, I'm going to show you that it's not as hard as you think. (And if you need to do some more work on your own money memoir, head back to chapter 3.) As the saying goes, the best time to start investing was yesterday; the second best time is today.

Understanding how investing can grow your money

Imagine you have one little tomato with only a few seeds inside. You want to grow more tomatoes, so you start preparing and replanting those few seeds. Soon you'll have more tomato plants bearing fruits that *also* have a few seeds each. Now you can choose to eat these tomatoes, sell them or harvest the seeds and plant them too. That's the basic principle of investing. You can probably see how starting small in the beginning, just with one little tomato, can turn into something much, much bigger if you keep planting the seeds! Eventually you can start eating some, because you know you still have enough planted and growing that you won't run out. And maybe you also start planting carrots, onions, basil or anything else you fancy so that you've got a nice diverse harvest from which to make a meal, without having to worry that a cold snap will ruin your tomatoes.

Investing, by definition, is basically just a commitment of resources into something expected to gain value over time. Beyond tomatoes, it's about putting your money into assets such as shares or property, with the expectation that they'll grow and generate profits or income over time. So how can you use your money to make more money? Well, you have a few options:

- *Invest regularly:* This might seem obvious, but buying investments regularly means you'll have more of them over time. This is why you need a conscious cash flow plan that has money allocated and automated to your long-term goals. (Remember your 'later joy' money from the previous chapter? That's usually what you use to create your freedom fund.)
- *Aim for capital growth:* This is a fancy way of saying that something goes up in value. For example, say you bought a property for $400 000 and now it's worth $550 000. You now have $150 000 in capital growth. Or if you bought 10 shares for $40 each and they're now trading for $50 each, you have $10 in capital growth per share, or $100 in total.
- *Focus on income:* Some investments pay you money while you own them. This income could be from the profits made by a company you're invested in — otherwise known as 'dividends', 'distributions' from an investment fund, or rent you receive from a property you own.
- *Take advantage of compounding:* This is the secret sauce of investing. It's when the money you earn from your investments is reinvested to buy more investments. By doing so, you'll have more assets that can grow and/or give you additional income.

Investing options 101

Now you can see why and how investing can grow your wealth, it's time to take a look at some of the most common ways to invest, and the pros and cons of each. I cover retirement savings more broadly in the next chapter. (It's so important, it gets its own section — even though it's likely to be invested in many of the assets listed here.)

Cash

Generally when we talk about 'cash' in the investment context, what we are talking about is money sitting in a bank account — not cold hard cash stuffed in a mattress. Here are the pros and cons of holding cash:

- *Pros:* Accessibility — if an investment option arises, you can quickly access any cash you hold to take advantage of it. (Although this can also make it too easy to get your hands on!) Cash isn't linked to investment markets, so changes to daily share prices won't affect how much money you have in your account.
- *Cons:* It generally doesn't grow very much and the real value of your money may go backwards during periods of high inflation.

Shares

Shares are also called 'stocks' or 'equities' — just to confuse the fuck out of you! Buying shares is like buying a slice of ownership in a company. So are you buying a big slice or a small slice of the pie? Well, it depends on two things: the number of shares issued, and how many you own relative to that total issued number. Here are the pros and cons:

- *Pros:* You can cherrypick which companies you want to invest into. This asset has growth potential (if the share price goes up) and some will also provide income along the way via dividends. You can attend annual general meetings (AGMs) and vote on important matters (you are a part-owner in the business, after all). You can sell your shares and normally have the funds back in your account within a few days.

- *Cons:* Share prices tend to move daily, based on company performance or broader economic factors. Researching lots of different companies to decide which to buy into can be laborious, often leading to people owning shares in only a handful of different companies (meaning their portfolio is not well diversified). You usually have to pay a brokerage fee every time you buy (and sell) shares, meaning if you wanted to buy into 30 different companies, you'd pay 30 brokerage fees. Ouch.

Exchange traded funds

Exchange traded funds (ETFs) are pre-packaged investment options you can buy via the stock exchange. What you're actually invested in will depend on the type of ETF you buy (most are passive, simply following a target index, but active-style ETFs are available). Here are the pros and cons:

- *Pros:* Generally, ETFs give you the ability to invest in lots of different companies through one investment product — kind of like buying a mixed bag of lollies. Usually, they have low fees and, just like shares, you can sell them and have your money back within a few days. It's easy to invest in ETFs via an investment platform, where you can look at the different options and choose the one that matches your goals. You then buy ETFs directly through the app or portal.

- *Cons:* ETFs don't allow you to cherrypick the companies you invest in. If you like the sound of an ETF product but don't want to be invested in a handful of the companies they have inside the product, you can't ask them to remove those companies for you. You'll either need to find a different ETF that excludes them, or accept that you're going to be invested in them all. Like shares, the price of the ETF will move up and down based on the investment market. You will likely still have to pay brokerage fees every time you trade (but you might make fewer trades because you're accessing a pre-mixed option and don't need to buy each company individually).

Managed funds

In a managed fund, a fund manager pools your money with other people's and buys assets on your behalf. You don't buy or sell your holdings directly on the stock exchange. The pros and cons of managed funds are as follows:

- *Pros:* Like ETFs, you have loads of different options to pick from that are pre-packaged, so you won't need to buy into each asset or company individually. You're spreading your risk and the potential for growth and/or income (depending on what you're investing in).
- *Cons:* Most managed funds have a minimum investment amount to open an account and may have higher fees than ETFs. They also generally take longer to have the funds returned to you. (In some, rare, cases the fund may be 'frozen', preventing you from withdrawing your money for a period of time. This is generally done in moments of acute market stress to protect members from selling assets at low prices.)

Property

Property as an asset includes houses, apartments or even commercial property that you (and the bank, most probably) own. Here are the pros and cons:

- *Pros:* Property is a physical asset and most people are able to borrow (that is, take out a mortgage) to get one, meaning any growth you see comes off a higher base number. As your equity (ownership percentage) grows, you may also be able to borrow against this equity to buy additional properties or other assets. If the asset is an investment property with tenants, you'll get rental income and some of your costs will be tax deductible. If you live in the property, once the mortgage is paid off, your annual expenses will reduce (unlike rent, which generally increases annually due to tight supply and inflation).

- *Cons:* Property is expensive to buy (and to sell!). You'll have ongoing costs, and if it's an investment rather than a home, you might face periods of time where the property is empty. Will the rent received cover all your costs? If not, it's called a 'negatively geared asset', and you'll need to be able to fund the cash-flow shortfall. Property is not what we call a 'highly liquid' asset — that is, if you need money quickly, you can't just sell a bathroom. Selling a property can take a lot of time. And while we have seen significant growth in property prices in Australia, not all of them go up in value at the same rate. (Annoyingly, houses generally are the most expensive to get into, but generally grow at a much higher rate than units or apartments because of the land they're on.)

Bonds and fixed income

Bonds and fixed-income products see you act like a bank for governments or companies (weird but true). You give them money, and in return they give you an interest amount (called a 'coupon'), plus your original money back at the end of the term. Here are the pros and cons:

- *Pros:* They can provide a predictable income and are typically considered a safe (albeit conservative) investment.
- *Cons:* Fixed-income products tend to have a lower return than growth-style investments. And the risk of inflation being higher than your return is also something to be mindful of. Most countries and companies will honour what they 'owe' you, but not always. There have been some high-profile examples where bond holders were screwed when a company collapsed (for example, Lehman Brothers) and some countries have defaulted in recent times too (for example, Greece, Argentina and Russia).

Other investments

Lots of other types of investments are possible — including in gold, private equity, crypto and alternative commodities. These are not the most common assets most new investors go into, and some are riskier or harder to access if you don't have a certain level of wealth or knowledge. (You might wonder why some cryptocurrencies have flown while others have flopped. It seems news and social media play a large part.[1]) Because this isn't the kind of speculative investing most new investors want to get started with, these options aren't covered here.

What to know and look out for when you're investing

In this section, I cover some basic investment theory and some of the potential risks.

Time in the market versus timing the market

The longer you're invested, the more you'll benefit from your investments compounding. Time really is your friend with investing, and the earlier you start the better. The approach of starting and staying consistent with regular contributions and reinvesting income has a track record of working in the long run. So rather than trying to pick the 'best' time to invest — perhaps when prices are at their lowest — just get started.

Buy and hold

One of the easiest ways to grow your money is to buy diversified portfolios, set up auto-reinvest functionality (meaning any money you make as income from the portfolio is reinvested to buy more of it) and hold steady. Buying and holding for the long term is a proven and very effective way to build your wealth. Plus, it doesn't require a huge amount of ongoing intervention.

Look for performance

While historical performance is never a guarantee of what an investment will do in the future, it's the best we've got to go off. Always look at the past performance over the longest time period possible.

(Don't just look at how a share, ETF or managed fund performed over the last year, for example.) See if you can find the 'net return' — this is the actual performance of the investment after taking the fees out.

Ideally, you should be aiming for returns at around the CPI plus 2 per cent for more conservative assets, and around the CPI plus 6 per cent for high-growth assets. For reference, the average Reserve Bank of Australia (RBA) cash rate was just 1.98 per cent[2] over the past 10 years. Over the same period, the average annual returns from the S&P/ASX 200 were around 10.2 per cent (as at June 2025) while returns from the US S&P 500 were about 13.6 per cent per annum (as at August 2025). In the last five years alone, property in Australia has on average grown by 43.2 per cent in the combined capitals (major cities such as Sydney and Melbourne), and by 59.3 per cent in combined regional areas such as Newcastle.[3]

Watch fees

Make sure you know how much you're going to pay for the privilege of investing — and this includes fund manager fees and any other fees or charges from your investment platform. Keep an eye on these, but don't choose an investment based on low fees alone — because while it's great you aren't being charged much in fees, you still want to make sure you're getting good returns.

Use dollar-cost averaging

Dollar-cost averaging (DCA) is buying investments at regular intervals, irrespective of the price. Trying to pick 'the best day' to invest is futile (unless you have a crystal ball — even the experts get it wrong, and often!). By buying regularly over time, you'll end up averaging out the purchase price of your assets — another reason it makes sense to regularly automate your investment purchases!

The following table provides an example DCA strategy.

Example of DCA strategy with monthly contribution

Month	Additional contribution amount	Unit price	Number of units purchased
January	$1000	$54	18
February	$1000	$38	26
March	$1000	$61	16
April	$1000	$47	21
May	$1000	$63	15
June	$1000	$73	13
	Total contributed = $6000	Average purchase price = $56	Total units purchased = 109

Consider your investment platform

Think of investment platforms as being similar to an online marketplace where investments are bought or sold — they're like an online shopping app that sells all different brands, but for investments. Options include Sharesies, Pearler, NAB Trade and CommSec.

Look for a platform that offers a broad range of investment options, charges low fees (or, if fees are higher, also offers additional services or support) and has good reporting functionality. Also look for no or low minimum investment amounts and auto-reinvesting functionality (giving you the ability to set up regular buys or auto-reinvest rules for any income you receive). Importantly, make sure the platform is easy to use — and, of course, that it's regulated and reputable. In Australia, this means they must hold an Australian Financial Services (AFS) licence.

Look at the tax implications

When considering your investments, it's also important to remember the tax implications. Most people don't love the idea of paying tax but, if you think about it, you're making this payment because you've made money. That's a good thing. Taxes also help fund things that all of us use, from roads to healthcare systems. Sure, we don't want to pay more than we have to but, generally, you'll pay tax on any income you receive from your investments (even if you reinvest the money straight back into your portfolio). And when you sell an asset for a higher amount than you bought it for, known as making a 'capital gain', capital gains tax (CGT) is usually applicable. In Australia, if you hold an asset for more than 12 months, you generally get a 50 per cent CGT discount. Property can also be subject to tax if you make a profit when you sell. Your primary place of residence (your home) is generally not subject to CGT — but it's always best to do your research and check.

If you make a shed load of income from your investments and you've invested it straight back into your portfolio, you will need to consider if you need any additional cash on hand when it comes to tax time. (This reinvested income is still part of your assessable income.) But you can seek professional advice to help you minimise your tax bill and make sure you don't pay more than you have to.

Ignore hype, fads and FOMO

Don't get sucked into investing in something because it's the trend of the moment. If something sounds too good to be true, it often is. Nothing is wrong with wanting to look into such options; however, especially for highly speculative investments, my general stance is only invest what you would be willing to lose and keep the main portion of your portfolio invested in assets that have a proven track record of performance.

Tread carefully with the DIY approach

If you are planning on buying individual shares to build your portfolio, you'll need to do a lot of research to decide exactly what companies to invest in. Have a think about all the aspects that give a company a competitive edge. Are they making money, for example? Is the company growing? Do they have a history of paying out dividends? Is the share price fair compared to the company's valuation? This is known as a price to earnings, or PE ratio (which has nothing to do with school sports). To determine it, you need to grab the share price, find the earnings price and then divide the share price by the earnings price. Some sectors have different average PE ratios, so you'll need to look into that too. As you can see, handpicking shares one by one is a lot of work (remember time is your most valuable asset and the life-swap hourly rate you calculated in chapter 6). It may also mean you need to do additional work to ensure your portfolio is well diversified. For these reasons, it's not something I generally recommend to first timers.

Read all those PDSs & TMDs

Repeat after me: 'This is my money. I need to know what I'm investing in'. And remember this when you're thinking of ignoring the boring as batshit but super important product disclosure statements (PDSs) and target market determinations (TMDs). A PDS will have all the info you need to know about a product (think: nuts and bolts of how it works) and the TMD will tell you the type of person the product suits best. Will they put you to sleep? Yes. Will they help you understand exactly where your money is going and if it's a good fit for you? Also yes. To try to make the task somewhat less tedious, I pretend the text was written by a pompous 18th century aristocrat and I read it with an accent that matches. This approach makes it easier to go through — and stops me from screaming, 'Why don't you just use plain English, for fuck sake!!'

But isn't investing risky?

Perhaps, even with all this information, you still have one core fear: that investing is risky and you'll lose all your hard-earned money. Let's remember risk exists everywhere. It's why we have seatbelts in cars or passwords on our email account. Risk is why we text our friends the name, profile pic and phone number of the person we are going on a first date with (and text them again when we get home safe). To be frank, anytime I attempt using liquid eyeliner immediately becomes a risky situation. We can never get rid of all of the risks in life, but we can do things to mitigate them.

Keeping money as cash in the bank can feel like the smartest and safest option, but you now know that's not always the case (thanks, inflation). Money in a bank account earns interest. While it's a pretty predictable return, in most instances it isn't anything to write home about. Park it there for long-term goals and you're probably not going to get the level of growth you could have achieved had it been invested elsewhere. This creates opportunity cost — meaning, you may have left money on the table or buried in the garden.

Does your rate of return really make that much difference in the long run? *Spoiler alert:* Yes! Where you invest your money can see you with very different financial outcomes. Here's an example. Let's travel back to 1995 (fittingly Coolio's 'Gangsta's Paradise' is at the top of the charts) and imagine you had $10000 to invest. Let's also assume there were no transaction costs and that you reinvested all your earnings (income) back into your investment to compound. How much would this initial $10000 be worth 30 years later? Here are your returns, based on what you invested in[4]:

- *Cash:* $33677.
- *Australian bonds:* $49451.
- *Australian shares:* $143786.
- *US shares:* $214332.

Having $33000 would no doubt feel good, but knowing it could have been over $200000 if you'd invested it differently for the goal time frame is a *big* wake-up call. So how do you identify your goal time frame when you're investing? We dive into that in the next chapter.

Money in the Wild: Cheryl (she/her)

- **Age:** 61.
- **Situationship:** Single.
- **Income:** $100000.
- **Current savings:** $30000.
- **Current relationship with money:** Excited, cautious, overwhelmed.

What does life look like right now?

Home is a full nest at the moment. My 89-year-old mother is staying with me while we transition her into retirement living, so I am helping her clear her house and get it ready for sale. She is not a hoarder, but has been in the house for several decades and has lots of things in cupboards. I also help with my grandchildren—one day a week I pick them up from school and day care, do the dinner and bath, stay overnight and do the drop off the next morning. Both parents work fulltime and arrive home about 7 pm. I believe this is called the 'care sandwich'!

Do you save or invest?

I do save a little bit and I definitely have a plan to invest. I went on a big holiday for my 60th last year to Europe. I had a bunch of girlfriends join me and family for two weeks in Tuscany. I then continued on a big world trip. It was so worth it but it took all my savings and any money I might have invested. So next year is the investment year!

What is a past money decision you're proud of?

Adding to my super after my divorce, and after my separation from my partner a few years ago.

What's one piece of money advice you wish you knew sooner?
I knew I needed to save and invest earlier in my life but kept putting it off. I have done a lot of research, courses and study, but I failed to launch.

What was your biggest 'ouch' money moment, and what came from it?
I built a storage studio/shed under my house and it cost three times what I had thought it would. I didn't know how to stop the build; it had to be finished. It wiped out my savings buffer and left me feeling scared, very fearful, and not safe or secure.

What does 'financial wellbeing' mean to you?
Being aware of my financial situation, what options are available to grow wealth, and still sleep well at night. Enough money to go on a holiday, pay my bills.

Did you have a big 'oh shit' moment that made you realise you had to learn more about money?
When we technically went bankrupt. My husband was a barrister but didn't like paying tax. The ATO was the main creditor. I had to go back and study bookkeeping and take over the finances. It was a tug of war for years to try to manage the money.

Anything else you'd like to share?
I wish I had believed in myself earlier and taken charge of my own finances. I was married at 23 and had a baby at 24. I thought life was great—my husband was earning a good salary, and we drove nice cars and had great holidays. I worked part-time through my marriage but didn't regularly contribute to super. Then I got divorced.

During my second relationship, I thought we would be together forever. I trusted him and joined all our finances. I was really burnt this time and had to fight in court for a year to get a share of the finances. He truly believed it was all his. I am okay now but I should be in a better position. I encourage my daughters to be financially literate and responsible.

GROW

How to cultivate long-term financial freedom through investing and super

Il faut cultiver notre jardin.
[We must cultivate our garden.]

—*Voltaire*

You've now got your head around investment basics and have an idea about some of your options. Perhaps you've even started to get your hands dirty and planted some seeds. Maybe some of those seeds have started to sprout.

In this chapter, I'm going to take you through my six-step GARDEN investing framework (because, of course that's what it's called). But first, you need to have a think about your investment time line, and whether you want your investments to grow within your retirement fund or within what I like to call your personal 'freedom fund'. Don't worry if you haven't really thought about this decision yet — because that's what the start of this chapter is all about.

Saving for retirement versus your freedom fund

Now you might have already decided that you are investing for your future specifically within your retirement account — your superannuation fund if you're in Australia (or perhaps within KiwiSaver if you're in Aotearoa New Zealand). And that's perfectly fine. You might be at an age where retirement is not too far away and the tax perks make investing via super the most appealing option. Or, you might want your investments to be more accessible, if the time frame for your goals mean you need the money *before* you can generally access it within the regulated retirement system. So you might choose to invest extra money in a personal investment account instead. I call this building your personal 'freedom fund' (because that's what it's growing to give you), and I cover how to make it happen later in this chapter.

Either way, it's important you remember that your retirement savings (particularly if they are held within your super fund in Australia) could end up being one of your biggest assets — if not *the biggest*. So no matter your age or stage, learning how to look after these investments now (even if retirement age is way, way far away) will ensure all systems are a-grow until that time comes, if you know what I mean!

It might still be a completely weird thing to think that one day, hopefully, you'll be old. Carrying wrinkles that show the map of your life, and laugh lines you built over many joyous moments. Who might you be then?

Hell, you might go *wild* and backpack around South America with your grandkid, get a tattoo to celebrate surviving breast cancer like my mum's retired friend did, or join a sea shanty choir. (I have a weird fascination about doing this one day, despite being neither a sailor nor a singer.) Or, you might choose a quieter, simpler life — your ideal retirement might include tea, books, pastries and as many rescue animals as you can squeeze into your home. Or maybe you'd like to have grandchildren squealing thunderously as they race around your kitchen and you prepare your weekly 'all in' family meal.

Whatever life you end up creating, you're likely to spend a pretty big chunk of it in retirement even though, it must be said, the idea of permanently leaving the paid workforce at a certain age is a very culturally constructed and financially contingent concept; one that looks very different for all of us, especially folks with disability, chronic illness and caring responsibilities. And that's part of why planning matters. With medical technology rapidly changing, who knows exactly how long each of us will live? However, in Australia today, the average life expectancy is 85.1 years for women and 81.1 years for men,[1] meaning if you access your retirement savings at 67, you'll, on average, need between 14 and 18 years of living costs to ensure you don't run out of money before you run out of days. For Aboriginal and Torres Strait Islander people, the average life expectancy is 75.6 years for women and 71.9 years for men.[2] We also know life expectancy is lowest among those in the least advantaged socioeconomic areas. This is not okay. Far too many people (especially older women, people with disability, and First Nations peoples) are living their supposedly twilight years in poverty.

According to a 2025 report from Super Members Council (SMC), Australian women currently entering retirement (that is, those aged between 60 and 64) are doing so with approximately 25 per cent less superannuation savings than men.[3] Many factors influence this, from the gender pay gap to unpaid care burdens and the opportunity-cost ripple effect that follows. The bottom line is this: many of us will need to put extra care and thought (and money) into our long-term plan, so we aren't left with an income shortfall in retirement.

Working out how much you need to retire

When trying to determine just how much you need to retire, the most annoying thing is that *it depends*. I realise that doesn't feel helpful, but everyone's situation and retirement goals are different. How much you want to spend every year (and how long you'll live for, which is clearly an unknown) will determine how much you'll need. Another — and important — factor is whether you'll own the home you live in. Not owning a home to live in, debt-free, leaves you more vulnerable and less financially secure once you retire. Perhaps unsurprisingly, the superannuation system itself was designed by *men*, for *men* (hard to believe, I know) and predicated on the idea of full-time paid work and home ownership. Super inclusive, if you catch my drift. So, if you think you won't live in a home you own when you retire, you'll likely need to have more investments to cover ongoing rent costs and increases.

Most people use the first 'phase' of retirement for adventures. Your days in the formal (paid) workforce are behind you and you're now (hopefully) entering your footloose and fancy-free era. The catch is: fancy ain't free. But that's okay, you've literally been saving your whole life for this! Of course, the tricky part is — while some living expenses go down thanks to fewer nights on the town — funds are often needed to cover medical care costs and home modifications (or moving into an aged care facility, which can be eye-wateringly expensive).

So the honest answer to 'how much?' is normally — the more retirement savings you have, the better. But I can sense that probably isn't what you want to hear, even though it's the truth. So let's look at the Association of Superannuation Funds of Australia (AFSA) Retirement Standard. These annual expenditure benchmark guides provide a breakdown of estimated expenses for both 'comfortable' and 'modest' lifestyles, for couples and singles. The following table shows the ASFA Retirement Standards for 2025.

ASFA Retirement Standards 2025: Total annual expenditure required for retirees aged 65 to 84

	Modest lifestyle (renters)	Modest lifestyle (homeowner, no debt)	Comfortable lifestyle (homeowner, no debt)
Single	$49044 a year	$34522 a year	$53289 a year
Couple	$66296 a year	$49992 a year	$75319 a year

These numbers include some *big* assumptions about what you're prepared to do, or do without, during retirement (including your holidays, leisure activities, health cover and ability to replace worn out clothes).[4] So feel free to amend the amount based on your own expenses if you think they will be similar to what you'd want in retirement.

It's likely your superannuation fund (or retirement fund provider if you're based outside Australia) also has calculators within their portal that can show you, based on your current income, retirement balance and contribution amounts, how much you're likely to have by retirement age and how much income you could draw down (take out to live off) annually without running out. (Often, these calculators can also show you when you're likely to run out and, in Australia, have to rely on the age pension.) This stuff can be scary as hell, but I promise you're not alone. And hopefully by the time many of us get there, we'll have created a much fairer super system, or created some version of my dream cantankerous cat lady coven (broomsticks optional). I would always recommend using these tools to show you, even well ahead of time, what you're on track to have.

Caring about older badass (and maybe bad hip) you

Most of us want to set ourselves up for success in the long run (even if we can't quite imagine a version of ourselves with dentures, a dodgy knee or a weekly blue-rinsed perm). However, we're often just *so* busy trying to get by in the here and now that we figure 'future us' can wait a bit. Suddenly, we look up and retirement is in sight and, frogs on a log, now we have to race to make sure we are sorted.

The easiest way to connect with future you is, you guessed it, by imagining a persona or character for retired you. Sometimes we are better at caring for others than ourselves, so this exercise is all about using that (terrible) trait to your advantage. You want to love, care for and protect that cute little (or bold and badass) old person. Make sure they live as close to their best retired life as possible with lots of adventures, access to top healthcare or new knits whenever they need them. Imagine that older, retired version of you, and start looking after them now by taking super out of the too-hard basket.

I've named my future retired self 'Isa the Indomitable', after the Marchioness of Mantua, Isabella d'Este. While being far from perfect, the Marchioness was nonetheless opinionated, smart and savvy. She was a woman who bargained hard to build her art collection (during the Italian Renaissance, no less), loved dogs, books and writing, and allegedly designed headdresses to distract everyone from her double chin — sounds like a fab retirement to me!

As a fiercely independent and security-driven person (hello, core values), I want my retired life to be one where I live out my days in a wonky (debt-free) home, filled to the brim with curios from a lifetime of adventures and scavenging. I want to have enough invested to do fun stuff—like sustaining my book, pooch and travel pleasures. But I also want enough for the serious stuff—like not being financially dependent on others, or living in a cold house because I can't afford heating, or being forced to sell up if I have a health issue that I can't afford treatment for. Since I've been making extra contributions to my superannuation since my early 20s, my balance is on track to support my retirement goals.

Activity: Answer the 'how much?' retirement question for yourself

Here's how to start to have more of an idea about just how much you might need in retirement, in two simple steps.

Step 1: Connect with retired you

Give retired you a name and persona that encompasses your goals and values. Start to connect with them by asking yourself the following:

▶ How much are they likely to need to cover annual expenses? Will it be similar to what you spend now? More? Less?
▶ What financial risks might they face, such as housing insecurity, expensive health issues and/or running out of retirement savings?
▶ What do they need to live their best life—that is, without a mortgage, with access to quality healthcare and with enough money to fly business class if they want to?
▶ What's one thing you could do to help them right now?

Studies have even shown that digitally aging a photo of yourself makes you more motivated to save for your retirement[5] (and probably start using night cream, I assume). So if you're really struggling to think about yourself as an old person, try it!

(continued)

Step 2: See if you're on track

Next, check if you're on track to meet your retirement needs by answering the following:

- Where are your retirement savings held (likely within superannuation if you are in Australia, or perhaps KiwiSaver in New Zealand)? Do you know which specific fund you are invested in? Do you have multiple accounts? Is that strategic and intentional, or just because you haven't merged or consolidated them?
- What is your balance? Imagine this as wads of cash on your dining room table. If I just came in and took (some or all of) it, wouldn't you want to know where the hell it was going? Yes. You. Would.
- What are you invested in? Don't trust the name of the fund's investment option (trust me!). What amount, for example, is allocated to growth versus conservative assets within the investment product you are in? For example, many 'balanced' funds are not balanced at all, so this is worth checking.
- Are you taking too much risk, or not enough, for your goal time frame? (I cover this in more detail when I outline the GARDEN investment framework, later in this chapter.)
- What fees are you being charged?
- What's the historical performance of that fund?
- Who is your beneficiary? Are they up to date and valid? Is it a binding nomination, and will it lapse? (Has it already lapsed?!)
- Are your contact details correct?

> ▶ Do you have insurance within your account? What kinds and how much?
>
> ▶ Did you have time out of the workforce? If so, did your partner (if you had one) split their retirement savings with you for that period?
>
> ▶ How much are you currently on track to retire with? Go into your fund's member login portal and run your numbers.

Boosting your retirement fund

No-one I've ever met has told me they are sad they have too much invested for their future — *ever*. What I have heard — over, and over, and over again — is people wishing they had sorted it out and started doing something, *anything*, sooner.

Employers have a legal obligation to make contributions into your retirement fund on your behalf. This is known as the Superannuation Guarantee (SG), and it's calculated as a percentage of your ordinary earnings (currently the minimum amount is 12 per cent). (If you're self-employed you need to do this yourself.)

Lay of the land: tax and super

In Australia, the superannuation system is the most tax-effective vehicle for growing your retirement savings. Generally, superannuation earnings are taxed at 15 per cent — rather than your marginal tax rate, which is usually higher — and benefits paid are generally tax-free in the retirement phase.

Concessional contributions made to your super fund are usually taxed at 15 per cent. These include payments made to your superannuation by your employer. At the time of writing, the cap for concessional contributions per financial year is \$30 000. If you know your employer isn't reaching this annual cap, you can also choose to add more to your super as an additional pre-tax contribution.

You can ask your HR team to set up a 'salary sacrifice' — meaning you're sacrificing, or foregoing, some of your salary so it can be paid directly into super, before it's taxed. Or you can add money from your bank account (which has already been taxed) into your super account and claim a tax deduction.

If you're going to use money already in your bank account, you can do so in two different ways.

Concessional contributions (from pre-tax income)

Making a concessional contribution means you get to claim a payment to your super, made from money already in your bank account, as a tax-deductible contribution. To get the deduction, you'll *need* to complete an S290 form via your super fund. If you don't complete this form and send it to your super fund *before* you complete your tax return, you won't be able to claim the payment as a tax-deductible contribution!

You still must ensure any additional money you add keeps you under the $30 000 annual cap. However, an important factor to note here is if you didn't hit your annual contribution cap over the last five financial years and your balance is under $500 000, you can carry forward unused concessional contributions — or basically 'backfill' into one or all of those prior five financial years.

You can check how much you've contributed for prior years on the ATO portal (available via your myGov account, once you've linked your services). If needed, your accountant can also check this for you. Note that the annual cap changes, so you need to check what the cap was for any prior years you want to carry forward.

Non-concessional contributions (from after-tax income)

You can't claim a tax deduction when you make non-concessional contributions — but you're still putting your money into a very tax-effective environment. The cap for 2025–2026 for non-concessional contributions is $120 000 or up to $360 000 under the 'bring-forward' rule, which lets you bring forward your non-concessional cap for two years if your balance is under a certain amount. (This doesn't include any 'downsizer contribution' allowances, which may apply if you're close to retirement age and want to contribute proceeds of the sale of your home into your super.) If you have a large amount of money you want to put into super, I always recommend getting professional financial advice to help you assess all your options and balance considerations.

At the other end of the spectrum, you might only have an additional $10 a week you can spare — and that's okay too. It's still money that will compound over time. As your income grows, ask yourself, 'How much would I not miss this week?' and use that as your rough yardstick on how much to put in (again, assuming you're under the contribution cap).

Activity: Growing your super

Let me show you how 'small', seemingly insignificant changes can make a huge impact over time. Let's say Daisy wants to boost her super. Here's her current situation:

▸ **Age:** 30.
▸ **Income:** $100 000 (before tax).
▸ **Current super balance:** $65 000.
▸ **Employer contribution:** 12 per cent of income ($12 000 pa).
▸ **Fund:** Balanced investments (average net performance of 7 per cent pa).
▸ **Fees:** 1 per cent pa (of total balance).
▸ **Additional contributions:** $0.
▸ **Expected retirement age:** 67.
▸ **Expected retirement savings:** $733 152.[6]

Now, let's say Daisy has done some research online and compared funds and fees. She's found a better investment option for her superannuation and has been able to:

▶ decrease her fees from 1 per cent to 0.5 per cent
▶ change her fund from balanced investments to a high-growth option with an average annual return of 9 per cent (so 2 per cent higher than the original fund)
▶ salary sacrifice an additional $100 per week.

When we run the numbers again, Daisy's outcome looks quite different:

▶ **New expected retirement savings:** $1 779 412.

That's more than a *million dollar* increase in retirement savings! Yes—by acting early and making a few strategic changes, she's more than *doubled* how much she'll have in retirement.

While $100 of pre-tax money missing from your pay is a lot for some, I have also worked with plenty of people who tell me they spent a lot of money without even knowing where it's going. Ask yourself: would you actually miss this amount each week?

Working out just how much you need in your freedom fund

While investing within retirement structures such as superannuation should *absolutely* be an important part of your overall financial freedom game plan, it's important to keep in mind you usually can't access these funds until you reach retirement age. (For superannuation funds in Australia, this is known as your 'preservation age', and is 60 years old if you are born after 1 July 1964.) But if you've got goals you want to achieve before then, you'll also need to build what I call your personal 'freedom fund'. But how much do you need for this fund?! If I had a dollar for every time I've been asked for the specific dollar amount to target, I'd already be retired.

If your goal is to retire early, but have no idea how much money you should be aiming to have, the strategy I'm about to outline does give you a clear target. The most commonly used methodology for working out how much you'll need is the 'rule of 25' — that is, to retire, you need 25 times your annual spending amount. That means you can withdraw 4 per cent of the total balance every year and (hopefully!) never run out of money. It's a simple idea and, of course, doesn't work for everyone, but it's a good place to start. Let's work through an example to see how it might work in practice.

Activity: Using the 'rule of 25' to determine your freedom fund amount

Rose is 25 and wants to be able to retire as early as possible, ideally by age 55. Her current annual expenses are $60 000 per year and she doesn't currently have any money invested (but does have her emergency savings and cash buffer sorted).

Using the 'rule of 25', based on her current expenses, Rose would need to have $1 500 000 ($60 000 × 25 = $1 500 000) in her investment portfolio. By withdrawing 4 per cent annually when she retires, she would have enough to cover for her annual expenses ($1 500 000 × 4 per cent = $60 000).

The following table outlines what Rose could do to have a freedom fund of $1 500 000 by age 55, based on the age she is when she starts investing.

(continued)

Age when she begins investing	Monthly amount to be added to an investment portfolio (assumed return of 8 per cent with all returns reinvested)
25	$1007
35	$2550
45	$8200

You can quickly see how time is one of your greatest investing assets. That's not to say that if you're closer to retirement age, all hope is lost. It's absolutely not; it's just a little trickier to get the compounding effect working for you. The earlier Rose begins, the more her money will compound and grow. The longer she leaves it, the more she will have to contribute to achieve her goal.

A few other important considerations

The quick calculations just provided don't take into account any tax (which can be a big consideration if you're investing in your name). They also don't consider whether Rose is renting or paying off a mortgage. If she's renting, does she want to do so indefinitely? Will her expenses go up drastically given historical rental increases? If she has a mortgage, she will need to consider how much she allocates to investing versus clearing her mortgage—and whether her annual expenses might reduce once she is mortgage free.

Another big thing to consider here is that, if Rose is working up to age 55, payments are also still likely being contributed to her retirement fund while she is still working. So does she really need that big a pot of money, if by a certain age she can start accessing that money? She may want to think about 'ideal retirement age' versus when she can access her retirement account, and how many years will be between them.

Based on the current rules at the time of writing in Australia, if Rose retired early at 55—that is, she ceased employment completely—she could access her superannuation savings at age 60. So she would have five years of annual expenses to cover before being able to access her super. If she decided to use all her personal freedom fund balance over the five years between 55 and 60 and then access her retirement savings, she might only need $300000 in her portfolio. This is still a lot of money, but only one-fifth of the number needed to stick within the 'rule of 25'. Of course, this decision should also take into consideration Rose's estimated super balance when she reaches age 60.

All this isn't meant to confuse you (and sorry if it has!). It's to show you that you have options. If one idea seems completely out of reach, what alternatives could you consider?

If you want to have a play around with what this could look like for you, ASIC's Moneysmart website has a range of great online money tools to help you figure out your figures—including a compound interest calculator.[7] You can use this calculator to determine the figure you could end up with based on how much you can invest, your assumed return and how long you invest for.

The GARDEN Investment Framework

Wanting freedom and taking the steps to build freedom are different things entirely. Most want, few do. But as Rudyard Kipling notes in his poem 'The glory of the garden', 'Gardens are not made by singing "Oh, how beautiful!" and sitting in the shade'. Building your freedom fund means you've got to roll up your sleeves and get your hands dirty. No more waiting in the shadows for it to all work out. Now is the time to get started, even if you feel scared—because freedom is what you'll grow if you do.

How to actually build your personal freedom fund is the main focus for this section, but keep in mind the six-step investment framework I cover here can also be applied to decisions you make within your retirement savings.

These are the six steps I teach to build your investment strategy:

- ✿ **G:** Goal.
- ✿ **A:** Assessment.
- ✿ **R:** Risk.
- ✿ **D:** Diversification.
- ✿ **E:** Ethics.
- ✿ **N:** Now, nearly or never.

G is for goals first

Start investing without clear goals and you'll have no idea if you've selected the right investments. Don't put the cart before the horse (a common investing mistake) and plot your *goals first*. Skip back to chapter 5 if you still need to polish yours but know this: your goals are the foundation for building your investment plan. Without them, you're walking on ground that can feel uneasy underfoot.

Knowing your goal, your time horizon and your financial target will help you decide how much money to contribute every pay or every month and how much risk you're comfortable taking (which will, in turn, help you pick the right investment products).

A is for assess your strategy

For your money to grow, you have to feed it. You need money allocated in your cash flow plan to your goals; otherwise, they will starve. You have two main options:

- *Freedom-first:* Figure out how much money you'll need to allocate every payday to achieve your goals by your target time frame. (You can use the Moneysmart goals calculator to determine the amount you need.[8]) This will ensure that money is allocated first to your goals, before it gets eaten up by other costs (goals aren't dessert, remember?). You might need to find ways to cut back on other costs to make it work, but this option does put you in the best position to make your goals happen.

- *Freedom-last:* From your income, deduct all expenses and then invest what's left. This might mean tweaking your goal if you end up not having enough cash left after expenses to achieve it. You can start with what you have spare and increase it over time without changing any of your existing costs. This one's the easier option because it doesn't require much sacrifice — except, of course, the thing you might want the most.

Whichever you decide, make sure payments to your investment account are set up as automatic, so you get out of your own way and don't have to remember to do it. You want this thing to grow without you needing to bust out the rake and trowel every month!

R is for risk-y business

You've figured out your goals and assessed how much you can invest each pay. Now it's time to consider what percentage of your funds should be allocated to investments that are lower risk versus investments that are higher risk for each of your goals. What will give them the best conditions to thrive?

Different asset classes (which is a fancy way of saying different categories of investments, such as property, shares or cash) tend to have different levels of risk. They can generally be split into one of two camps: defensive or growth assets.

Defensive or conservative assets

Like the names 'defensive' or 'conservative' suggest, these aren't assets that will grow like wildfire. They are designed to give you stability and income. Generally, the risk of losing money with these investments is lower. 'Okay', you might be asking, 'so why don't I just pick those?!' They also tend to have lower (but more predictable) returns. This means money invested in these types of assets isn't likely to grow as much as others, but it's not likely to be as volatile either.

Examples of defensive or conservative assets include cash, term deposits, bonds and fixed-income products. (Refer to the previous chapter for more on these assets, including their pros and cons.)

Growth assets

The job of a growth asset is to, well, grow. 'Oh', you might now be saying, 'that sounds fab. Why don't I just choose those ones then?' While they have potential for higher returns, you might be in for a bumpier ride — because they tend to move up and down more in value. So you've got to make sure you're playing the long game.

Examples of growth assets include shares (both domestic and international), property (residential and commercial) and ETFs. (Again, refer to the previous chapter for a rundown on these assets.)

Most managed funds are also heavily weighted to growth assets (but you need to 'get under the hood' and see what any particular product is actually invested in because it can be lots of different things).

The following table provides an example of one investment fund manager's portfolios. You can see the percentage split between defensive and growth assets for each of the portfolios, and the average return, minus management fees, of each investment product. Of course, previous performance isn't guaranteed in the future.

Example asset splits and average returns for different investment fund options

Portfolio	Percentage split	Average historical annual return after fees (based on the last 10 years)
Conservative	Defensive = 70%; growth = 30%	4.45%[9]
Balanced	Defensive = 50%; growth = 50%	6.20%[10]
Growth	Defensive = 30%; growth = 70%	8.02%[11]
High growth	Defensive = 10%; growth = 90%	9.80%[12]

Deciding on your risk level

Ultimately, you need to consider what level of risk you are comfortable with in order to get the return you're looking for. However, what I often see is new investors being too conservative for long-term goals. Often, this is due to fear. Their brain knows they have decades until they need the money, but they are scared by the idea of investing a higher percentage in growth assets.

The very general risk-rule is this: the shorter the time horizon on your goal (one to two years), the more conservative or defensive you want to be with your investment selection. The longer you have to achieve your goals (more than seven years), the more heavily (generally) you should be invested in growth-style assets — because you have time to ride out investment market ups and downs. Medium-term goals (between three and seven years) are often the trickiest to decide what to do with. While it's still a little way off, investment markets can take a while to recover if they fall (sometimes several years — as we saw after the 2008 global financial crisis). You want to find a balance between not taking enough risk and taking too much (Goldilocks strikes again!). This may mean you look to have investments that are a balanced mix of growth and defensive assets.

D is for diversification

The most abundant, resilient and flourishing ecosystems in the world are so because they are diverse. Take the Amazon (the rainforest, not the company, and before humans started clearing it for profit). Each of its inhabitants contributes to the system's growth and survival, and not everything grows at the same time or pace. You want that with your investment portfolio.

Diversification is about building your own investment ecosystem. It's about investing in many different things so you spread your opportunities (and your risk). That way, if one company, sector or country doesn't perform well, the performance of others can help balance it out.

When looking to diversify, you have two primary approaches, active or passive (index-based) investing:

- *Active portfolios:* This is where either you or a fund manager actively handpicks what to buy, hold and sell within a portfolio. Choosing individual investments requires a lot of time and effort, and more frequent changes may be made to your portfolio. So adopting and managing this investment style typically costs a premium.
- *Passive or index-based portfolios:* These funds are more passive in the sense that your money is invested in all the companies within a particular category. Usually, this is based on an index — for example, the S&P/ASX 200, which brings together the top 200 companies on the Australian share market. Similarly, you may have heard of the S&P 500, which is an index composed of the 500 biggest companies in the United States. Buying into a fund that tracks an index means you'll invest in all of these companies. No-one is actively picking which specific ones are held; instead, the percentage held in each company is simply based on its weighting in the index.

Because index funds are efficient in how the companies are selected, they normally have low fees and high levels of diversification. Warren Buffett (one of the most respected investors in the world), once said, 'By periodically investing in an index fund, for example, the know-nothing investor can actually out-perform most investment professionals'.[13]

The easiest way to get loads of diversification in your investment portfolio, without having to become a full-time stock broker, is to look for what are known as 'pre-mixed investment products' or 'diversified portfolio' options. These allow you to invest in different companies, countries, sectors and asset classes efficiently. (They're the grazing platter of the investment world, if you will). ETFs and managed funds all have various pre-mixed options for you to select from.

E is for applying an ethical lens

Our money is one of the most powerful tools we have to shape the world, and it's often said that every dollar we invest is a vote for the kind of future we're funding. Before you pick exactly what you want to invest in, consider which companies, industries or countries you do — or don't — want your money invested in.

Ethical investing is becoming more mainstream, meaning more fund managers are now offering more ethical pre-mixed options. This is great news, but it comes with a catch. No *one* definition exists for what is 'ethical'. What feels ethical to you (say, avoiding fossil fuels or supporting companies with strong human rights records) might look totally different to someone else's version (such as prioritising animal welfare or only investing in companies with a woman on the board). That's why it's important to dig deeper than the label and define what kind of investor you want to be. Next, check what's *actually* in the fund, how decisions are made, and whether this truly aligns with *your* values.

It's your money, and you get to decide what kind of companies you want to contribute to. Here are some different ethical investment options you could consider:

- *DIY active portfolios:* You can pick exactly which companies meet your ethical requirements and invest in them directly. This can be extremely labour intensive, because you're going to have to sit down and research a whole bunch of companies without necessarily knowing what to look for, and you might end up building a portfolio that isn't well diversified, or that under-performs in a purely financial sense, or costs you a lot in trade fees. But this approach can also be deeply personal, purposeful and flexible, because you can divest (sell your asset) immediately — without waiting for a fund manager to catch up.

- *Ethical active funds:* In this option, investments are selected because the fund managers believe they are going to perform well *and* they meet their ethical philosophy framework. These generally cost more, because a team of people are deciding what gets added and removed from the fund and applying what's called an 'ethical screen', or a set of criteria to decide which companies or industries are included or excluded from an investment portfolio.

- *Activism-based investing:* We are starting to see a 'Trojan horse' style of investing emerge, whereby investors pool their money to buy shares in companies they want to change. As shareholders, they can then vote as a bloc at AGMs and push the board for specific outcomes (be it on environment, social or governance issues, otherwise known as 'ESG'). It's literally buying a seat at the table, albeit you have no guarantee you'll be successful — and you're still invested in companies you might not ethically align with.

- *Ethical index funds:* While this seems counterintuitive (given an index-fund philosophy generally means investing in an entire marketplace), but some fund managers do offer specific ethical index-based investment products (for example, an ethical index ETF). These take all the companies from an index and then put them through the manager's ethical filter or screen. Any that meet their criteria will go in the portfolio, while those that don't will get left out.

Ethical investing is the act of choosing to put your money where your values are, even in a world that doesn't always make that easy. Choose wisely. Ask questions. And remember: doing good and making money don't have to be mutually exclusive.

N is for now, nearly or never

Through this book I talk a lot about time horizons and choosing different approaches to grow your money depending on how long you have. When it comes to investing, you generally have three basic time frames for when to begin your journey. You pick which works for you:

- *Now:* You've sorted your savings, cleared all bad debt and worked out a clear goal you're ready to start working on. You've figured out how much you can allocate from your income to your retirement and/or your freedom fund. The only thing that's missing is the brave first step. If this is you, the time is now!
- *Nearly:* You really want to get started, but know you can't just yet. That's okay. If you have to get on top of some other financial items first, set a date when you know they will be done by. (You should have a clear date for them if they are a financial goal.) Add the date to your diary. Because that's the time to celebrate

your achievement and then move to your next goal: investing. That's exciting; you're nearly ready to start!

- *Never:* Read this book, hide it on the shelf and decide you never want to invest or grow your wealth. It's too hard and you don't even care about freedom, or living your best life anyway. (Said no-one, ever.) Never say never, remember? Go back and pick from one of the two preceding options (you will thank me later).

By using the six steps just outlined, you have a framework to follow to get started with investing. Of course, you may also have a bunch more stuff to learn about. Jump back to the previous chapter to make sure you understand the basics of what shares or ETFs are, what to look for when comparing investment options and how to not fuck it up down the track. If you think you're okay with those elements, take a breath, grab another cuppa and let's keep going…

Money in the wild: Sophie (she/her)

- **Age:** 35.
- **Situationship:** In a relationship; don't live together.
- **Income:** $120000.
- **Current savings:** $15000.
- **Current relationship with money:** Excited, abundant, hopeful.
- **Money monster's name:** 'Scarcity Sue'.

What does life look like right now?

I am almost two years into that mortgage-holder life. I bought my first home, a one-bedroom apartment, on my own and I am keen to pay this down as aggressively as possible, while still living an enjoyable lifestyle. Now that I have ticked off a list of financial goals, which all involved me hustling pretty hard, I am working on trying to learn how to have the balance between investing for the future and wealth building, and using my money for fun things like travel, fancy food and bevs, renos to the apartment, and upgrading some of the things I refused to buy for the last three years, like clothes and linen. I also have a Tabby cat named Delilah, who gets fed higher quality food than I do (haha).

What was your biggest 'ouch' money moment?
When I was 19, I received a $75000 inheritance from a relative, which I have nothing to show for anymore. I so badly wish that someone had told me at the time that I could use that money as a house deposit or invest it. Instead, all I can recall using it for was a new car, laptop and some travel. I am grateful for those things but, in hindsight, and with all of the knowledge I now have, it's a bit of a bummer.

What has shaped your relationship with money the most?
Family and experiences. Growing up, my dad had a real scarcity mindset, always worried that there was never going to be enough. Having said that, we lived a very comfortable life and so on reflection there was no reason to have that. I think I have adopted the scarcity mindset. It is becoming particularly apparent recently, now that I am in a relatively comfortable situation, but there is still a fear that one day I won't have enough.

I also went through a breakup with a partner four years ago along with a job loss at the exact same time. That situation left me with basically no money to my name outside of super. This was a scary and stressful time, and I moved back in with my parents to recover. This experience was the catalyst for me to really assess how I was living my life, and I realised that I needed to financially set myself up *on my own*.

What does 'financial wellbeing' mean to you?
Financial wellbeing for me means safety and abundance. Safety is knowing that I will never need to move back in with my family. Abundance is having enough money to comfortably pay all of my bills, keep building wealth, and at the same time be able to be a little bit frivolous every so often.

You win the lotto. What do you do?
All of the travel (business class, of course) and I'd like to travel around the world and visit all of the Michelin star restaurants. I'd also love to give extremely generously, in a way that could really change someone's life. Deposit on my next home.

What's one outrageous thing you've spent money on and did you regret it?
I bought a Thermomix for $2400, and I don't regret it for a second.

'Is it me? Am I the problem?!'

One of the biggest risks to any investment portfolio is the person making the decisions — and, yes, that would be you. Remember how our brains don't like things that make us feel scared and unsafe? In these situations, we choose between fight, flight, freeze and/or fawn — which might be smart for survival, but it's shite for investing. Because when we see or hear headlines like, 'Billions of dollars wiped off share markets' or, 'Worst day on the share market in over five years' (usually with some apocalyptic image attached), it can be easy to panic.

Here's a basic 'how-to' guide for behaving like an irrational investor:

1. Discover investment markets have gone down.
2. Immediately panic (and perhaps call others to discuss catastrophic event). Given fear is contagious, potentially infect others with panic.
3. Log in to your account to confirm it's true, and then gasp.
4. Stare at reduced portfolio value as your brain confirms it had good reason to panic.
5. Irrationally decide the smartest thing to do is sell all your investments to avoid the potential of more losses.
6. Quickly mutter, 'Fuck, fuck, fuck, fuck, fuck' as you figure out how to sell down holdings.
7. Place trade to sell — either at a loss, or for considerably lower than the price was even just a few days ago. This doesn't matter, because you must exit this hellscape immediately.
8. Park money back in cash (phew), and shake fist skyward at investing gods for screwing it up.
9. Tell yourself you never will invest again. (Clearly, it's tooooo risky!)
10. Keep money in cash and (if it doesn't accidentally get spent) wait for markets to rise again and then say, 'Okay, maybe I will give it one more go'.
11. Buy back in at a new, higher price.
12. Wait for the next market dip, repeat.

This, my friends, is an example of loss aversion. We are wired to feel the pain of losing something (à la money) much more intensely than we feel the joy of gaining something. People tend to panic sell when markets go down because their survival factory setting has overridden their ability to think logically in the heat of the moment.

Avoiding panic selling—and thinking long term

Firstly, you haven't 'lost' anything if you don't sell your investment when the market dips—it's just that the *value* of that investment has decreased. It's a *paper* loss. (I mean, it's digital, but you get the idea.) The only time it becomes a *real* loss is when you *actually* sell the asset. Until then, you still hold the same number of assets. Selling when prices are low and buying again when they are high is, when you think about it, a bizarre yet all too common strategy.

Diversifying your investments will also help to protect you. If you invest heavily in a single company that goes belly up, then, yes, you've lost that investment. But if that was one of many diversified investments, you can be protected by the others that are still holding strong.

If you are investing for the long term, you can expect markets to go down at some point. You can reassure yourself this is all part of the cycle and that you have invested correctly for your goal, which is still years away, so it has time to come back and continue to grow. Many of the best days in the share market happen soon after some of the worst. By selling out, you are not only getting out when prices are lower, but you're also potentially missing any gains that may soon follow.

As an example of this, let's say you invested $100 000 from 2014 in the S&P/ASX 300 for ten years. Here's how much you would have in total if you held your investment portfolio for the full ten years, versus what you'd have if you'd missed out on some of the best days on the share market:

- *Invested all days:* $213 072
- *Missed 10 best days:* $136 594
- *Missed 20 best days:* $104 154
- *Missed 30 best days:* $83 233
- *Missed 40 best days:* $68 289.[14]

Don't wait for the bear

It pays to make plans to mitigate risk *before* an adverse event happens. No-one's going hiking in bear country without packing bear spray. So it makes sense to plan ahead with your investments too, right? A 'bear market' is when prices of shares or units in other investments drop by about 20 per cent. (On the other side of the coin, a 'bull market' is when prices rise by about 20 per cent. The easiest way to remember the difference is to think of a bear moving its paw downwards (market downturn) and a bull raising its head and horns up towards the sky (market rise). You are welcome.) So if you know the 'bear' is likely to make a visit at some point and that you are likely to freak out when it does (I get it; they're scary), let's get on the front foot and build your own survival plan, well before any signs of its arrival.

By writing out your answers to the questions in the following activity, you can make sure you're invested in a way that is going to work for you. You can also review these questions (or your answers) if you need to give yourself a good talking to when the bear gives you a scare.

Activity: Working out your survival plan

Answer the following questions to work out, and perhaps revise, your bear-market survival plan:

▶ Do you currently have enough emergency savings that you feel comfortable if share markets went down? If not, how much extra would you need to save?
▶ If your investment portfolio dropped by 20 per cent, would you still be able to sleep at night?

> ▸ Would you be more comfortable taking on less risk (that is, having more conservative investments in your portfolio) and be okay with less opportunity for growth?
>
> ▸ Imagine the share market has gone down, media speculation is swirling about a looming recession (with more ominous stormy imagery!) and you feel yourself starting to wobble. What does that version of you need to remember in that moment so you don't panic sell your investments?
>
> No answers are right or wrong here. Your survival plan needs to be based on what's going to make sure you can survive your bear encounter—without leaving the forest completely.

What to do when share markets go down

If you've invested in index funds with solid historical returns, when share markets go down, in most cases you should do nothing! Remind yourself that you're investing for the long term and that the ups and downs are normal.

Here are some further tips to help you avoid trading out of panic, stress or even boredom:

- Go back and review your goals if you need to, so you remember why you invested in the first place.
- If you need to, take your investing app off your phone (and so make it harder for you to log in and spiral!).
- Consider cutting back on spending and stashing some extra cash into your emergency savings account. This will help you feel like you have more financial wiggle room should anything happen to your income (so you don't need to sell your assets at a time they've gone down in value to pay your bills).

- Buy instead of sell! If you have additional spare funds that you don't need access to for anything (meaning you have emergency savings and your cash buffer is sorted), you may choose to buy more of your chosen investment product when prices are low. Think of it like your favourite (investment) shop is having a sale.

Importantly, if you see others panicking, remind them (and yourself) that history is full of examples of downturns and 'crashes'. While markets took a while to bounce back from some of these downturns, history shows they always did. Over the last 150 years, for example, the US market has not only always recovered, but kept soaring to new highs.[15]

Growing the garden

Investing is your ticket to freedom. Once you have your goals and emergency savings sorted, and no longer need to pay down bad debt or focus on other priority goals, you can use the GARDEN framework to build out your plan. Life is always going to have competing priorities and starting is often the hardest step.

By taking the right level of risk for your investments, you'll be calmer during any investment storms and not jump ship. You'll also get the right level of growth to achieve your goals.

Where to grow from here

Now it's time to really get your hands dirty. Ask yourself:

- What are your next steps to get invested? You might have a big list of next steps — and that's great!
- Have you got a clear number you're going to invest every pay towards your 'freedom fund'?

- Do you still need to decide which investment style and risk profile fits you and your goals best?
- When are you going to complete these steps?
- Who is going to keep you accountable to make sure you *actually* do them?
- What additional research do you need to complete so you can pick the right investment product for you?
- When you invest for the first time, how are you going to celebrate it?! Write a little note to yourself saying why you're doing it, and perhaps tell your friends you've started. (Doing so might motivate them to as well.)

Garden tasks for existing investors

You always have something to do in a garden, even if what you have planted is growing well. Here are some things to think about if you're already an investor:

- Review your current investments to make sure they are still fit for purpose for your goal. Check the asset allocation, fees and long-term net performance.
- Is the current asset allocation of growth versus conservative assets correct, or do you need to rebalance your portfolio? And be sure to consider the tax implications of doing so.
- If you are on a dividend reinvestment plan, could this mean you end up with too much invested in one company? If so, you may choose to have those dividends paid to you instead, so you can invest them in more diversified investment products.

By working through the concepts in this chapter, you can start planting the seeds for long-term freedom and know how to keep it growing for years to come. Just as night follows day, however, winter is always coming — and any good gardener knows to prepare for it. So that's what we delve into in the next chapter.

10

WINTER

Your plan for financial shit storms: insurance, savings and frosty relationships

I'm not afraid of storms, for I'm learning how to
sail my ship.

—Louisa May Alcott (Little Women)

Content warning

In this chapter, I discuss illness, death and estate planning,
and financial abuse. Some of this chapter might make you
uncomfortable, and parts may confront you or even bring back
painful memories. I hope you stick with me, even through the
hard bits, but absolutely do what you need to do to take care
of yourself, and feel free to come back when you're ready.

Up until this point, we've been focused on growing your money, but
unfortunately growth is only one side of the coin. Protecting it (and
you!) is the other.

Certain seasons of life, like winter, can be brutal. Times that feel so
bleak, bitter, dark and stormy — you wonder if the sun will ever come

out again. All of us will endure the brutish force of winter at some point in life. Yet, unlike the somewhat predictable flow of nature's changing seasons (thanks climate change), unfortunately we never know exactly when *our* winter will make an unwelcome arrival, or how long it will last for. Accidents, illnesses, job losses, conflicts, abuse, divorce and death all carry financial consequences, many of which can be very serious.

Even if we might wish to, it's not possible to live in a sunny, temperature-controlled microclimate indefinitely. We also can't naïvely tell ourselves 'winter' happens to other people; it won't happen to me. The reality is that everyone you've ever met has endured bad weather (and if they haven't yet, winter is coming). So how do we prepare if we don't know when it's going to hit? In the wise words of John F Kennedy, 'The best time to repair the roof is when the sun is shining' — and not when it's hailing golf balls outside. He's right; we need to build our own safety shelter (ideally!) before the inevitable storm hits.

I know that we all want our perfect plans to play out, well, perfectly. Yet, I also know (from my own life and from the many people who have arrived at my office door, sodden from life throwing them an unexpected cold change), how much more awful it is when you haven't prepared for winter. Of course, no amount of financial safeguards can bring a loved one back or make serious illnesses go away. But you can do certain things to make sure these terrible times don't come served with a side of financial ruin. You don't need more shit when you're already eating dirt.

So how do you do that? How do you mitigate risk and make sure your money, yourself and what you love is protected? First things first, your financial shelter is built bit by bit. Getting it all sorted might take a bit of time, so the most important advice I have is to keep at it. To help you on your way, I've split this chapter into themes, with areas to review and things to be aware of, consider and action. But let's start with a story...

One of my many 'oh shit' storms

In February 2024, I headed out on what was meant to be a fun-filled Saturday. My friends had bought me an oyster farm experience on the Hawkesbury River (Dyarubbin), about an hour's drive from Sydney (Gadigal). There we were, waist deep in our water-proof overalls, sipping wine and shucking fresh oysters, thinking how great life is. About halfway through the day, I started to feel a bit, well, *off.* As the day progressed, I got worse — much worse. Head out the window like a dog so I didn't spew all over my friend's car, kind of worse. By midnight, I was at the emergency department. Assuming a bad oyster was the culprit, the doctor gave me pain relief and sent me home in the wee hours of the morning. A few days later, still not feeling better, I reluctantly skipped out on some meetings to see my GP and get some stronger pain relief. She took one look at me and told me, in no uncertain terms, to head back to emergency — immediately.

I knew rather quickly something was wrong when I was given what I affectionately called the 'honeymoon suite' (an enclosed private room) and the head of the emergency department was assigned to me. As you've probably guessed, turns out, it wasn't a bad oyster — I had a blockage in an organ that had turned septic. All of a sudden, an emergency surgeon (and a surprisingly large entourage) burst into the room, explaining my infection was life-threatening. But the blockage couldn't be removed until they had the sepsis under control. The ICU had no beds, so I was sent to a ward for around-the-clock care. Bags of antibiotics and fluid coursed through my veins to flush and fight the fucker out of me. The sepsis had caused my heart rate to drop to a dangerously low level, meaning I also needed my blood pressure checked every 15 minutes. Not fun, when all you want to do is sleep.

Looking back, it's funny (funny weird, not funny haha) what I thought about in those initial days — chained to a drip and hoping the volunteer therapy dog would soon do his rounds. My first thoughts were

251

a panic about work. I didn't have time to be sick. We had just opened the doors for our first program intake of the year, plus I'd committed to several speaking events. Cancelling would not only let people down but also lose precious revenue for my fledgling business. I worried about my dog, the washing I'd left in the machine and the upcoming weekend away I had booked. At a time when arguably all of my focus should have gone into getting better, I also worried about money. I had a team, a mortgage and bills that needed paying.

On the night of my 36th birthday, as I watched the lights from the P!NK concert happening just down the road from my hospital bed, my thoughts changed. I started to reflect on how fucking grateful I was that I had built a very solid financial shelter, over many years.

And let me tell you — the level of relief I got from knowing my ass was covered is something I will never be able to fully articulate. For me, the feeling was like a combination of taking off an uncomfortable bra after a long day, releasing your hair from a tight bun, falling into a comfy lounge after your plans got cancelled and finding a giant wad of cash under the cushion — all at the same time. Never have I ever felt more gratitude for past me for putting things in place to make sure I could withstand a financial winter. If I could go back in time to each of the moments I did one of these things, I would squeeze the shit out of myself and ferociously say 'thank you, thank you, thank you'.

Here's what I had in place, and what I was so thankful for:

- *Emergency savings:* Thankfully, I had a decent chunk of emergency savings stashed in my offset account.
- *Income protection insurance:* This would cover any reduction to my pay, if I needed to take time off for surgery and recovery.
- *Will and power of attorney:* Honestly, I got a morbid sense of comfort knowing if shit slid any further south, I had already appointed a power of attorney, medical guardian and executor of my estate (who had a list of my assets and account numbers).

- *Life insurance:* If the worst happened, I reminded myself I had enough life insurance to clear my mortgage and, as per my will, distribute assets to the people I love. I'd included instructions for loved ones on things such as organ donation.

My friends and family were already across my very specific instructions (demands) for the cheapest casket, fanciest champagne, most delicious canapés (no soggy sandwiches to send me off!) and a DJ to play nostalgic bangers everyone must dance to. Yes, these really were the things my brain buzzed with as worry and panic (and sepsis) fought to take a stronghold of my body.

Spoiler alert: I did survive, albeit minus an organ and a rather large amount of my savings. I also gained a pretty serious oyster aversion. I was lucky, on many levels. And not for the first time, either, was I glad I had planned for stormy weather. My life has been far from smooth sailing, and as much as I hope you don't have to navigate any choppy waters, let's get you set up, too — just in case.

Building your financial bedrock

The 'bedrock' layer is the foundation that lies quietly deep underneath the soil. Its job is to hold steady and, literally, be rock-solid. You need a financial version of this foundation too, to weather any shaky life events.

If you've ever built a house, you'll know laying the foundation is a fair bit of work and effort. It's also not cheap. It can feel criminal to have a giant chunk of your money go to metal pilings or an ugly, grey, boring slab that no-one 'oooohs' and 'ahhhhs' over. But, during bouts of bad weather, knowing something sturdy is underfoot is reassuring — and you will be grateful you looked after yourself. You'll also thank your loved ones if they lay the same kinds of foundations — and don't leave you to pick up the pieces in the aftermath of a life-altering storm. The same goes for your finances.

I'd like you to think about each of the risk-mitigation strategies in this chapter as forming a solid bedrock your money can grow on. You may not need all of them right now and, as life changes, they may need to change too. But it's a good idea to have at least some, at all times. So let's start with the most important first step.

Emergency savings — your cash stash

Bees prepare for winter by stockpiling enough honey to survive the months when resources are scarce. They know sunny, flower-filled days won't last forever. Clever little buzzers! We need to do the same. Having access to on-demand 'liquid' assets (cash) is key to helping get you through difficult times. I know I've mentioned it throughout this book, but I'm going to say it again: no matter how old, young, healthy or not you are, you need access to emergency savings. Yes, even if you have a job, lots of annual leave, sick leave, a partner with a job, or a donkey with a large social media following and an affiliate link. I don't care — you need it anyway.

Ideally, you should have enough funds to cover at least three to six months of expenses, sitting in a high-interest or offset account for easy access. This is your ready-whenever-you-need-it honey pot. If you own a business, work seasonally or can't access insurance, you may want to consider having a higher amount on hand. Importantly, this should be in an account in your name — meaning only *you* can access it. Not even a partner (if you have one) should be able to access it.

If you don't currently have emergency savings, your first task is to save $1000. From there, build out a plan to get the amount you need, as soon as possible. Get these funds together before saving for holidays, buying a new car or starting a renovation. These aren't emergencies. Sorry (absolutely not sorry).

Why do you need a cash stash?

You need these funds to be able to pay for any large, unexpected situations, or cover your expenses if something goes wrong (that is, a genuine financial emergency). Be it you lose your job, the cat needs expensive surgery, a family member overseas suddenly becomes gravely ill or your car breaks down, these funds are there to cover unexpected, unplanned life events that require money, fast.

What happens if you don't have emergency savings?

If you don't have easy access to emergency cash and the shit hits the fan, the alternatives are costly. You might use a credit card (which normally comes with double-digit interest rates), you may have to borrow from family and friends (which can be messy and complicated, if it's even possible), or need to sell assets quickly (which may see you sell them at a time where the value is down and might create tax implications).

Plus, selling assets reduces their compounding effect for your future, or may mean you can't get back into a market. For example, if you sell your property, the bank may no longer offer you a mortgage for the same, or any, amount if you no longer have a job. Then, of course, you might face the very real threat of experiencing homelessness, going hungry, or not having the freedom to leave a situation that's no longer safe or tenable.

Don't have emergency savings, and emergency strikes?

Firstly, that fucking sucks. I'm sorry. Before I get practical, a gentle reminder that your worth isn't linked to your bank balance. You're in the eye of the shit-storm but, like the weather, it's not permanent. It won't last forever.

The very first (often hardest and most confronting) thing to do is be proactive. Cancel all non-essential costs, immediately. Get rid of them, now. Call your bank, utility providers and real estate agent (if you rent), explain the situation and see what support they can offer. Banks have financial hardship teams you can speak to that may be able to pause or reduce your repayments. If you have a credit card or personal loan, they may be able to reduce or waive interest for a set period.

If you are entitled to any government support or crisis payments, apply for them — that's what they are there for! You may also be able to access your superannuation; however, very strict rules apply as to when you can do so (and, of course, any amount you take out will impact your long-term retirement balance). The trustee of the super fund will review your hardship application and may give you access to a small portion of your balance to help you stay afloat.

If you're facing a medical event like I was, be sure to check if you have any insurances or covers in place you may be able to claim on. Consider if you can bring in any additional money — from selling anything you no longer use, or by doing any kind of paid work (if you can work). Look to reduce as many expenses as possible and find ways to bring money in — without needing to resort to loan sharks, or trying to sell pictures of your feet online (unless you want to — in which case, you do you!).

What to consider for future planning

Here's a summary of what to keep in mind as you start, build and maintain your emergency savings:

- Have you got enough emergency savings right now to cover three to six months of expenses?
- If not, how much more do you need to make you feel comfortable?
- Is this a financial goal and part of your conscious cash flow plan (refer to chapter 7)? If it isn't, add it in!
- Who else can access it?

- Do you need to define what an 'emergency' is? This may be so you don't spend it on something that isn't a genuine emergency, but also to give yourself permission to use it when one does arrive.
- Do you need to open a separate bank account specifically for this money?

I hope you never need to touch your emergency savings. I hope you look back on your life and think what a waste it was to have that money sitting idly — because no emergency ever landed in your lap. Wouldn't that be grand?

But emergency savings normally only stretch so far. Cash to cover a few months, stashed away for the rainy day generations gone by warned us about, is one thing — but what if you need more? What if you get sick and can't work for *years*, or perhaps never? Or have huge medical expenses? Or, worse, what if you weren't around anymore? Could your loved ones financially survive without you? This is where insurance comes into play, which I cover in the next section. But first, let's keep an eye out for lurking dangers.

Activity: Watching out for scams and red flags

Scams are becoming increasingly sophisticated. Always protect your passwords, change them regularly and add multi-factor authentication requirements. Basically, never trust anything and always go back to the source (for example, don't click on a link from your 'bank' and instead go directly into your banking app). If you get an email that requires action, call the bank and make sure it's legitimate.

And if ever someone is giving you advice that feels not right or too good to be true, listen to yourself! Get a second (and even third) opinion. Never let anyone bully or belittle you into making

(continued)

> any financial decision, or try to force you to act when you're not comfortable doing so. If needed, report them to the Australian Financial Complaints Authority (AFCA). And if someone tells you they can help you make bazillions of dollars with no risk? Head for the hills as fast as you can.

Adding the protective roof with insurance

Maybe you think you've already got your insurance all sorted. Indeed, I have had clients who had the car, the cat and the couch covered, but forgot about themselves. This isn't ideal, to say the least. To show you why, let me run through a scenario. Let's say you forgot everything I have taught you so far and went and bought a brand-new car for $2.4 million. I know — fancy car, right? Before you drive it out of the showroom, would you insure it? What if the car (*only*) cost you $1.5 million? Would you still bother getting it covered in case you were in an accident, or it got stolen? Yes! Of course you would.

In 2013, $2.4 million was the estimated lifetime wage for a 25-year-old Australian man. For a woman, it was almost a million bucks less at $1.5 million (blergh).[1] Today I'm sure lifetime wages are much higher than that (although the gender pay gap still most definitely exists). But my point is this: why are we so good at insuring our stuff, but not ourselves? Are things more important than you? Could you keep the car (or the cat!) if you had no income or had huge medical expenses? Probably not. Whoever coined the term 'she'll be right mate' needs to be made aware that, in some instances, she absolutely bloody won't be.

So, beyond our cherished possessions and pets, what insurances might you need? When are they needed? What level of cover should you get? What should you look for? I'm going to give you a general rundown of the insurance 'must knows', but it's important to do your research because policy terms and conditions change regularly.

Generally, it's best to get an expert to help set these up for you. An insurance specialist or financial adviser will be across the policy options offered by all the companies, which one is most likely to offer you cover, and which options, benefits and structures are going to work best for you. They can also be the liaison between you and the insurance company to help you apply and (hopefully never) claim on the policy.

Fair warning: The next few pages are a bit on the dry side, but they can also be pretty heavy. As mentioned at the start of this chapter, I discuss serious illness and injury, and death (including of a child). Skip these sections if you need to, and come back when you can.

The information provided here is most useful for protecting yourself and/or your family. I don't cover business insurance (which can have different considerations, and various ownership and tax implications). I'm also not an accountant or a lawyer, so make sure you run anything past your own accountant or lawyer as needed.

Okay, let's go through the different types of personal insurances.

Income protection

Also known as 'salary continuance' (especially inside superannuation), you should very, very strongly consider having this type of insurance in place if you have an income and don't have enough assets (yet) to replace your salary — and especially if it's a long time until you retire.

How does it work?

You receive a regular monthly amount for a set period of time, generally a specified percentage of your pre-tax income, if you aren't able to work due to illness or injury (not normally redundancy).

Note: You won't be paid 100 per cent of your income and your monthly benefit amount is generally paid in arrears. For example, if you have a 30-day waiting period as part of your policy, you generally won't get your first payment until day 60 — an important consideration when making sure you have sufficient emergency savings.

Important terms and information

The 'waiting period' is (usually) exactly what it sounds like — how long you need to be off or unable to work before you can make a claim. The 'benefit period' is how long you'll be entitled to get a monthly 'benefit' (amount of money), if you meet all the other criteria.

For example, if you have a '90-day wait' and an 'age 65' benefit period, and you're unable to work due to illness or injury (and meet the definition), after 90 days you could be paid a monthly benefit (in arrears) for every month you can't work until you reach 65. But if the benefit period is only two years, you are only going to get your claim paid for two years, irrespective of whether you're still unable to go back to work.

Ownership and tax considerations

Your monthly benefit amount will be subject to income tax (so that needs to be considered to make sure you have the correct level of cover). The costs for most income protection policies that are paid from your after-tax income (meaning the money from your bank account), are tax deductible — but check with your accountant to confirm. You can also hold this policy inside your superannuation (in which case, the premiums for the insurance come out of your super account). Income protection policies that are held through superannuation are usually less comprehensive than outside super options, because the cover needs to meet specific superannuation legislation.

Trauma insurance

If you've ever been sick, you'll know it's expensive (even with private health insurance and access to public healthcare services). This cover, also known as critical illness cover, helps people who don't have bucketloads of financial resources to support them, and don't want to sell assets in a hurry or go into debt if they have a serious illness.

How does it work?

You get a lump sum of money if you suffer from a listed critical illness. The big ones that often get claimed on are cancer, heart attacks, strokes and coronary bypass surgery, but normally quite a long list of other specified medical conditions are also covered.

Important terms and information

This cover is all based on whether you meet the medical definition in the policy. You don't usually have any requirement to be off work, as with income protection. But you only get paid if you suffer one of the listed conditions, at the level defined. For example, you might have a skin cancer removed, but it may not be at the level where it is covered under the melanoma definition.

Lump sum amounts of money are either paid via a 'partial payment' if you are diagnosed at an early stage for a covered condition or a 'full payment'. Payments are not drip-fed to you in monthly instalments like with income protection.

Many people consider having a small amount of this cover (even though it can be quite expensive, due to the high statistical likelihood of claim!) to make up for any gap between their current income and what they'll get from any income protection for a period of time.

For example, if someone on a salary of $100 000 has an income protection policy that covers 60 per cent of their pre-tax income, they may decide they need $80 000 of trauma insurance as well to cover the gap between their wage and their income protection for two years.

You can also choose to add an amount to cover some out-of-pocket medical expenses (because private health insurance usually has a gap and public wait times or options may not be suitable). For example, the lifetime cost of having a heart attack is estimated to be $95 728, while breast cancer is estimated at $41 260, and prostate cancer is $42 130.[2]

Ownership and tax considerations

In Australia, you can't hold a trauma insurance policy inside superannuation, so it needs to be paid for with money from your bank account. Generally, this cost isn't tax-deductible; however, benefits paid to you are tax-free.

Total and permanent disability cover

This cover, also known as 'TPD' is again for people who don't have the funds (or don't want to drain their assets) in the event of a serious, life-altering medical event.

How does it work?

This insurance is to cover you if, due to illness or injury, you're *never* able to work again. These situations are serious and not generally ones you will recover from. The examples that get used a lot are a surgeon who permanently loses function of their hands, or someone who becomes a quadriplegic and can no longer work.

Important terms and information

Okay, so TPD is harder to claim on than, say, trauma insurance (which is based on whether you suffered a medical event that's covered) because it looks at your ability to work, ever again. Doctors need to be confident you permanently won't be able to work in order to sign off on this with the insurer — but there's a catch. When choosing your cover, you can pick from two different definitions of 'permanent incapacity'. One is generally wayyyy more expensive than the other, because how they assess you for each definition is quite different. Here are the two options:

- *Permanent incapacity in your own occupation:* Can you work in your own occupation ever again?
- *Permanent incapacity in any occupation:* Can you do any job that you have education, training or experience in, again?

Does it really make that much of a difference? It depends on your job, experience and what happens to you (which, annoyingly, you won't know until it happens). But let's take the surgeon example. If their hand injury meant they couldn't perform surgery ever again (as signed off by a doctor), and they had an 'own occupation' policy, their claim would be paid out. However, if they had an 'any occupation' policy, the insurer would look to see if they were still able to do other duties that fit with their experience and education. If they could, they likely wouldn't be paid out.

You can probably imagine that for many people who experience something like this, it's a lot to deal with. They may not be able to live in their current house, or need significant modifications made. They may need support to carry out basic daily activities beyond what's provided in the public health system. And while you may have part of your income covered (if you've taken out income protection insurance), costs can add up quickly.

Ownership and tax considerations

You can own TPD cover inside superannuation, but only 'any occupation' policies are available. If you know that's not the definition you want, speak to a professional. You may have the option to split part of the cover inside super and some outside to help reduce costs. (Keep in mind that premiums paid via super are paid from your retirement funds, meaning your balance will be reduced.)

If you do get paid out via a policy inside your superannuation, it likely will be subject to tax. If you own the policy outside of superannuation, payments are typically tax-free.

Life insurance

Also known as 'death insurance', this cover is generally useful for anyone who has debts they want cleared when they aren't around anymore, or someone who has financial dependants and wants to ensure any costs relating to them (such as school fees, childcare and support at home) are covered. No-one wants to inherit debt or face sudden and unexpected costs after a loved one dies. If you don't have debts, a partner or kids, and don't see them in your future, you may choose not to take out life insurance.

How does it work?

This cover, while covering your life, is actually about financially supporting the people around you when you are no longer here.

Important terms and information

Think about who would be financially impacted if you were no longer around. Would your partner be able to cover the full mortgage and all the other costs? Or would the bank call the loan in? Would your kids have to leave their school? Would money be needed to pay for someone to pick them up from school and do bullshit life stuff (such as the groceries, cooking, cleaning and gardening) if you weren't around?

Over the years, I worked with a few couples where one of them would say, 'I don't want it'. My response to this was always,

'No worries. We won't get life insurance for your partner then'. They would often be confused by this, so I would explain: 'Because your life insurance is actually going to look after your partner when you're not around, we don't need to get your partner life insurance because you'll be able to cover it — right?!' They would very swiftly realise they probably couldn't cover the cost of their mortgage and life (especially if they had kids) without additional funds. Life insurance can go a long way towards financially protecting those left behind. My life, and my mum's, would have undoubtedly been different if my dad had taken it out before he got sick.

Many life insurance policies also cover and provide an early pay out for terminal illness. This means you can sort out your financial affairs before you go — or, you know, live your last days however the fuck you like.

Ownership and tax considerations

You can own this policy within superannuation or own it personally. Paying for cover through super may assist your personal cash flow, but (as noted previously) it will reduce your retirement balance because premiums are paid from your retirement funds. If the cover is held in super and the beneficiary is considered a tax-dependant (there are strict criteria in Australia for who this includes), payments are generally tax-free. If the payment goes to others, it will be taxed. If you own it personally, payments will generally be tax-free to whoever you want to give them to.

Child cover

Also known as child trauma cover, this insurance might be taken out by parents of children aged between 2 and 17 who want to make sure they have sufficient money if their child is seriously unwell. (Note that a parent's income protection won't usually give them an income if they have to take time off to look after a sick child.)

How does it work?

This insurance covers your child if they suffer a serious medical condition (such as cancer, severe burns or open heart surgery). It also usually covers death.

Important terms and information

Most policies allow children to be covered from age two and many of them automatically convert to an adult trauma cover policy when they turn 18 years old, without any additional medical assessment.

Ownership and tax considerations

This insurance can't be held inside superannuation and needs to be paid for personally. Benefit amounts are paid out tax-free.

Getting insurance in place

As already mentioned, sometimes you might get insurance automatically as part of your superannuation plan. Normally, what's offered is basic cover, at low levels. To access more comprehensive or higher levels of cover, you need to apply for it (usually through an expert) — and if you think your neighbour is nosy, you ain't seen anything yet.

The process of applying for insurance (called 'underwriting') can feel like you're applying for a job in the FBI. Insurance companies want to know everything about you — like, *everything*. You'll need to detail your medical and family history, job history, sexual history, pastimes, if you smoke, have ever taken drugs or are on any medication... it's a lot. But they need all this information because most of these policies will automatically renew, without any additional medical info ever needed. Underwriters are like the security guards at the hottest club in town, with a strict list of who can and can't get in. But, once you're in, you're in! They can't kick you out if you keep paying your premiums.

It's important to disclose everything on your medical record, because the last thing you want is for them to decline a claim due to a pre-existing condition. They may choose to cover you for all the standard conditions (although, in my experience, that is very rare), or they may exclude certain conditions. The most common exclusions relate to back and mental health conditions. If you've ever had a problem with these, it's likely they will be excluded from your cover. Or they may choose to charge you more if they think you're an additional risk (they call that a 'loading'). In some instances, they may decline cover completely. Ideally, your insurance expert will find out ahead of time if you're going to be declined, so they can try another company or withdraw the application so it's not on your record.

If they do decline you, ask them if it's for a certain period of time or until a particular situation occurs. This could be after you've had scheduled surgery, for example, or your blood pressure is below a certain level for a certain period of time. Or it might be a specific amount of time since your last symptoms and treatment for a condition. Other times, they will say they won't look to review it. In the situations where you can't get cover, you need to consider if you need additional emergency savings or could consider accident only cover. (Sure, it won't cover illness, but many claims are paid because of accidents every year!)

Still with me? Because here's an important point, and I want you to sing it with me: 'life insurance is a non-estate asset, a non-estate asssssssssset'. Okay, what the hell does that mean and why do you need to sing it? Life insurance being a non-estate asset means the benefit payment goes to whoever is nominated as your *beneficiary*.

Why does that matter? Well, let's say your ex-partner is your listed beneficiary (because you forgot to update it), but now you have a new partner and maybe you've got children (or you're still single, but would rather see hell freeze over than give your ex your life insurance payout). If you die, your new partner and kids won't get the money.

Even if that's what's stated in your will! Because… *sings*… 'life insurance is a non-estate asset'. Instead, the payment will go to your listed beneficiary, even if your situation has completely changed since you nominated them. Have a friend going through a divorce or separation? Sing this at them! Or, at the very least, make them aware of it.

You can appoint your personal legal representative on the policy so it can be handled via your estate (more about this later in this chapter). Nominating beneficiaries on your insurance can be useful if you have a complex situation and want certainty on who gets the money. Generally, you can have multiple beneficiaries and can split it into different percentages.

I know you have a lot to get your head around, so here are your next steps:

- Review what insurance you currently have, if any. What types of cover do you have, what are the waiting periods, and how much are you insured for?
- If you are looking to consolidate your superannuation, be sure to check if you would lose any insurance (or no longer be covered for any specific conditions).
- Consider what gaps exist, or where you are covered for less than you think you should be. (Get help to work this out if you need it.)
- Look at your policy terms and conditions! It's better to find out now that you're not covered for what you thought you were. The devil is in the details with insurance.
- Find a qualified and licensed financial adviser or insurance expert and book a chat to find out more about what they do and how they charge. Many will charge a small up-front fee to prepare your application and then the rest of the fee is paid from the insurer once your application has gone through (similar to charges for mortgage brokers).

- If you have a partner, ask them to review their cover (or use a scheduled 'money date' to do it together), or grab a friend to make the entire thing as less-terrible as possible.
- If you have a scheduled call with an insurance company for your application, be in a private place and have all your medical info on hand.
- A financial adviser or insurance specialist can also do an anonymous 'pre-assessment' to see if anyone can offer you cover, before you submit an application.

Read this before cancelling your cover!

As you get growing, you might reach a point where you feel you don't need to be covered anymore, or you may want to reduce the level of cover you have. Before you do — my *general* advice is to go and get a full medical first (including full bloods). The last thing you want is to cancel your cover and a week later find out you have a medical condition you could have claimed on.

If you're thinking about cancelling because of the cost, you may have other options. Ironically, when you have the least amount of money is probably when you have the most need for insurance (because you have limited financial wiggle room). Some policies offer 'premium holidays' — yes, your cover takes a vacation (perhaps to a Greek island?). While you won't need to pay for that period, it's not on the clock either — so you won't be able to make a claim during that time. But you may get to keep your cover, without going through the application process again, and give you some financial breathing space. You can also look to reduce your cover amount to better fit your cash flow plan. Obviously, doing so means you won't have as much protection, but sometimes something is better than nothing.

Thank you for sticking with me, and maybe go and hug your kids, pets or partner. Message your bestie and remind them you love them. And promise yourself you'll do what's needed, at the very least, to take the financial burden off those you love if anything horrible happens. Ask your loved ones if they are covered too. Sharing this knowledge will help them cover any gaps they may have too — because, remember, it may impact you.

So now you've got the bedrock foundation (emergency savings) and the roof on (insurances), let's see how else you can insulate yourself from any other shitty financial weather events.

Protecting your ass-ets

Before we get into this, know that laws vary (and change) from state to state in Australia, let alone country to country, so I always suggest you get a qualified legal expert to help you and provide specific advice based on where you live. And I still advise seeing an expert, even if you don't think your situation is overly complicated or you have 'enough' financial assets to warrant it.

Listen: families can be 'interesting' at the best of times. But, let me tell you, things get way more 'interesting' with blended families, family disputes or differences of opinions on what your wishes are, if they aren't explicitly stated. You probably don't want to leave your loved ones with 'sadmin' as your parting gift. Consider each of the ways I outline here to protect yourself. Ask yourself, do you need them right now? What would happen if you didn't have it in place? Who would that impact and to what extent?

Now let's dive in.

Protecting existing assets: Binding financial agreements

Everyone's got assets. Maybe you're a whiz in the kitchen or a genius at the trivia table. Or maybe you have the most glorious head of hair anyone's ever seen. But when I talk about 'assets' in this sense, I mean the financial ones. A property, a car, a share portfolio, even your superannuation is an asset. If you bring financial assets to a relationship, protecting them normally requires a legal agreement. In Australia, we call this a 'binding financial agreement' but most people know them as a 'pre-nup' or 'separation agreement'. They aren't 100 per cent watertight, but are generally recommended.

Arguably, the best time to create this agreement is before any sticky relationship situations arise. Some people have very strong feelings about these, seeing it as a 'destined for doom' alarm bell. But, if you think about it, what it actually says is you're each there for love, not money. Romantic, right?! Now, if your situation changes — perhaps you have children and take time out of the workforce, or have a lower income for an extended period of time — it's worth getting this agreement reviewed (or perhaps checking what would happen to the agreement in the event of such changes as you're getting it set up).

Having loan agreements in place

If you lend anyone money, get a legal agreement drafted. The only reason not to get an agreement in place is if you're perfectly okay with never getting the money back. (In which case, it's not a loan. Instead, it's a gift and may have implications to you receiving government pension payments if it's more than $10 000 per financial year, or $30 000 over a five-year period.)

Setting up a trust

Some people want to grow their wealth inside a trust structure. If you're considering this, get help from an accountant. You need to understand a fair bit about the options available and how they work. Trusts normally aren't cheap to create and maintain, but they can provide additional protection or options for whoever the money is distributed to.

Naming your superannuation beneficiaries

In Australia, you have different options when nominating who gets your super when you pass away, and strict conditions as to who is considered a 'valid' beneficiary. The problem is most funds let you put whoever you want down and only check if it's valid when actually needed.

Here's who you can nominate:

- a spouse or partner
- your children
- someone who you have an interdependency with, or a financial dependant
- your estate or legal representative.

A common mistake is nominating your parents or siblings as your beneficiaries, even though they don't fit any of the preceding criteria. Doing so means, if the time came for your nomination to be reviewed, it would be classed as invalid. If you don't have anyone who fits the above listed criteria, you're generally best to nominate your legal representative.

Also note the following definitions:

- *Binding death benefit nomination:* This means the trustee must pay your super to the nominated beneficiaries (assuming they are a valid nomination). Note that many super funds have requirements for these to be renewed after a certain time frame (in most cases, three years — but it's always best to check).

- *Non-binding death benefit nomination:* This is more of a general preference or a suggestion on where you'd like the payment to go. However, the trustee will be in charge of making the final decision on who gets it, according to the law.
- *Lapsing nominations:* These expire after a specified amount of time. Find out how long that period of time is and update your nomination when it lapses.
- *Non-lapsing nominations:* These won't generally expire, but it's important that you revoke or amend them if your intended beneficiary changes.

Estate planning

Okay, this is another area people usually put off thinking about. But, again, you don't want to leave a mess for your family and loved ones to clean up after you're gone. So let's start with the big one — planning your will.

Wills

This is a legal document that lays out your final wishes. It covers who gets what and who's in charge of making it happen (your executor). Your will can also include other elements, such as who will become the guardian of children, your funeral wishes, and any charitable donations or bequests. Even when you have a will, it can be contested. So, if you have small children, you might also want to consider if you need a 'testamentary trust', which comes into effect upon your death and will appoint a trustee to look after your assets — and any payments from the trust — until your beneficiaries can access them (that is, when they reach a certain age).

So what happens if you die without a will? It's often a very shite experience for everyone who's left behind to have to deal with (on top of the emotional turmoil). Dying 'intestate' (meaning you've died without a valid will) means you don't have any say over who gets your assets. Every state and territory in Australia has a different process in this situation, but it's normally a long, painful and stressful journey.

In my experience, you want the most logical and pragmatic person in your life to be your will's executor. Tell them if you've appointed them (it surprises me how many people don't!). Let them know who your legal representative is, give them a copy of your will and a list of what and where your assets are (for example, banks, super funds, investment platforms and insurers). You should probably also discuss your stated wishes with your loved ones, because no-one wants to be kept in the dark.

Power of attorney

This varies a lot from state to state within Australia, but generally a power of attorney (POA) allows an appointed person to make financial and legal decisions on your behalf. Depending on the type of power of attorney you have, if you're unable to make decisions for yourself, they may be able to make decisions for you. You can also appoint a specific medical power of attorney to make medical decisions for you. (This isn't the same as a general POA and doesn't need to be the same person.)

Advanced healthcare directive

Sometimes called a 'living will', an advanced healthcare directive outlines your wishes for medical treatment in the future, according to your needs, values and preferences. For example, you may have particular spiritual, religious or cultural practices you want to happen before or after you die. Do you want to donate your organs or tissue?

Do you have a particular definition of 'quality of life'? You can add this to your health record, so doctors can view it in the future. Depending on where you live, you may need to complete a specific form.

As Benjamin Franklin noted, nothing in life is certain except death and taxes. None of us is getting outta here alive. So while I don't recommend getting this stuff sorted over a festive lunch, you do need to get it done, and you should also have these conversations with your family members.

Here are some questions to consider:

- What protections do you already have in place? Are they up to date and valid?
- What needs to go on the list to learn more about or get started?
- Who do you need to chat to or book a meeting with?
- When was the last time you checked your super beneficiary? Is it valid and up to date?
- Do you know if your close family or friends have a will or insurance sorted? What happens if they don't?
- Allocate time to your diary *now* to at least take the first step (which could even be just checking what you do or don't have sorted).

Considering inheritances

Over the coming decades, it's estimated that trillions of dollars will be transferred from one generation to the next. So let's cover what to do if you receive an inheritance — be it a few thousand dollars, many millions or any amount in between.

For most people, this is an emotionally complicated time, because money is normally received due to someone they loved dying.

Many feel a sense of guilt — while it's given them financial options, someone died for that to happen. This may not be spoken about often, but it's common. You can feel both grateful and be grieving at the same time.

Another tricky aspect is that inheritances sometimes have strings attached, even if they're only heartstrings. If you're not in the headspace to make a decision on what to do with the inheritance yet, give yourself some breathing space. Set a date for when you want to pick this back up. (Don't let yourself delay making a decision on it forever.)

Most people fear doing the 'wrong' thing with the money. Go back to your goals. Which ones can now be advanced or completed because of the inheritance? I also think it's worth considering (depending on your relationship with the person who died, of course), if you want to use a portion of the funds to do or create something in memory of them. This could be something you know they would love to see the money go towards. For example, the mum of a close friend of mine inherited a small amount of money from their beloved nan after she passed away at the ripe old age of 100. They put the money in a dedicated account and used it to buy birthday and Christmas presents, from Nan, for all the grandkids and great-grandkids until it ran out. It became the ultimate gift that kept on giving!

Finally, make sure you check with your accountant on the tax implications of any inheritances.

Protecting yourself in a relationship

Choosing a partner (if you choose one) is one of the biggest decisions you'll ever make. It's also one that can carry huge risks — to both your money and wellbeing, but also your safety. This is especially the case for women, and especially for women in relationships with men.

The way I see it is this: no one person in a relationship should be 'in charge' of all the financial responsibilities, no matter their gender. Not only is this responsibility way too much to expect one person to be able to shoulder alone, but, on the flip side, abdicating from making those decisions also puts you at risk. You have far too much to lose to not be across and have a seat at the (dining room?) table where decisions are made. It needs to be a team effort.

The best analogy I've heard is around parenting responsibilities. Imagine you have a partner and kids. And your partner casually says to you, 'I've been thinking. It seems like you're just naturally better at this whole parenting thing. So I think it makes sense that you do it all. Don't worry — I support your decisions. I trust you. You just seem to 'get it' so it makes sense you do everything that comes with it'. Yeah, no — fuck that! The same goes for your money.

Of course, you may think this isn't an issue you ever need to worry about. Well, to borrow a line from Katie Charlwood (one of my favourite historians and podcast hosts), why don't we slip into some context? Here's the reality:

- In 2024, the divorce rate in Australia was over one-third of the marriage rate (120 844 marriages compared to 47 216 divorces).[3]
- According to 2023 figures, one in six Australian women and one in 13 Australian men has experienced financial or economic abuse.[4]
- Women who earn more than their male partners have a 33 per cent increased risk of experiencing partner violence and a 20 per cent greater risk of experiencing emotional abuse.[5]
- Men are statistically more likely to leave their female partner when she becomes seriously unwell.[6]

- Women are twice as likely to say financial stress impacts their physical wellbeing.[7]
- Men are likely to have an increased incidence of psychological distress when their wife or partner earns 40 per cent of the household income, with distress reaching the highest levels when men are economically dependent on their wife.[8]
- In my own research, I found 36 per cent of couples report that they fight about money at least monthly.[9]
- In Australia, three in five people accessing homelessness services in 2023 and 2024 were women. One in six was a child under the age of 10.[10]
- Leaving a violent relationship and starting again costs an average of $18 000.[11] Up to 7700 Australian women a year are returning to violent partners while 9120 women are forced into homelessness after escaping violent homes because they have nowhere else to go.[12]

These statistics are horrifying.

Not one ounce of me relishes sharing these with you. But they are real. This happens — every day. Your income, education level or postcode doesn't make you immune from it. I don't care what gender you are. We all should care that this happens in our communities, on our street, and perhaps even under the roof of someone we love. Much more awareness is needed, along with conversations about the warning signs of financial abuse and coercive control, and what steps to take, if or when needed.

What should you look out for? Here are some relationship red flags:

- not having oversight, autonomy or access to financial resources
- not being included in important financial decisions
- being asked to take out debt in your name for your partner

- being given an 'allowance' of money
- being coerced into any financial decision (be it becoming a company director for a business you are not involved in, selling or buying an asset against your will, forcing you to quit your job, sabotaging your ability to go to work, or accessing your assets without your permission)
- emotional manipulation ('if you loved me, you would do this for me') or threatening access to money, custody of children, divorce or physical harm if you do not do as requested.

If you need help and you're in Australia, here are some wonderful places to access support and resources:

- *1800RESPECT:* The 24/7 national helpline for domestic, family and sexual violence counselling, information and support. (Call 1800 737 732 or text 0458 737 732.)
- *The Orange Door:* Local support for adults, children and families experiencing or using family violence. (Check online for locations near you.)
- *13YARN:* Crisis service for Aboriginal and Torres Strait Islander peoples. (Call 13 92 76.)
- *InTouch:* Dedicated support for migrant and refugee communities. (Call 1800 755 988.)
- *Rainbow Door:* Support services for LGBTQIA+ communities (Call 1800 729 367.)
- *MensLine Australia:* A counselling service for men, both victim-survivors and those using violence. (Call 1300 789 978.)
- *Men's Referral Service:* Support for men wanting to stop using violence, operated by No to Violence. (Call 1300 766 491.)

Money in the wild: Dana (she/her)

- **Age:** 40.
- **Situationship:** Single parent.
- **Income:** $200 000.
- **Current savings:** $50 000.
- **Current relationship with money:** Good, proud, empowered.
- **Money monster's name:** Umm never thought about it. I don't think I have one? I usually only splurge on health-related things, which I see as essential or an investment.

Have you ever had to use your emergency savings, and how did it make you feel?

Not yet but I will soon likely need to use all or most of it for legal fees, which is infuriating. It made me feel secure for now, proud and grateful.

What does life look like right now?

Renting, hoping to buy and worrying about whether it will be possible due to legal fees.

Do you save or invest?

Both. I don't have a super high knowledge, but I know it's safer to spread across multiple avenues.

What is a past money decision you're proud of?

Paying off all my credit card debt several years ago, and pushing hard in my career to earn an income much higher than most of the country, as a person who never went to uni, and a woman.

What's one piece of money advice you wish you knew sooner?
People say there is more to life than money, except money makes life better in every way. I've gone from hunting for coins to have enough petrol to get to work before payday to not worrying about bills.

What was your biggest 'ouch' money moment, and what came from it?
Not fully understanding work share schemes and how they are taxed. It's really screwed me over (though overall, of course, beneficial; it just ruined my forecasting).

What has shaped your relationship with money the most?
Family—growing up with not much money made me drive to ensure I am in a better position than my parents were.

What does 'financial wellbeing' mean to you?
Not worrying about bills, being able to afford a home, having savings as a backup.

You win the lotto. What do you do?
Buy a beautiful family-sized home, get the *best* lawyer, and go on some overseas holidays.

Anything else you'd like to share?
No-one talks about the financial impact of domestic violence, particularly after you leave and particularly if you earn over the minimum for Legal Aid and so on. I am so incredibly grateful to have money and my story would be so different if I didn't. However, this situation may mean I cannot buy a home and in the short term it impacts my every thought and decision because of what it might mean for my case or how it might affect outcomes.

A final word on withstanding winters

We can't stop winters from coming. All we can do is best prepare ourselves, and then hope they never arrive. If it does arrive, we can take heart from the wisdom of icon Dolly Parton, who said, 'Storms make trees take deeper roots'.

I don't know what life has in store for you. But I do know that you are strong and capable of growing and protecting yourself and your money simultaneously. I know you can dig deep when you need to. And when the winter fog lifts, I know you can get your hands dirty growing the life you want, once again.

When things get bumpy, here's what to consider:

- Have you taken steps to make sure you are safe (physically and financially)?
- Must you make a decision right *now*? If so, find independent experts you can lean on to support you (and challenge you), to make sure you're making the right call — not only for right now, but also for later you.
- Let your values be your North Star and your goals help shape your next move.
- Get your most blunt friend (I can say this because I am usually that person) and ask them to help you put together a pros and cons list of your options. You want someone with practical, logical and level-headed thinking. Your comfort friends are to soothe, and your pragmatist friends are there to help you solve. You need both.

- Never do it alone. If you don't have a big support network, get online and find one. Loads of community spaces are full of people who have been exactly where you are now, and can help you understand their journey and what insights they have. If you want one dedicated to money, you can learn more about our community at the back of this book.
- Set your 'D Day'. If you have been able to give yourself a bit of space, it's now time to set a 'decision date'. This will avoid you procrastinating forever on making the decision. Get someone to keep you accountable to making the decision by this date.

FLOURISH

A love note to your growth and everything it makes possible

I am rooted, but I flow.

—Virginia Woolf (The Waves)

Well, my friend, you've made it! You are now officially part of our money-growing community. I need you to believe with *everything* you've got that you were never put here to merely survive. You deserve to *flourish*. Seriously, how can anything made from literal stardust (you!) be anything other than magic?

You deserve to grow, change, take up space, evolve, blossom and financially thrive. You're allowed to want stability, security, safety, choice and freedom in your life. And now you know what to do with your money to make that happen.

Hopefully, by now you also understand that it's not your fault if you were never taught anything about money, because that's literally how the systems were designed — to keep people from accessing greener pastures. Hopefully, you also understand why you may have had money stories, monsters and habits that stifled your growth. You now know how to harvest your cash to grow those big goals of yours into existence. And you know that investing in and protecting what you're building is how to make sure you can reap something solid and self-supporting.

To truly flourish, you must do the things that scare the shit out of you. You must break out of the shackles of shame and comfort and accept there will be moments that feel really fucking scary. And when that happens, you must keep going. Sure, rest is important too. But then it's time to get your boots back on and get back out there!

If you're feeling like you're on shaky ground as you begin taking bold action with your money, know that I and this money-growing community are all right there with you. None of us was born knowing this stuff.

But the feeling of hitting milestones and achieving goals is so worth it (in every sense). Consider this your permission (and a kick up the backside) to do it imperfectly and refine as you go. Start now, and as you are — wild, imperfect and human, or as a wildly imperfect human. Imagine what life is going to feel like when you do. How will it feel in a year? Or ten years? When you've retired? As you take your last breath? Imagine what planting the seeds now and tending to them with all you've got is going to give you. Hold on to that picture and let it push you when you need a nudge.

My hope is that, as your life inevitably changes, and when you need to realign, relearn or take your money to the next level, this book will be here waiting for you. Let your core values guide your decisions, and your life circumstances shape your goals and your game plan — because you and money are in a lifelong situationship.

You now have knowledge that *no-one* can ever take away from you. Your job is to put it to good use, creating a ripple effect of change for yourself and those around you — one that spreads wide and far, outlasting us all. Share your insights generously, talk about money enthusiastically, do the work tenaciously, and tell people about your journey with humility — be the money role model (or alter ego!) you wish you had. You may just inspire action for your friends, kids, niblings, grandkids and neighbours — perhaps even that random person you met at that BBQ who you ended up having a deep chat about money with. Maybe you'll find yourself singing 'life insurance is a non-estate asset' to your bestie who's mid-separation.

Because isn't life better when we all grow and support each other? Yes, yes, it absolutely is. You can be the change the money world desperately needs right now.

So what are you waiting for? Go — get growing.

Jess x

ACKNOWLEDGEMENTS

Giving my gardening crew their flowers

When I was first approached about writing this book, I'm not going to lie... I was filled with unbridled fear. The (brilliant) publisher looked at me, sitting sombrely on the other side of the table at my local cafe in Sydney after signing on the dotted line, and said 'you look terrified'. And I was.

See, I didn't do this so I could smugly add 'Author' to my LinkedIn profile, or so I can gloat in a nauseatingly posh voice '*I am a published author daaaarling*' when someone asks what I do at a dinner party. I wanted to write something that would help change people's life trajectory with money.

Knowing now what I feared then — that writing a book is a feat of superhuman proportions — I feel like these acknowledgements are actually the most important part of this book. It's impossible to ever truly communicate just how many people it took to bring this book into existence, and at the risk of flogging the garden metaphor past the point of no return, they all deserve their flowers (and some).

Admittedly, before embarking on this process, I guess I assumed the proverbial sea would part and I would step into a land and time where my washing, inbox and all other responsibilities dare not follow. Like those authors in movies who whimsically hire a crumbling chateau in a far-flung place, or cabin deep in the woods, I thought maybe I could leave the world behind and forget about everything except the task at hand. Instead, much like managing money itself, I wrote this book on top of my real life. With real responsibilities, major unexpected life events and while running a fledgling business full-time. To be truthful, I often felt like I was both flailing and failing at everything, all at once.

There were many moments where I experienced many of the same hang-ups people tell me they have with money — self-doubt, fear, overwhelm and a genuine concern that I had absolutely no idea what I was doing. I was tempted (on more than one occasion) to burn it all to the ground and start again. And, if anything, this process was a reminder that you can feel uncomfortable, and still do it scared anyway.

I am the person who always reads acknowledgements but never could quite understand why it seemed authors were thanking everyone they've ever met. Now I know why. And unless this somehow becomes the biggest bestseller the world has ever seen, then this is me one and done — so there are more than a few people I want to thank.

Firstly, to Lucy Raymond at Wiley, thank you for convincing me that I could do this and believing in me, when I didn't yet believe in myself. Your support and care throughout this process made me feel that I was always in safe hands. To Leigh McLennon, who shepherded and guided me with such care and grace. Your immense skill in patiently supporting me to make this into something that has some semblance of structure and order is remarkable. Thank you for backing my wild ideas, challenging others and metaphorically holding me whilst I came to grips with the reality that not all my ideas could possibly fit into one book. I said to you from the beginning that my hope was to not be your most hated author to work with — and given I missed *every* single deadline, I would absolutely understand if I failed in that task.

I will miss our meetings where I tell you I am sure it's all terrible and I need to start again and you tell me it's not and to keep going.

To Charlotte Duff, who was tasked with painstakingly wordsmithing and fact-checking absolutely everything in this book — thank you for your incredible skill, care and fastidious attention to detail. To Chris, Renee and the entire Wiley team — thank you for supporting me to bring this book to life and making sure as many people know about it as possible.

To my beyond brilliant and mostest cleverest friend Carmen Hawker — who has had eyes and (perfectly painted) fingers over every inch of this book. I am eternally grateful for your *monumental* generosity of time, skill, insight, humour and help in making this book what it is. You have taught me about empathy and compassion in ways I never thought possible and I'm in awe of how much you embody the spirit of what it means to show up (with lamingtons) for people when they need it most, even while running your own business (seriously people ... CARMEN GET IT!). The world would be an infinitely better place if everyone had a friend like you.

To the wonderful Anita and Tony — I am enormously proud of what we get up and do every single day at work. I've thrown a lot of curveballs your way over the last few years, thank you for catching them all and making sure they don't shatter on the floor. I'm very lucky to have a team that cares so much about helping people build better stories and outcomes with their money.

I feel incredibly lucky to have the equivalent of a forest full of people who helped, hyped and held me throughout this process. A big thank you to every single one of you — Joris, Claudia, Kyra, Selina, Erin, Kyle, Charlie, Grace, Anna, Danni, Josh, Ryan, Yana, Maddie, Anastasia and Nathan. A very special thank you to Stef (who jumped on a plane last minute to help me to get this finished), Greg who scoured this book for imperfections and Ange from My Goals Squad who is my *literal* cheerleader in life (thank you for your positivity, motivation, kicks up the toosh and help trying to figure out how to get everything done without falling apart). And to Chandel, thank you for everything you do for Ladies Talk Money and your sincere and unwavering determination to make the world a better and safer place for all women and gender-diverse people.

To my family — Mum, Dad, Chris, Ben, Robyn and Matt. Thank you for always being an unwavering support crew and letting me share our stories with the world. And for the food parcels, dog-minding, sleepovers and babysitting required to get this finished. My family (some of whom are no longer earth-side), have always given me support, words of wisdom and the courage to back myself. I love you all.

I think one of the most special parts of this book are the real-life stories that show us how non-linear money journeys often are. A huge thank you to each 'Money in the wild' contributor for being vulnerable and letting others know they are not alone. Also, a big thank you to Nicole Haddow for your generous insights on how to navigate goals in a relationship. To Glen James, thank you for all your help and support (and the podcast) and to Molly Benjamin for backing this book. And to all the people who have shaped my career and relationship with money, but especially Glen Hare who co-founded Fox & Hare Financial Advice with me. Even though the 'Fox' took herself on a wilderness adventure of her own — I am still enormously proud of you and the business we created. Thank you for everything you did to make that happen.

And how could I forget my Chief Distraction Officer, Olive — my working breed and allergic-to-everything Lagotto dog who, really, needs whatever is the opposite of an acknowledgement for actually making this book almost impossible to write amidst her constant chaos, attempts to send me broke thanks to eating everything she shouldn't, emergency vet bills and her explosive, house-quaking barks in retaliation to almost anything that dared move outside my home without her permission. Many have said their toddlers are easier to manage.

Doing the research for this book made me even *more* grateful to all of the women who came before us, who fought courageously for the rights and opportunities many of us now take for granted, me included. I would never have been able to write a book about money (or have a career in finance) and many of you wonderful readers would never have had access to financial independence or autonomy without their tenacious (and in many cases dangerous) pursuit for equity and justice. It reminded me that 'ordinary' women are capable of *extraordinary* things that can leave a lasting legacy. We stand in the shade of the trees you planted.

Finally, thank you to all of the magnificent people I get to help every day. From the amazing Greenhouse and Evergreen Money Club members, to the workplaces who invite me to teach their team about financial wellbeing and now also *you* as part of this money-growing community. I started this business so I could help more people learn and grow their money (without already needing a bunch of it) — it was genuinely one of the scariest and biggest decisions of my life. And to know just how many of you have told me that you, your life, your family and how you see wealth have changed because of the work that I do makes it all worth it.

And so, your next step starts *now*. Get those metaphorical money-manoeuvring gloves out and start growing a life that you will look back on with wonder, awe and gratitude. Because you *can* do it — I know you can. Your goals are waiting for you, so what are you waiting for?

KEEP THE GARDEN PARTY GROWING

Meet Jess and join the community

Meet Jessica Brady

Founder. Money educator. Slightly sweary financial fairy godmother.

Jessica Brady (she/her) is a money educator, former licensed financial adviser and speaker with two decades of experience helping people ditch financial overwhelm and build wealth on their own terms. She's worked with some of the biggest names in finance from Macquarie Bank to Zurich and CommBank, but her real passion lies in making financial education more inclusive, less confusing for women, LGBTIQA+ folks and anyone who's ever felt shut out of the finance world.

Named in the Financial Standard Power 50 as one of the most influential advisers in Australia, Jess co-founded award-winning firm Fox & Hare Financial Advice (a Certified B Corp) and Ladies Talk Money, a free online platform tackling financial inequality.

Today, Jess leads a flourishing community of money-growers through her digital programs, workshops and podcast, *Financially Fierce*. Down-to-earth, no-bullshit and grounded in the belief that you don't need perfect conditions to start growing wealth — you need the right tools, the right support and bucketloads of bravery.

About The Greenhouse

A judgement-free place to learn how to grow (and protect) your money.

This 10-week foundational program is where the money-growing magic starts. Learn how to untangle your money beliefs, get across your cashflow, and build a personalised plan to start investing, manage your super, and make confident financial decisions — checking the jargon and overwhelm at the door. Think bite-sized videos, actionable tools, live support and a seriously nurturing community cheering you on every step of the way.

The Evergreen Money Club

Keep your money plan alive and thriving.

Designed as the next step after The Greenhouse (or for folks who already have a plan in place), this monthly membership is your space for ongoing expert guidance, accountability, and community. With fresh content, timely prompts and regular check-ins, you'll stay connected to your goals and continue growing your wealth, season by season.

Ready to find your people and get growing?

You don't need to be perfect. You just need to start.

Join us, download free resources or learn more: jessicabrady.com. au/get-growing

NOTES

References and research

Introduction

1. Kelly, M (2013), 'Poor concentration: Poverty reduces brainpower needed for navigating other areas of life', Princeton University, www.princeton.edu/news/2013/08/29/poor-concentration-poverty-reduces-brainpower-needed-navigating-other-areas-life.

Chapter 2

1. Gerken, M, Batko, S, Fallon, K, Fernandez, E, Williams, A & Chen, B (2023), 'Assessing the legacies of historical redlining: Correlations with measures of modern housing instability', Metropolitan Housing and Communities Policy Center.
2. For a deep dive into this topic, see Stretton, T & Kesselring, KJ (2013), *Married Women and the Law: Coverture in England and the Common Law World*, McGill-Queen's University Press.
3. Blackstone, W (1765), *Commentaries on the Laws of England*, Book I, ch. 15.
4. Dolan, L (2018), 'Child marriage in early modern England', Australian Women's History Network, www.auswhn.com.au/blog/child-marriage/.
5. Unfortunately, for too many girls the idea of child marriage is far from ancient history. For more on the current start of child marriage, and the strategies to end it, see www.girlsnotbrides.org.

6. See 'Appointment of women to the Commonwealth Public Service — Note for Cabinet discussion', National Archives of Australia, www.naa.gov.au/students-and-teachers/learning-resources/learning-resource-themes/government-and-democracy/appointment-women-commonwealth-public-service-note-cabinet-discussion.
7. See, for example, Dumas, D (2025), 'Australian women are doing 50% more housework than men. It's creating "volcanic levels of resentment"', *The Guardian*.
8. Bahar, E, Bradshaw, N, Deutscher N & Montaigne, M (2023), 'Children and the gender earnings gap: Evidence for Australia', working paper, The Treasury, Australian Government.
9. See, for example, Weiss, C, Parkinson, D & Duncan, A (2015), 'Living longer on less: Women, paid work, and superannuation in Victoria, Australia', *SAGE Open*, 5(30).
10. Australian Bureau of Statistics (2022), 'Household income and wealth, Australia', www.abs.gov.au/statistics/economy/finance/household-income-and-wealth-australia/latest-release.

Chapter 3

1. For an in-depth discussion of this concept, see Whitebread, D & Bingham, S (2013), 'Habit formation and learning in young children', The Money Advice Service.
2. Vasih, A, Grossmann, T & Woodward, A (2008), 'Not all emotions are created equal: The negativity bias in social-emotional development', Psychological Bulletin, 134(3), 383–403.
3. Lagattuta, KH & Wellman, HM (2001), 'Thinking about the past: Early knowledge about links between prior experience, thinking, and emotion', Child Development, 72(1), 82–102.
4. Danes, SM & Haberman, HR (2007), 'Teen financial knowledge, self-efficacy, and behavior: A gendered view', Journal of Financial Counseling and Planning, 18(2).
5. As quoted in Lindzon, J (2019), 'How parents talk about money differently to their sons and daughters', Fast Company.
6. Available via my website at www.jessicabrady.com.au.
7. Available via my website at www.jessicabrady.com.au.
8. Duffy, C (2025), 'Financial literacy should be mandated in curriculum, teaching staff say', ABC News.

9. Kanji, S (2021), 'Summary report: Gendered representations of money in visual media, a study', Starling Bank and Brunel University London.
10. Ofem (2024), 'Impulse buying in the age of algorithms: A systematic literature review of psychological triggers leading to buyer's remorse', Research Square.
11. Davis, M (2023), '69% of Americans admit to emotional spending, pushing 39% of them into debt', LendingTree.
12. Jung, J, Kim, SK, Kim, JY, Jeong, MJ & Ryu, CM (2018), 'Beyond chemical triggers: Evidence for sound-evoked physiological reactions in plants', Frontiers in Plant Science, 19(January).
13. Caruso, EM & Gino, F (2011), 'Blind ethics: Closing one's eyes polarizes moral judgments and discourages dishonest behavior', Cognition, 118(2), 280–85.

Chapter 4

1. See, for example, Dweck, CS & Yeager, DS (2019), 'Mindsets: A view from two eras', Perspectives on Psychological Science, 14(3) 481–496.
2. Clear, J (2018), 'Identity-based habits: How to actually stick to your goals this year', jamesclear.com/identity-based-habits.
3. White, RE, Prager, EO, Schaefer, C, Kross, E, Duckworth, AL & Carlson, SM (2016), 'The "Batman effect": Improving perseverance in young children', Child Development, 88(5), 1563–71.

Chapter 5

1. Matthews, G (2007), 'The impact of commitment, accountability, and written goals on goal achievement', faculty presentation, 87th Convention of the Western Psychological Association; research summary available at www.dominican.edu/sites/default/files/2020-02/gailmatthews-harvard-goals-researchsummary.pdf.
2. Biology Insights (2025), 'What is the RAS and how does it affect your brain?', biologyinsights.com/what-is-the-ras-and-how-does-it-affect-your-brain/.
3. Jeannerod, M (1995), 'Mental imagery in the motor context', Neuropsychologia, 33(11), 1419–32.
4. That was me, Jess!

Chapter 6

1. Family Friendly Workplaces (2024), National Working Families Report 2024: The impact of work and care on Australian families, Family Friendly Workplaces.
2. Baxter, J (2021), 'Sharing of housework in couple families in 2020', Families in Australia Survey: Toward COVID Normal.
3. See jessicabrady.com.au for more.
4. Figures based on ASIC Moneysmart Mortgage Calculator (see moneysmart.gov.au/home-loans/mortgage-calculator). Assumes no interest rate changes and no funds in an offset account.
5. See https://firsthomebuyers.gov.au/australian-government-5-percent-deposit-scheme for more information on the 5% Deposit Scheme.
6. Figures based on Moneysmart Credit Card Calculator (see moneysmart .gov.au/credit-cards/credit-card-calculator).
7. ASIC (2018), Credit Card Lending in Australia, Australian Securities & Investments Commission.

Chapter 7

1. Prelec, D & Banker, S (2021), 'How credit cards activate the reward center of our brains and drive spending', MIT Sloan School of Management.

Chapter 8

1. Aysan, AF, Caporin, M & Cepni, O (2024), 'Not all words are equal: Sentiment and jumps in the cryptocurrency market', Journal of International Financial Markets, Institutions and Money, 91(101920).
2. Focus Economics (2025), 'Australia interest rate', www.focus-economics .com/country-indicator/australia/interest-rate/.
3. Cotality (2025), 'Home Value Index', September report, discover.cotality .com/hubfs/Article-Reports/COTALITY%20HVI%20Oct%202025%20 FINAL.pdf.
4. According to Vanguard; to see these figures as a chart, go to fund-docs .vanguard.com/AU-Vanguard_Index_Chart_poster.pdf.

Chapter 9

1. ABS (2025), 'Life expectancy: Health throughout life', Australian Bureau of Statistics, www.abs.gov.au/statistics/measuring-what-matters/measuring-what-matters-themes-and-indicators/healthy/life-expectancy.
2. ABS (2025), 'Life expectancy: Health throughout life'.
3. Ruting, B & Blane, N (2025), Economic Security in Retirement: How Life Events Affect Older Australian Women, prepared for the Super Members Council by Impact Economics and Policy.
4. See www.superannuation.asn.au/consumers/retirement-standard for more information and details on what's included in each breakdown.
5. Sims, T, Raposo, S, Bailenson, JN & Carstensen, LL (2020), 'The future is now: Age-progressed images motivate community college students to prepare for their financial futures', Journal of Experimental Psychology: Applied, 26(4), 593–603.
6. Figures based on Moneysmart superannuation calculator, moneysmart .gov.au/how-super-works/superannuation-calculator.
7. See moneysmart.gov.au/budgeting/compound-interest-calculator.
8. See moneysmart.gov.au/saving/savings-goals-calculator.
9. Vanguard (2025), 'Fact sheet: Vanguard Conservative Index Fund', fund-docs.vanguard.com/WS-Vanguard_Conservative_Index_ Fund_8132_FS_VCIF.pdf.
10. Vanguard (2025), 'Fact sheet: Vanguard Balanced Index Fund', fund-docs .vanguard.com/WS-Vanguard_Balanced_Index_Fund_8121_FS_VBIF.pdf.
11. Vanguard (2025), 'Fact sheet: Vanguard Growth Index Fund', fund-docs .vanguard.com/WS-Vanguard_Growth_Index_Fund_8133_FS_VGIF.pdf.
12. Vanguard (2025), 'Fact sheet: Vanguard High Growth Index Fund', fund-docs.vanguard.com/WS-Vanguard_High_Growth_Index_ Fund_8134_FS_VHIF.pdf.
13. Buffett, W (1993), 'Chairman's Letter', Berkshire Hathaway.
14. Russell Investments (2024), 'Value of an advisor study', Russell Investments.
15. For more on this, see Fredlick, E (2025), 'What we've learned from 150 years of stock market crashes', Morningstar.

Chapter 10

1. ACTU (2013), 'The gender pay gap over the lifecycle, www.actu.org.au/wp-content/uploads/2023/05/media96271Pay-gap-over-a-life-cycle-report.pdf.

2. According to Zurich's The Cost of Care, Volume 2, quoted in OnePath (2024), 'The hidden costs of illness and injury', www.onepath.com.au/customers/clarity/cost-of-care/the-hidden-costs-of-illness-and-injury.
3. ABS (2024), 'Marriages and divorces, Australia', Australian Bureau of Statistics.
4. ABS (2023), '1 in 5 Australians have experienced partner violence or abuse', Australian Bureau of Statistics.
5. Zhang, Y & Bruinig, R (2023), 'Female breadwinning and domestic abuse: evidence from Australia', Journal of Population Economics, 36, 2925–65.
6. Vignoli, D, Alderotti, G & Tomassini, C (2025), 'Partners' health and silver splits in Europe: A gendered pattern?', Journal of Marriage and Family, 87(4), 1639–63.
7. 2023: Gender and generation financial wellbeing report 2023 — available at jessicabrady.com.au.
8. Syrda, J (2019), 'Spousal relative income and male psychological distress', Personality and Social Psychology Bulletin, 46(6).
9. 2023: Gender and generation financial wellbeing report 2023 — available at jessicabrady.com.au.
10. AIHW (2025), 'Homelessness and homelessness services', Australian Institute of Health and Welfare.
11. Australian Women Against Violence Alliance (2021), Submission to the Committee, Inquiry into Family, Domestic and Sexual Violence, Parliament of Australia.
12. Equity Economics (2021), Nowhere to Go: The Benefits of Providing Long-Term Social Housing to Women that Have Experienced Domestic and Family Violence, commissioned by Everybody's Home.